The Campus History Series

Minot State University

Mark Timbrook

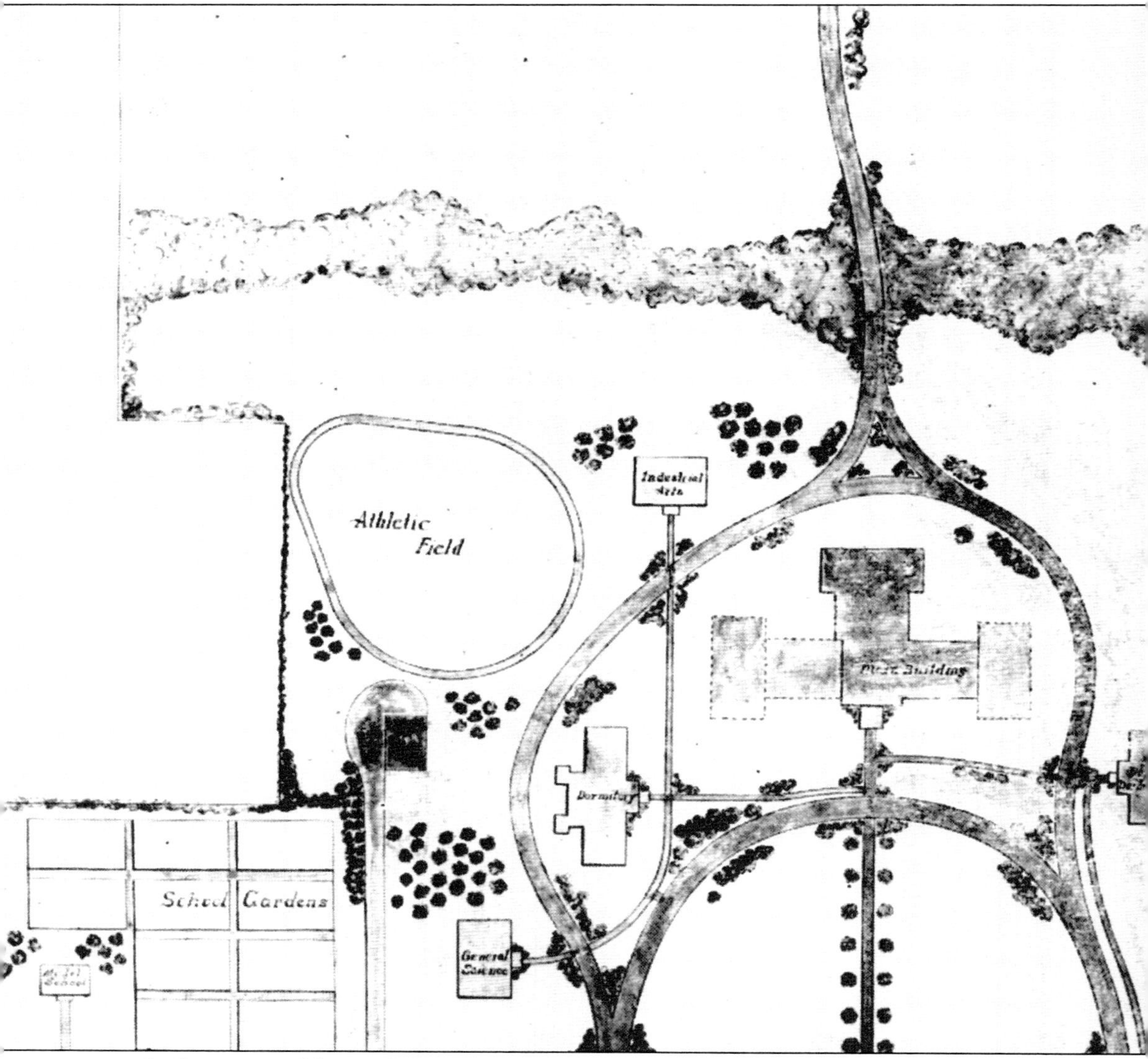

Prof. Clare B. Waldron of the North Dakota Agricultural College designed the original layouts for the grounds of the State Normal School at Minot in 1912.

On the cover: Old Main has been the centerpiece of the campus since its creation in 1913. The building was designed with three structural wings. The primary wings extended east and west, overlooking the river valley, and were intended to house classrooms, laboratories, and faculty and administrative offices. The third wing, on a centered, north and south axis, was warmed by the prairie sun and looked over the surrounding grassland. It was planned to contain the gymnasium, auditorium, and supporting facilities. However, the North Dakota state legislature in 1911 reduced funding for construction and only the east wing and the belowground gymnasium in the north wing were completed. The campus operated under these constrained conditions until 1924 when the west wing was added. The auditorium was funded in 1925. (Minot State University.)

The Campus History Series

MINOT STATE UNIVERSITY

MARK TIMBROOK

ARCADIA PUBLISHING

ISBN 978-0-7385-6047-2

Published by Arcadia Publishing
Charleston SC, Chicago IL, Portsmouth NH, San Francisco CA

Printed in the United States of America

Library of Congress Control Number: 2009925184

For all general information contact Arcadia Publishing at:
Telephone 843-853-2070
Fax 843-853-0044
E-mail sales@arcadiapublishing.com
For customer service and orders:
Toll-Free 1-888-313-2665

Visit us on the Internet at www.arcadiapublishing.com

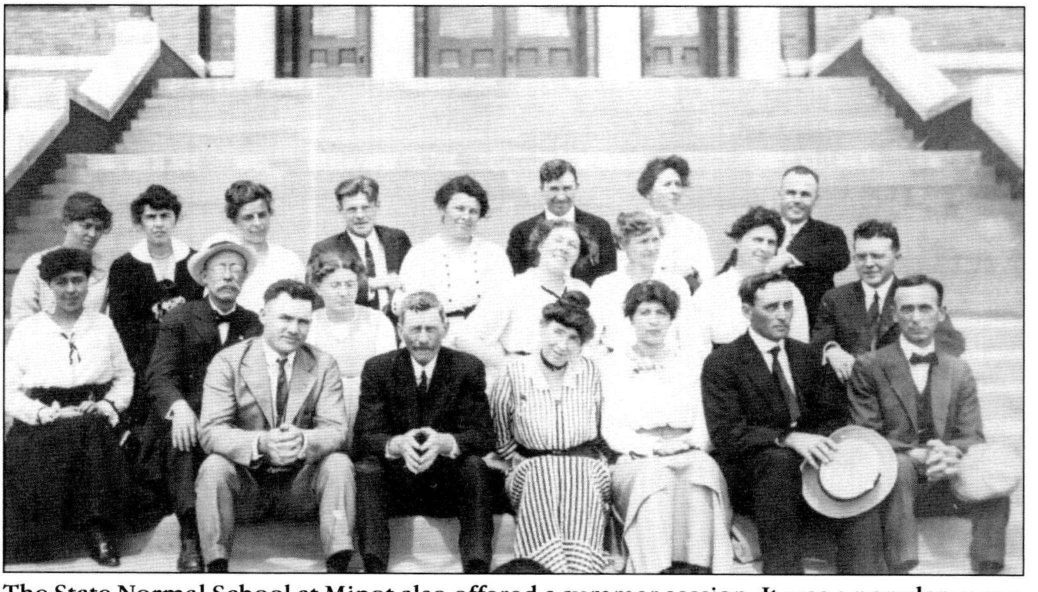

The State Normal School at Minot also offered a summer session. It was a popular venue for educators seeking additional hours or recertification. As shown by the photograph, with only 11 full-time educators, the large number of summer enrollments forced the institution to seek the assistance of additional staff. President Arthur Griswold Crane is in the first row holding his hat; William F. Clarke is to the right.

CONTENTS

ACKNOWLEDGMENTS

Much like the community of which it is part, Minot State University (MSU) has a rich and dynamic history. Being intimately familiar with the history of the community and surrounding region, I nonetheless found researching and preparing the early history of the campus a true adventure of discovery. As I walked in the footsteps of the institution's educators, administrators, staff, community leaders, and students, I have realized just how great the school's value has been to the state of North Dakota and the city of Minot. The story of the campus is inextricably tied to its location in the city of Minot, "the Magic City," and its place on the Great Northern Plains. As you browse through the collection of photographs, this "sense of place" will become apparent.

I wish to thank Susan Podrygula, MSU Gordon B. Olson Library; Anton Huether, network services; and Darla Weigel, student affairs, for their assistance with the collections and imaging. I wish to extend a special thank-you to Dr. Jonathan Wagner, history department; Dr. Kris Warmoth, Center for Extended Learning; and my wife, Eunice Timbrook, who served as proofreaders and patient critics. The State Historical Society of North Dakota archival staff deserves a special thank-you. I would truly be remiss if I did not extend my appreciation to Courtney Wankel, Alyson Parrill, and Abby Langehaug, Office of Instructional Technology student workers, for their assistance in the collection and the many trips across campus to the library. Lastly, I must thank President David Fuller for the opportunity to undertake this journey before the centennial celebration in 2013. The Dr. N. M. Lillehaugen History Scholarship Fund at Minot State University receives all royalties from this publication.

Unless otherwise noted, all images are courtesy of Minot State University.

INTRODUCTION

The city of Minot first appeared on the landscape along the Manitoba rail line in 1886. It was selected as a railhead and storage site for the 1887 westward push to Billings in the Montana Territory. The site soon supported 5,000-plus boomers and the gritty population that followed them. Surviving the first year, Minot attracted a variety of business. By the dawn of the 20th century, it had become the largest community in the region. During the second Dakota boom, the state's population soared. The surge of settlers in the sparsely occupied northwest region stressed the rural school systems, which were predominately one- or two-room schoolhouses. The two existing normal schools at Mayville and Valley City could not keep up with the demand for teachers. Minot's leaders saw this as an opportunity to acquire a normal school. However, this was a problem. The state's founders had established a limit of two normal schools in the state constitution. To build another school would involve changing the constitution. To do this, three consecutive legislative sessions and the electorate were required to approve. The political gauntlet was thrown down.

Despite the daunting political challenge, Minot's leaders launched the movement to change the state constitution and add a third normal school. Introduced and voted on in 1907, the first bill passed without difficulty. However, in 1909, Velva, Rugby, and Towner attempted to kill the second bill in committee and some legislators tried to obtain the school for their own communities. The bill passed only after Joseph M. Devine, ex-governor of North Dakota, and a committee of leading Minot business and political leaders provided convincing testimony of the school's need and Minot's ability to sponsor it. The bill passed the third and final time in 1911. In 1912, the citizens of North Dakota voted overwhelmingly in favor of the project. Flush with their victory, Minot leaders began the debate on the institution's location. This nearly led to its demise. In Minot, five different sites were considered for the school's location. The matter was finally resolved after the intervention of the State Board of Control and a straw poll of the community. The Erik Ramstad site on North Hill proved victorious.

While the location debate raged, the North Dakota state attorney Andrew Miller filed an injunction to prevent the construction of the normal school at Minot and to stop the financing of it. He argued that the addition of a normal school required a constitutional convention and that legislators had violated the state constitution in proceeding as they had. The matter went to the North Dakota Supreme Court in late 1912. In a climatic reading, the court under Chief Justice Burleigh Spalding ruled in favor of Minot and the normal school.

In the spring of 1913, construction finally started, but not before a late freeze ruined the first pour of concrete at the building site. Then, as if nature itself conspired against the school, a tornado hit the new location and nearly destroyed the recently built power plant. True to the pioneer spirit of the community and the school's first leaders, a temporary campus in the newly constructed armory in downtown Minot was established. Despite the setbacks, classes started on time for the fall 1913 semester. Until construction was completed, students roomed in the community, attended classes in the armory, and walked over one mile to the training school, which was adjacent to the campus grounds. Classes were not held on the campus until later in 1914 when the dormitory opened to students. Despite the odds, the State Normal School at Minot had become a reality.

During the years of the World War I (1917–1918), the normal school experienced declining enrollments, especially of male students. Many campus activities supported the war effort. These included rallies, parades, Liberty Loan drives, and Red Cross war work. Because the institution's first president, Arthur Griswold Crane, entered active duty with the U.S. Army Sanitary Corps, the institution's leadership was disrupted. In 1918, two of the normal school's students serving in the American Expeditionary Forces in France, Henry Finn and Otis Cooper, were killed in action. The campus established a memorial of trees, flowers, and two small, white crosses to commemorate their sacrifice.

In 1924, the State Normal School at Minot achieved collegiate status and became North Dakota State Teachers College at Minot. Despite the Great Depression and dropping attendance, campus leadership expanded campus facilities with the construction of a new training school (Model Hall) and a second women's dormitory (Dakota Hall). Other construction projects followed with support from the Depression-era Works Progress Administration (WPA). These included the first-generation student union and the president's house. At the outbreak of World War II, across the nation, enrollment plummeted as the nation dedicated its resources to the war. The military designed and initiated several educational programs on campuses to prepare America's men for the coming war. Minot State Teachers College adopted two such programs, the U.S. Navy V-5 and V-12 programs. These programs fostered the rapid development of new courses, increased enrollments, and the appearance of uniformed navy students, instructors, and administrators on campus. Navy personnel practiced their drills and ceremonies on the grassy ellipse in front of Old Main. An obstacle course was built adjacent to College Field for the physical training of navy cadets. A large *V* for victory appeared over the front of Old Main, and a navy anchor materialized on Pioneer Hall. Over the next three years, the school and surrounding community produced a number of navy aviators and officers. The momentum, generated by the war, also prepared the institution and its faculty for the growth that would follow in the postwar years, the arrival of the baby boomers, and the transfiguration of the campus and programs that were to become Minot State University.

One

The Early Landscape

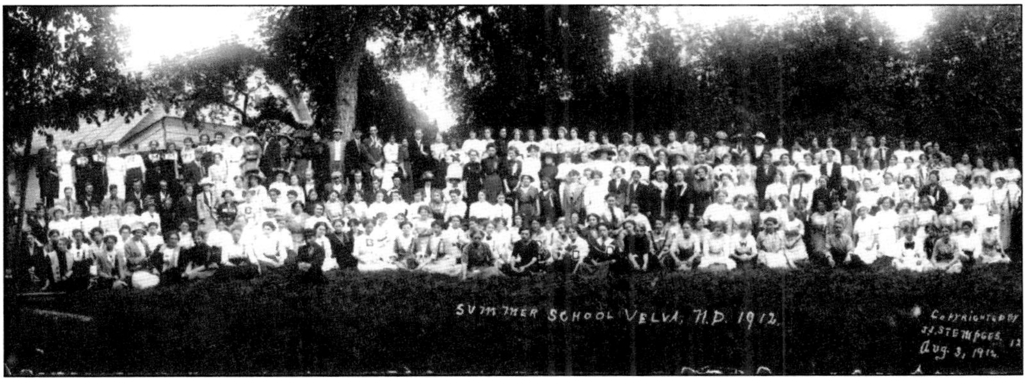

During the second Dakota boom, the need for teachers in western North Dakota resulted in a drive for a third normal school. Prior to the creation of the Normal School at Minot, the small community of Velva served the region, sponsoring summer sessions to advance teacher certification. When Minot's legislative representatives submitted a bill for the creation of the school in Minot, Velva's district representatives offered stiff resistance. Taken adjacent to the Velva pavilion in 1912, this photograph captures the last Northwest Teacher's Summer School held there. Thereafter, the State Normal School at Minot offered the sessions on its campus. Arthur Griswold Crane, the future president for the State Normal School at Minot, is standing to the right of the tree, holding his hat in his hands. He was an instructor at the time. (Wendy Thomas.)

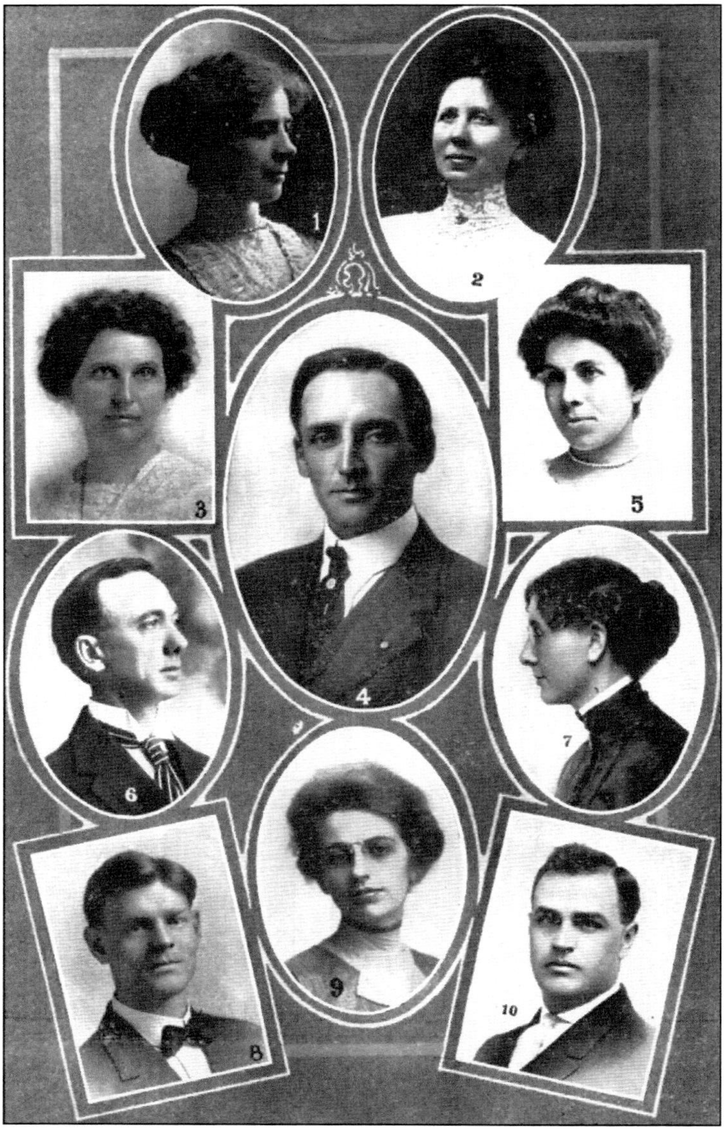

The original 11 faculty members of the State Normal School at Minot were as much founders as were the men and women who fought for the institution's creation. They created the "first impression" and established the institution's motto: Service First. President Arthur Griswold Crane (4) arrived in 1912 to start up the campus. He had served as the principal of the Menahga, Minnesota, schools; as the principal of Fergus County High School at Lewistown, Montana; and the superintendent of city schools in Minto and Jamestown, North Dakota. William F. Clarke (6) assumed responsibility for the Minot training school in 1913. When Crane departed in 1917 to pursue his graduate degree and wartime service, Clarke became the acting president until Dr. Asra Steele assumed the duties. When Steele resigned in 1918, Clarke again took charge until replaced in 1921 by Dr. Levi Beeler. Pictured are Elsie Cook (1), Julia McDonough (2), Amy Simpson (3), president Arthur Griswold Crane (4), Eula Miller (5), William F. Clarke (6), Huldah Winsted (7), George Altmann (8), Hazel McCulloch (9), and Charles Hammond (10).

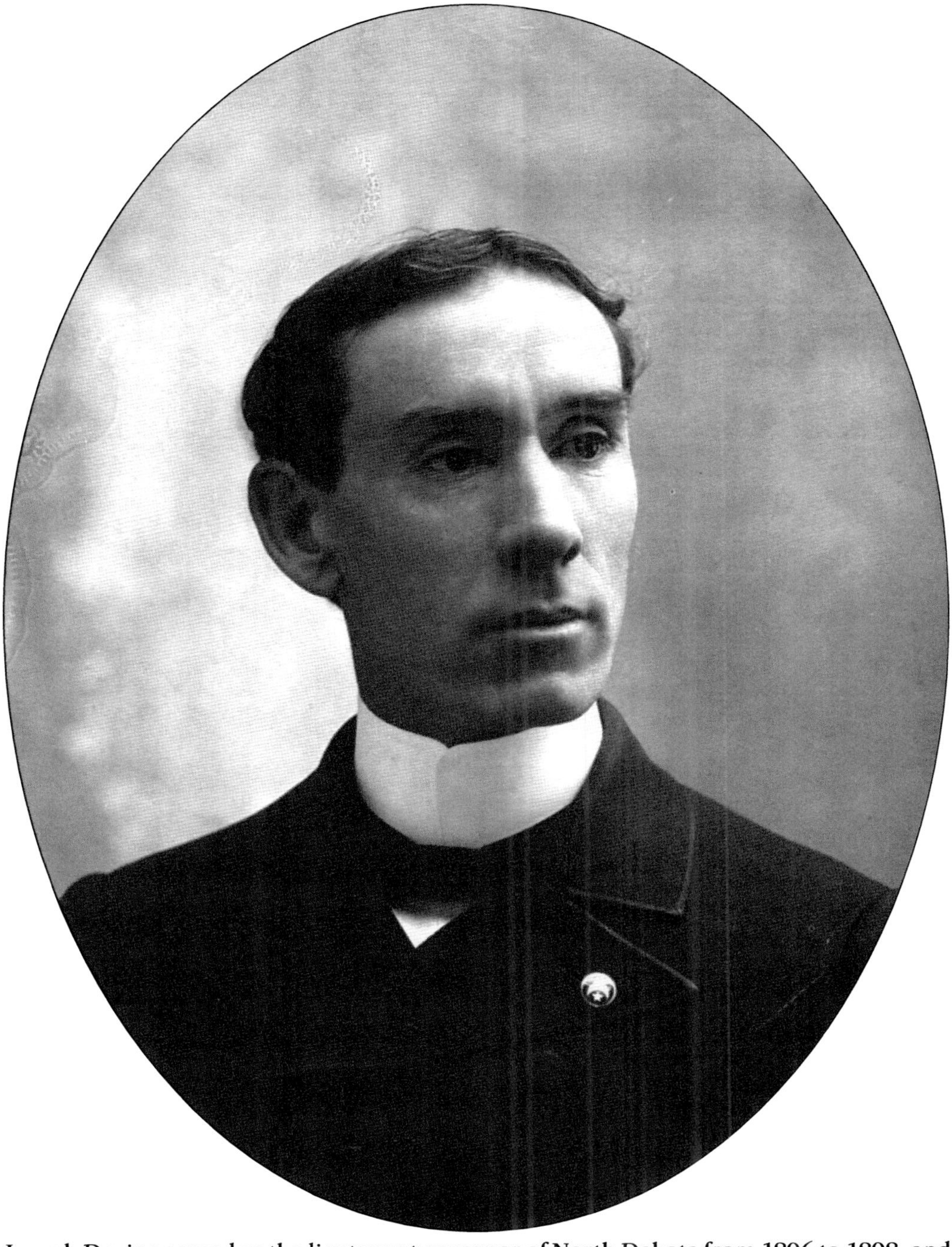

Joseph Devine served as the lieutenant governor of North Dakota from 1896 to 1898, and when Gov. Frank A. Briggs died in office, Devine finished his term. Devine served as the president of the North Dakota Education Association and as the state superintendent of schools. In the battle to secure the normal school at Minot, Devine testified before the state legislators in Bismarck and defended the community's right to have the institution. (State Historical Society of North Dakota.)

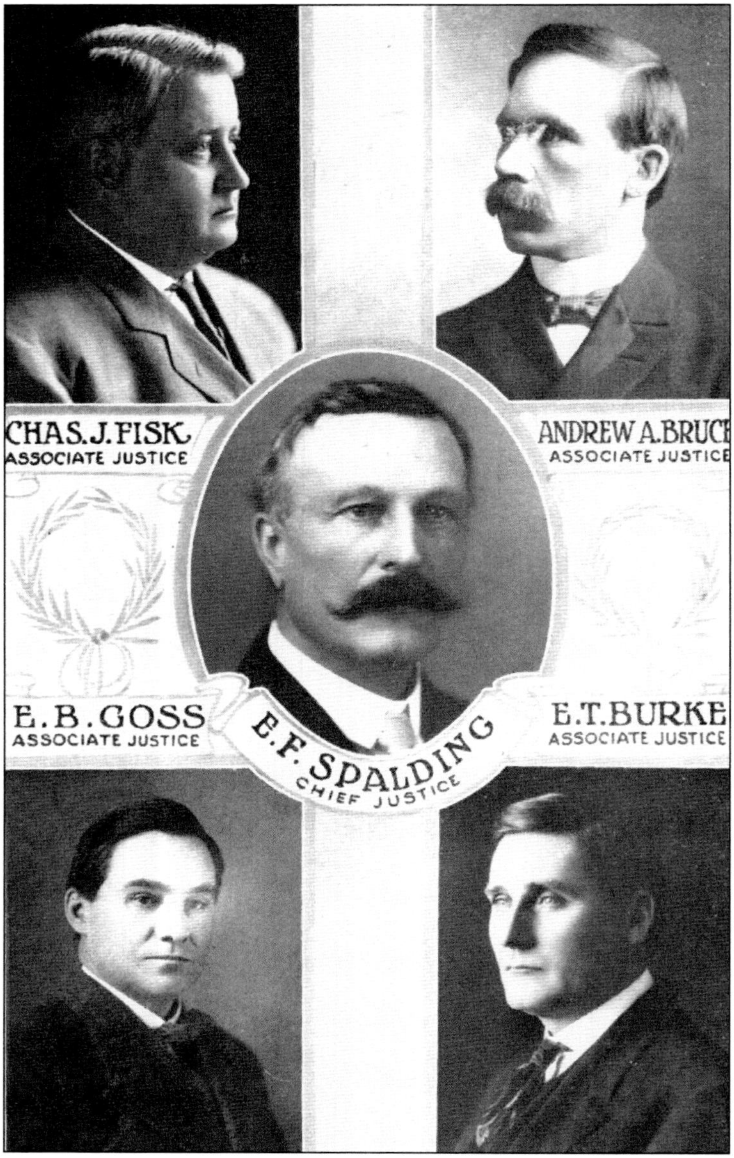

The North Dakota attorney general Andrew Miller filed for a "permanent injunction" to prevent the State Board of Normal Schools from locating the normal school at Minot. He also sought to prevent the "expenditure of any money belonging to the state of North Dakota for such purpose." His argument was simple. The state constitution stated a "revision" of the constitution would be required to add more than the legislated number of normal schools. Miller believed it required a constitutional convention. The debate finally came before the bench of the North Dakota Supreme Court. Minot attorney John Greene was the leading counsel for the citizens of Minot. The parties filed their briefs and then presented oral arguments. On December 18, 1911, Chief Justice Burleigh Spalding released the court's opinion in favor of the Minot Normal School. The temporary writ was squashed, and the application for permanent injunction was denied. Minot had a normal school. (Courtesy of North Dakota 1913 Blue Book.)

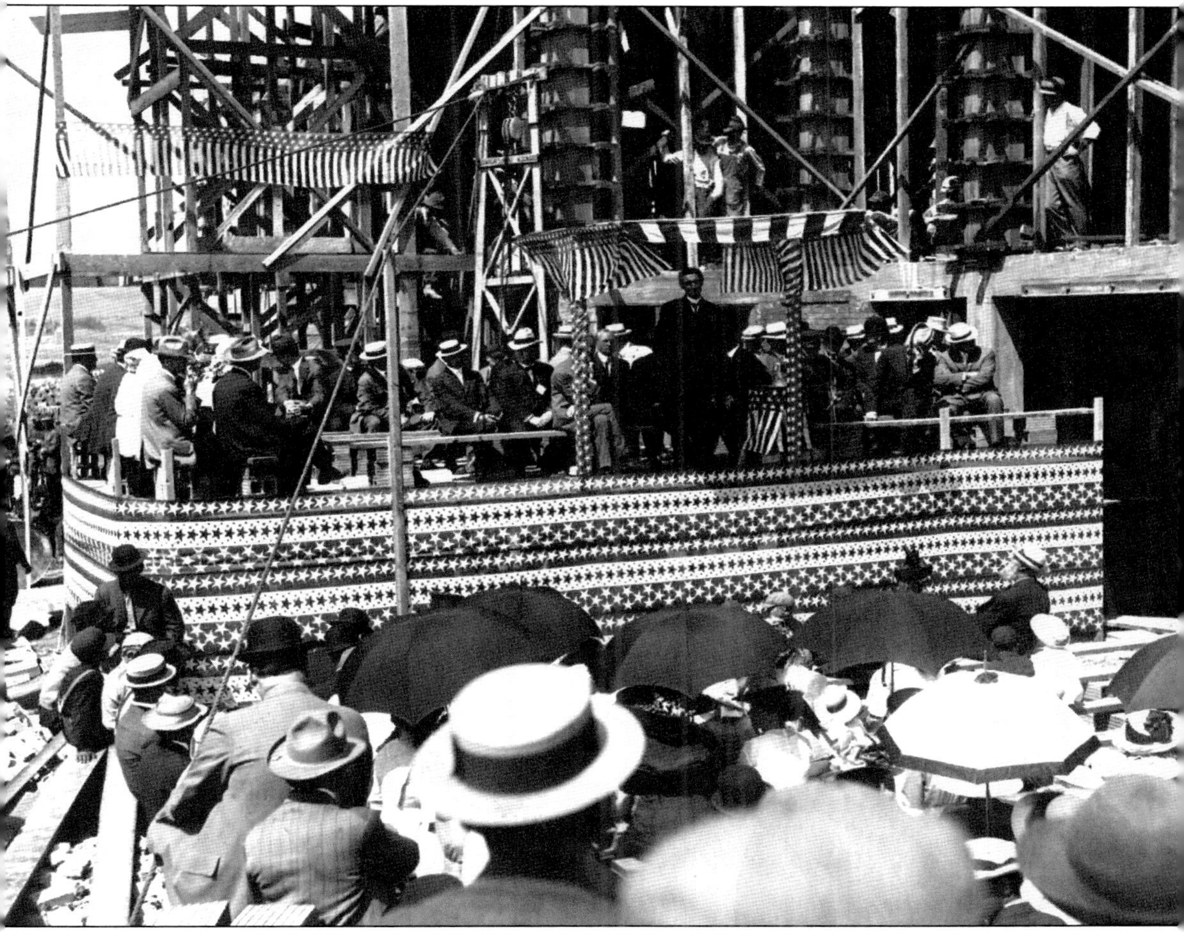

On July 25, 1913, following a parade that started at the Minot Elk's Home on South Main Street, the cornerstone for the main building was laid. Ex-governor Joseph M. Devine, who led the fight for the normal school, introduced Rev. P. W. Erickson, who opened the event with the invocation. Devine then commented on the series of challenges faced and overcome to secure the school and its Minot location. Edwin J. Taylor, state superintendent of schools, followed Devine and addressed the importance of the normal school to the Minot area. Then, with trowel in hand, North Dakota governor L. B. Hanna sealed the cornerstone in place. The cornerstone contained a time capsule. It contained various documents related to the creation of the school, local newspapers, and a brief history of the institution.

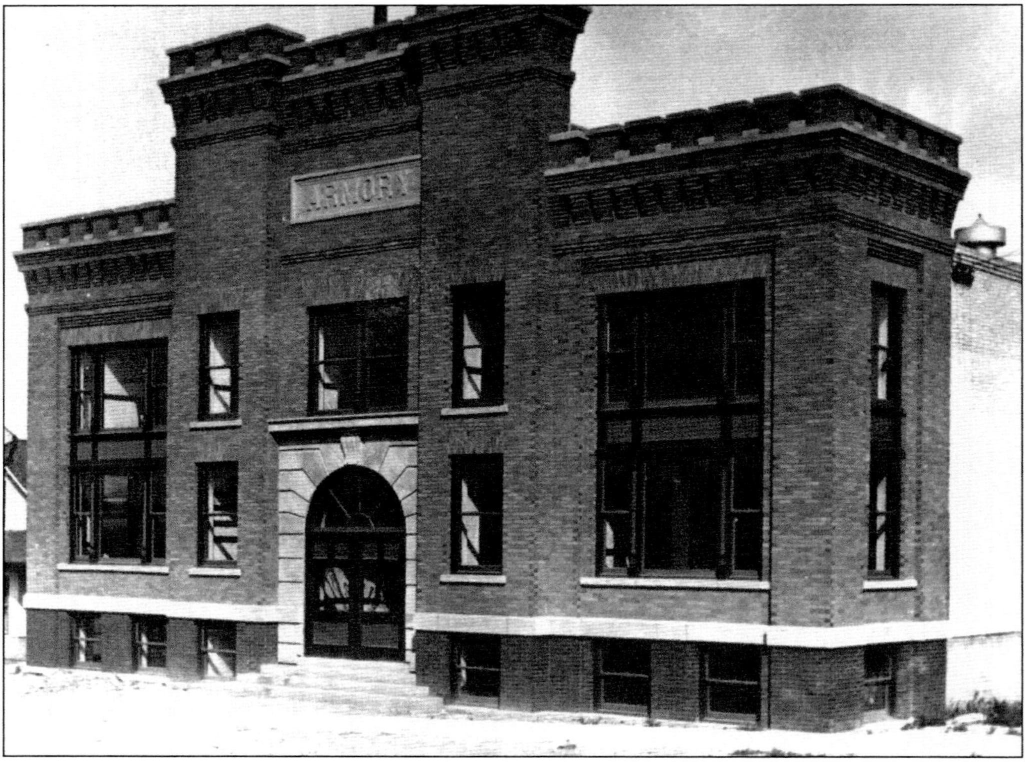

When construction problems delayed the opening of the campus, president Arthur Griswold Crane acted quickly to find other options. Crane appealed to the community, which promptly provided the normal school with the rent-free, temporary use of the newly constructed Minot Armory. (Minot High School.)

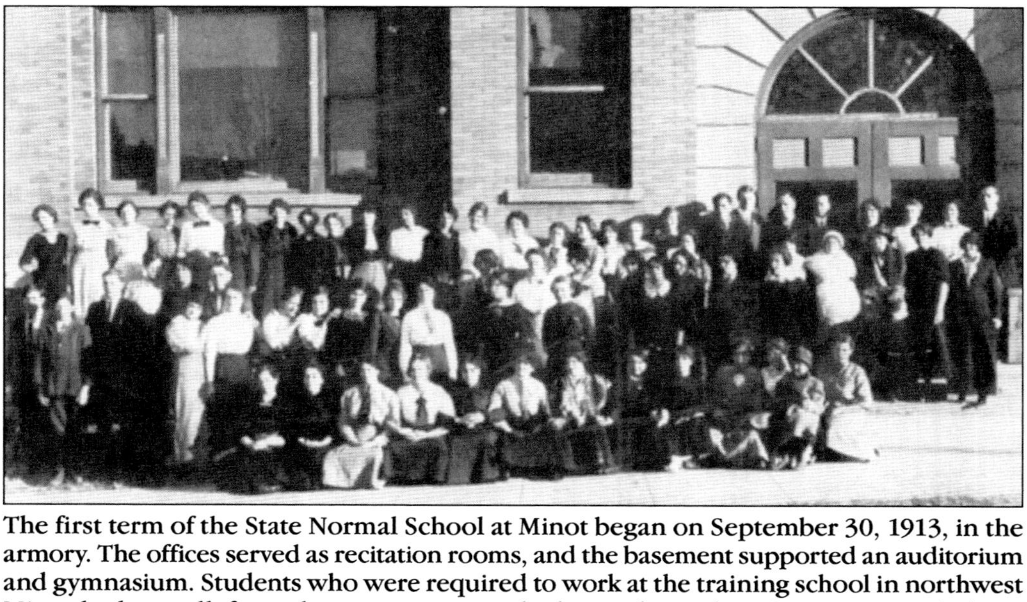

The first term of the State Normal School at Minot began on September 30, 1913, in the armory. The offices served as recitation rooms, and the basement supported an auditorium and gymnasium. Students who were required to work at the training school in northwest Minot had to walk from the armory or use the horse-drawn bus that was provided.

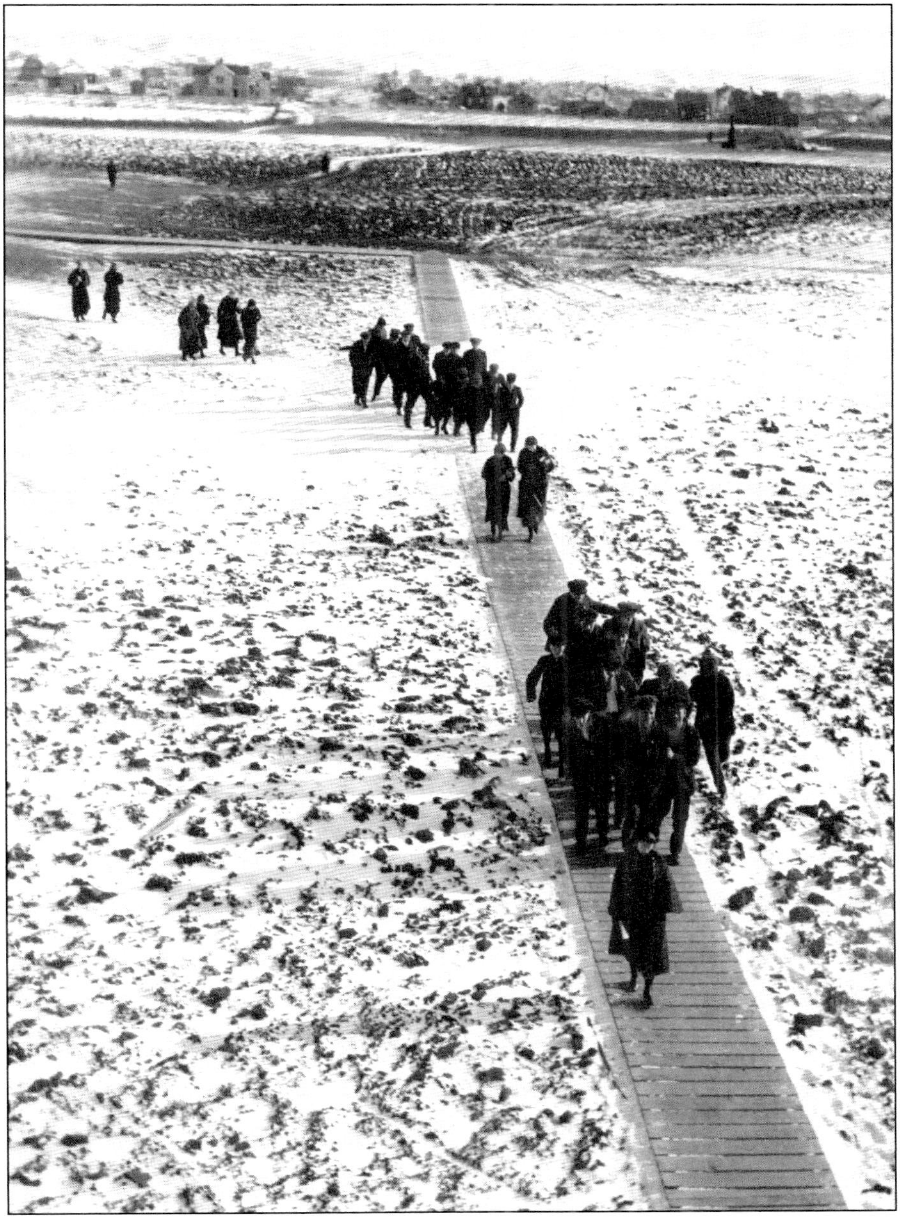

The walk from the Minot Armory to the training school proved to be a cold trip during the winter of 1913–1914. A horse-drawn bus was available, but it proved very unreliable and could not take everybody in one trip. Most students made the long, cold journey on foot. No trees or buildings existed to stop the icy winds that howled off the North Hill slope. Marion Wood, class of 1914, shared her memories of that first term at the armory, "Tho there were hardships that year, I am certain that none of us regret them. The classrooms in the Armory were small, but think of all the floor space for 'gym' work. When we assembled for chapel we did look pitifully few, but emptiness only made our singing sound the finer. We sometimes thought the walk to the model school was too great, but what better exercise could be found."

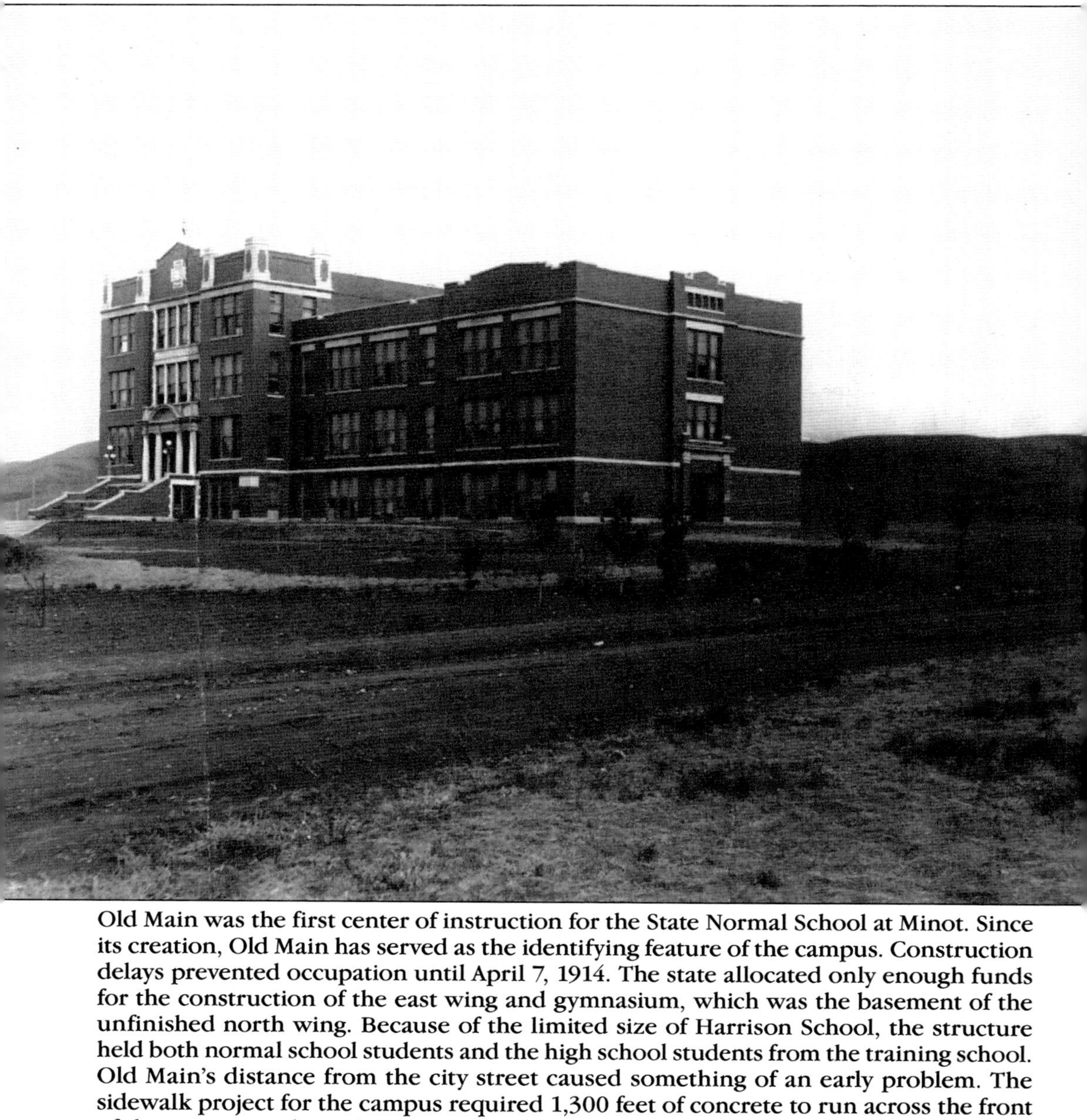

Old Main was the first center of instruction for the State Normal School at Minot. Since its creation, Old Main has served as the identifying feature of the campus. Construction delays prevented occupation until April 7, 1914. The state allocated only enough funds for the construction of the east wing and gymnasium, which was the basement of the unfinished north wing. Because of the limited size of Harrison School, the structure held both normal school students and the high school students from the training school. Old Main's distance from the city street caused something of an early problem. The sidewalk project for the campus required 1,300 feet of concrete to run across the front of the campus and another 800 feet to connect Old Main and the west dormitory with sidewalks. The cost delayed the concrete pour until the summer of 1915.

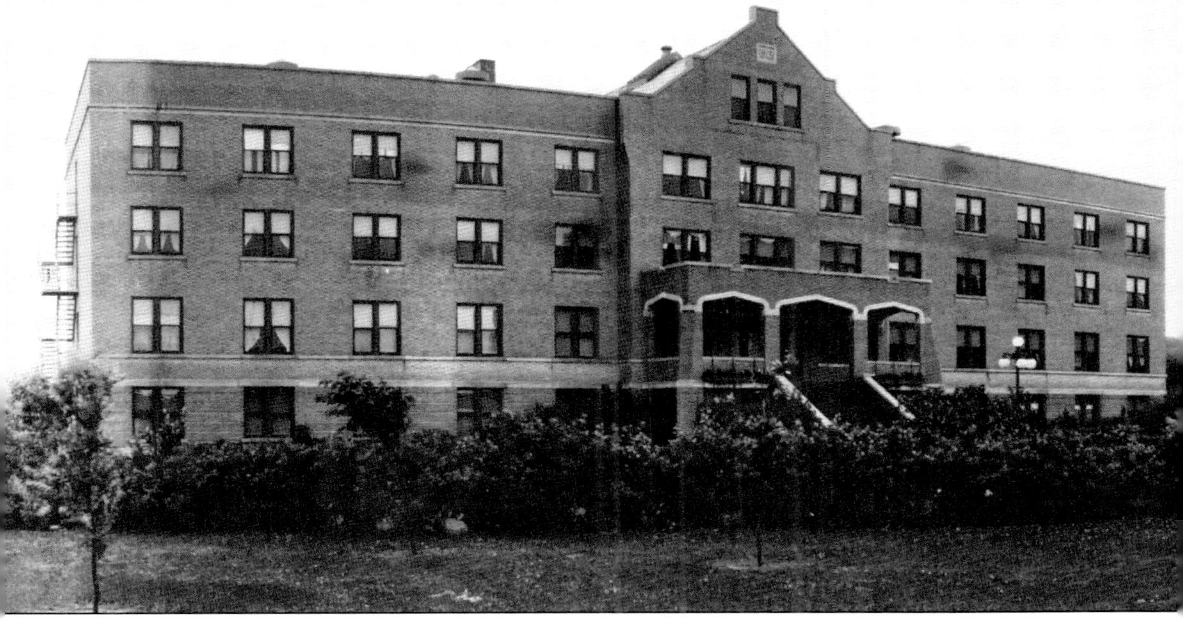

On March 5, 1914, the west dormitory was finally occupied. The fireproof, three-story structure with a basement was constructed of reinforced concrete and pressed brick facing. The basement possessed a splendid kitchen, cold storage rooms, a bakery, and all the modern conveniences to provide food for a large number of students. The west wing had a dining room capable of seating 200 diners and a cafeteria. The remainder of the dormitory consisted of 50 rooms for "roomers." At the request of the campus in 1933, the west dormitory was renamed Pioneer Hall. To a spectator looking toward North Hill, the dormitory appeared to be alone on the landscape. The hedge and lilacs used to line the ellipse drive came from the banks of the Mouse River, ensuring their success in the North Great Plains environment.

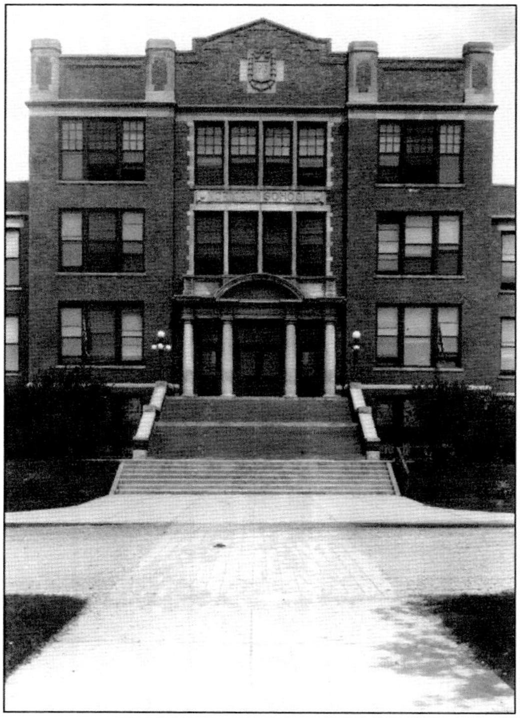

The frieze over the entryway of Old Main was engraved with "Normal School." The year of construction, 1913, was proudly displayed on the apex of the building.

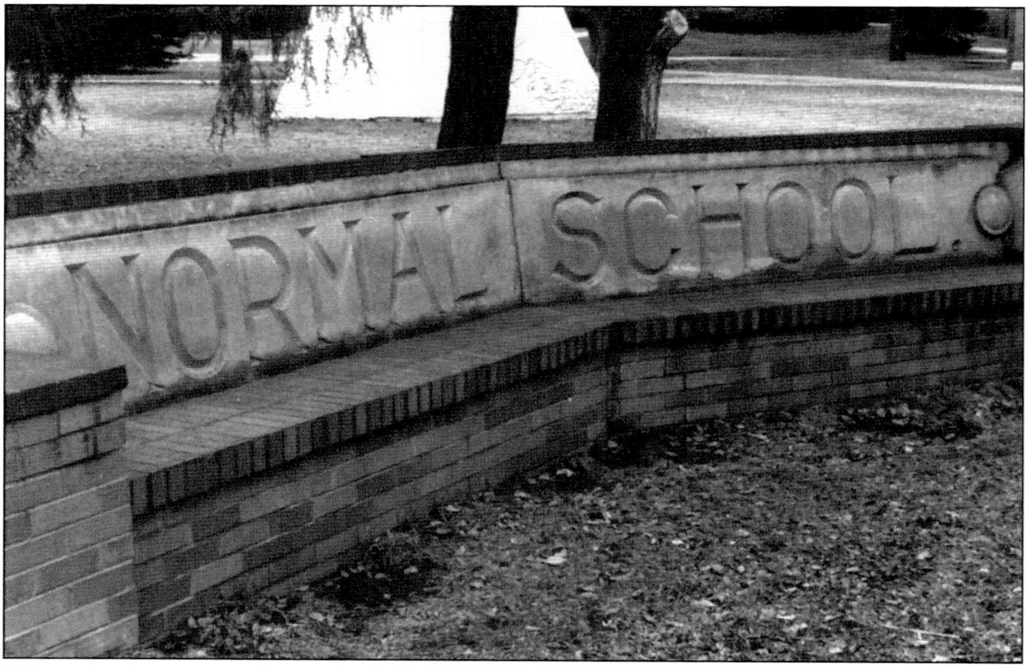

When the institution became the State Teacher's College at Minot, the normal school frieze was removed and replaced with a new engraving, "Teacher's College." The old normal school frieze was placed on the ellipse, where it has reminded everyone of the school's origins.

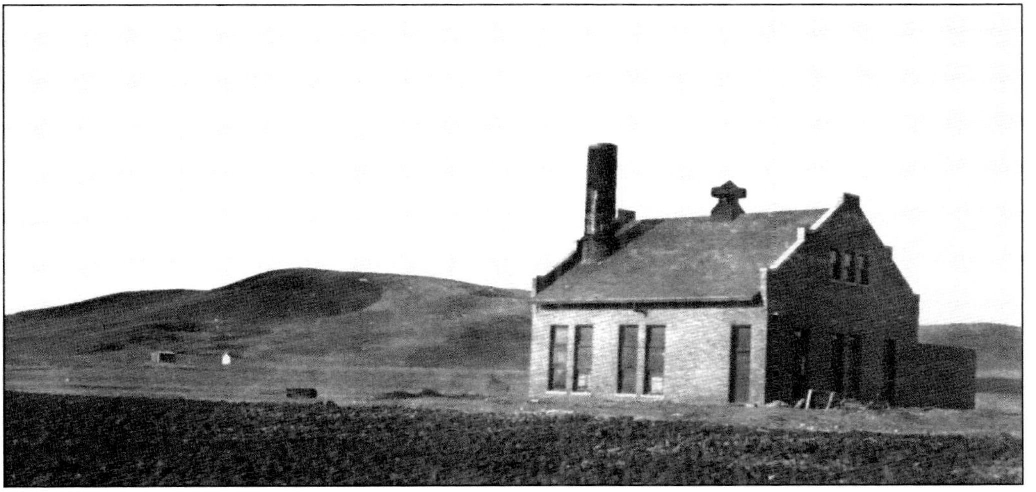

The heating plant was located on the northwest corner of the grounds. It heated Old Main and the west dormitory. In 1913, it received a direct hit by a tornado and required extensive repairs. The building housed a 350-horsepower boiler, which ran on lignite coal. The building also housed the engineering staff. A tunnel connected the plant to Old Main and the dormitory and contained heat and water pipes.

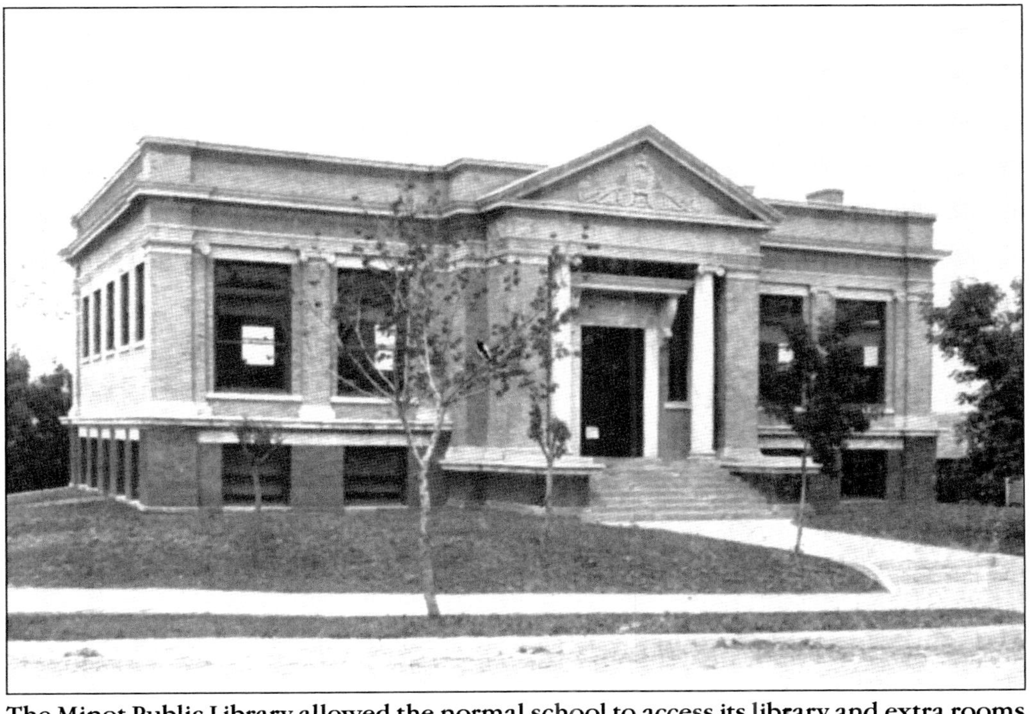

The Minot Public Library allowed the normal school to access its library and extra rooms for recitation. The library was only one block away from the school's temporary operation at the armory. The relationship continued after the campus was opened. Books from the city library were often loaned to the campus library.

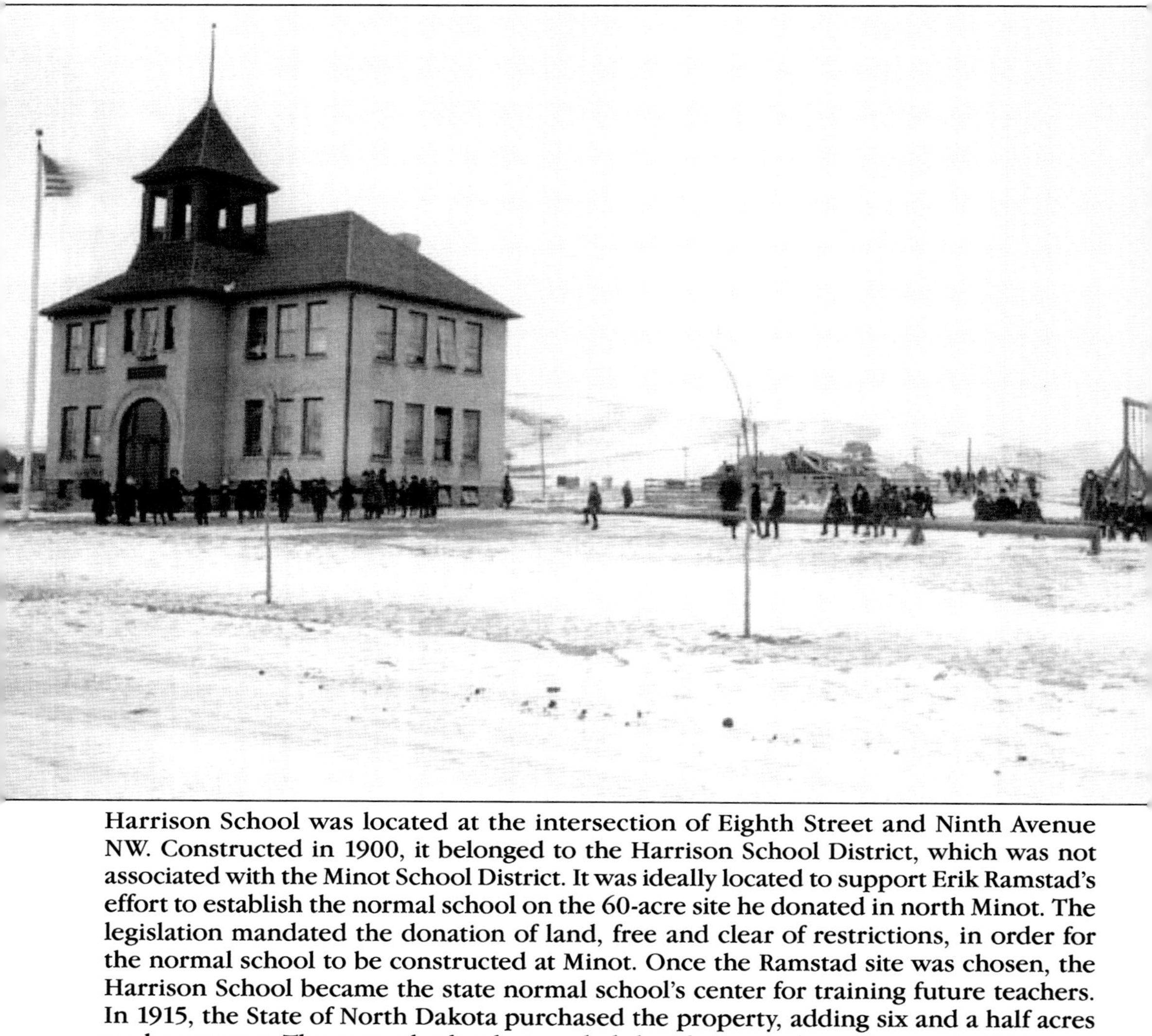

Harrison School was located at the intersection of Eighth Street and Ninth Avenue NW. Constructed in 1900, it belonged to the Harrison School District, which was not associated with the Minot School District. It was ideally located to support Erik Ramstad's effort to establish the normal school on the 60-acre site he donated in north Minot. The legislation mandated the donation of land, free and clear of restrictions, in order for the normal school to be constructed at Minot. Once the Ramstad site was chosen, the Harrison School became the state normal school's center for training future teachers. In 1915, the State of North Dakota purchased the property, adding six and a half acres to the campus. The normal school upgraded the playground equipment the following year. The school contained the primary grades through eighth grade, rooms for the critic instructors, and a small kitchen and cafeteria in the basement. The school gardens were located to the east of the playground.

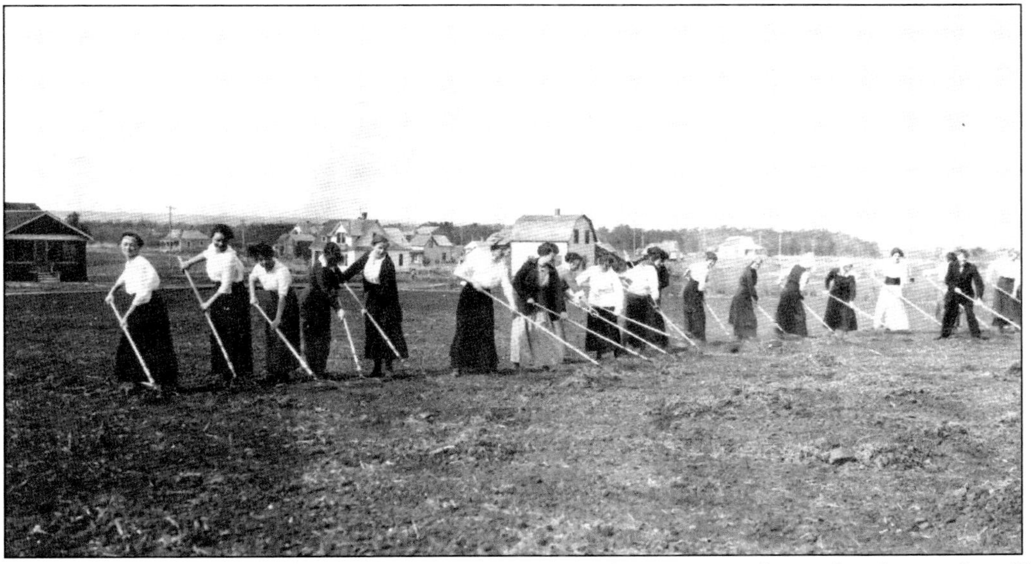

In 1915, the first full academic year on campus, enthusiastic students, faculty, and staff worked in shifts to pull up weeds, pick up and haul away stones, hand rake, and seed the five-acre ellipse in front of Old Main. None of the plants or trees in the original architectural design had been planted due to reductions in funding by the state legislation. The sidewalks had been completed in front of Old Main and leading out to Ninth Avenue, and most of the wooden sidewalks had been removed. Only the sidewalk across the front of campus on Ninth Avenue remained to be completed. Even though Old Main stood on the landscape with only the east wing and part of the north wing completed, everyone was excited and proud of the new campus. Minot had its normal school. President Arthur Griswold Crane is the first person on the right in the photograph below.

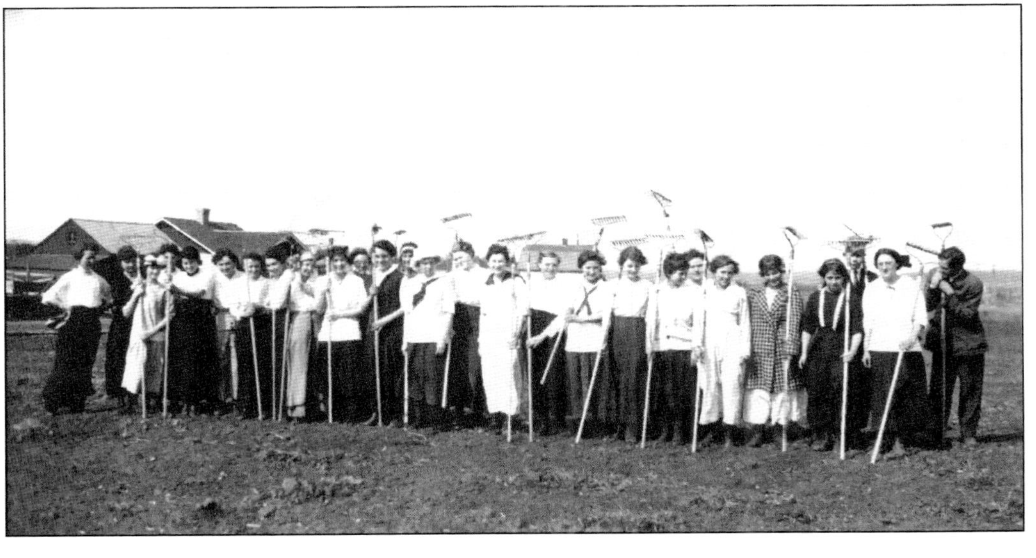

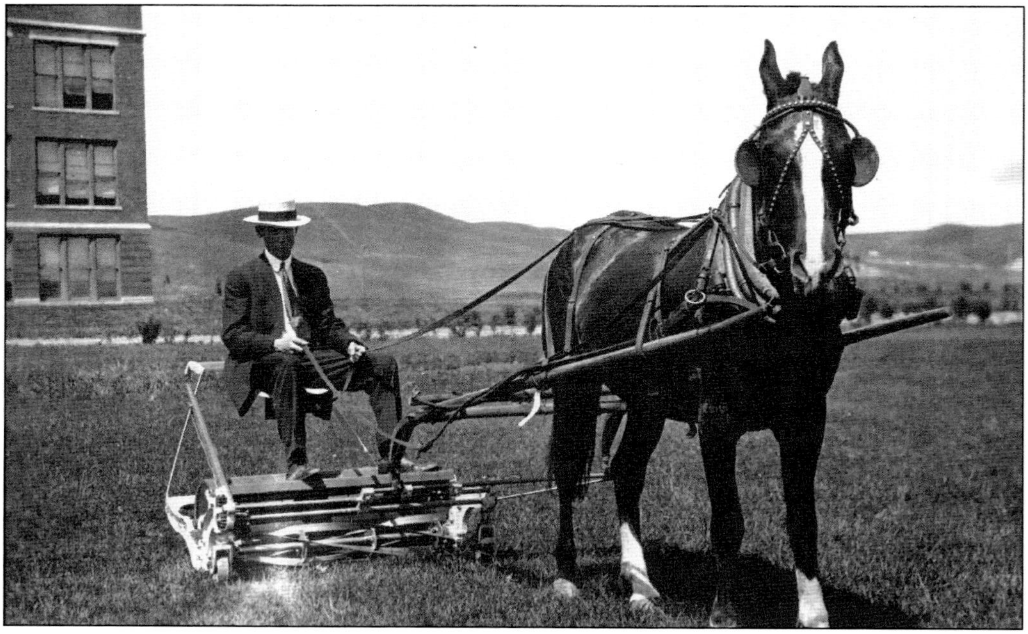

On July 5, 1916, James McArthur, the campus botany and agricultural instructor, took his turn cutting the grass on the ellipse. The area was used for sports, celebrations, and class activities. Note the blinders (blinkers) on the horse.

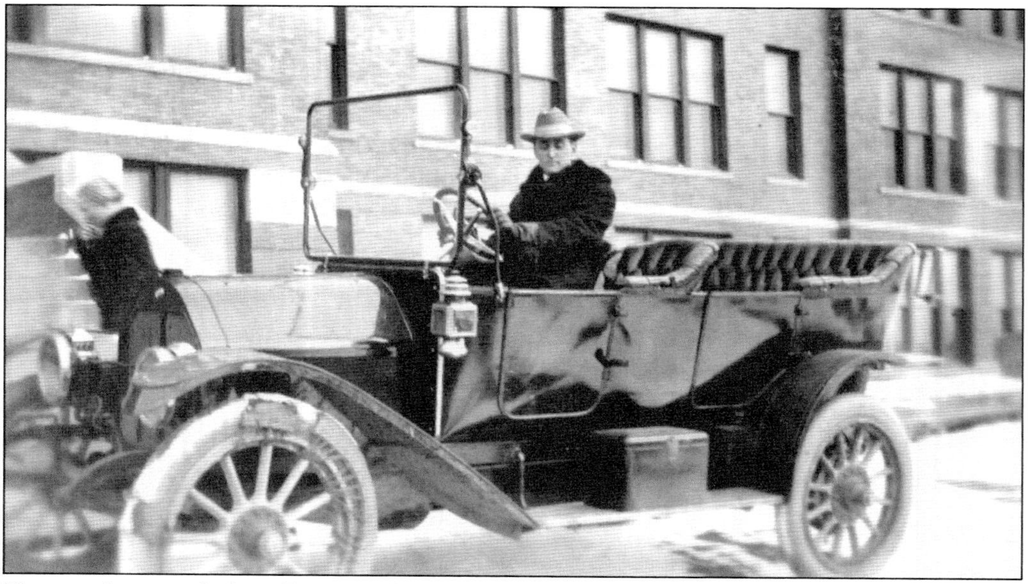

The road around the ellipse in front of Old Main did not always exist. Initially only paths and the concrete sidewalk to the west dormitory crossed in front of the building. Then, in 1914, president Arthur Griswold Crane drove his vehicle, an Overland model (as shown below), up the lawn and around what would become the ellipse drive, a feature on the modern campus.

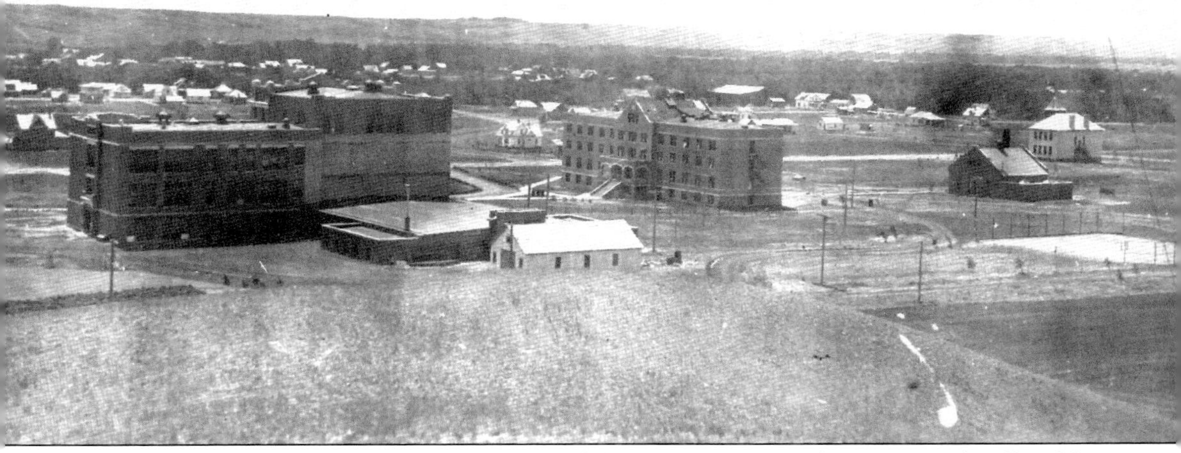

This fall 1915 photograph captures a view of the entire campus from Normal Hill. Old Main is visible to the left. Only its east wing and the basement of the north wing are completed. The west dormitory stands in the center. The power plant is on the right foreground. In the right background is Harrison School, which the state had acquired as the institution's training school. The edge of northwest Minot can be seen in the left background. The tree line across the photograph marks the location of the meandering Mouse River.

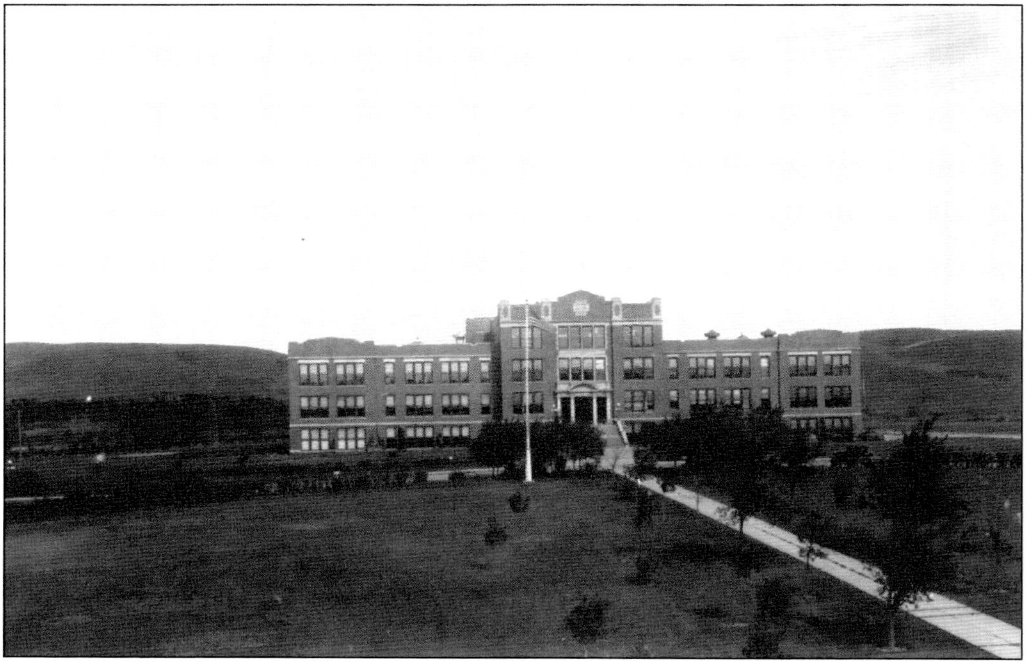

On March 24, 1924, the long-awaited west wing of Old Main was completed and many of the plants and trees enjoyed today were planted. These included Persian lilac, cranberry, coralberry, snowberry, alpine currant, flowering plum, cut leaf elder, golden elder, ginnala maple, Hansa rose, peonies, iris, and phlox. On the east side of campus, 168 fruit trees were planted. Only a few of the apple trees remain.

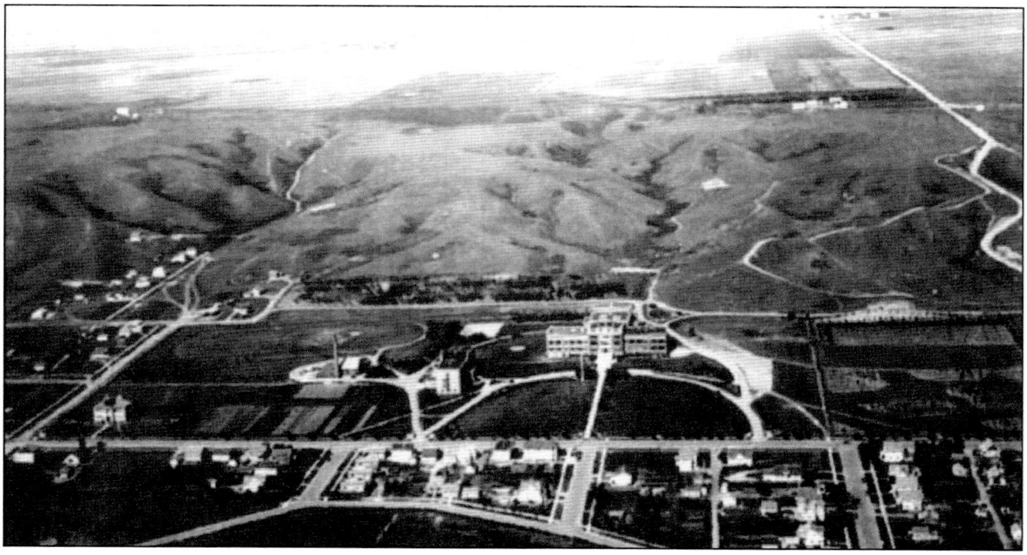

By the end of 1924, the campus layout as envisioned by the founders was finally achieved. The campus had Old Main, the west dormitory, the power plant, Harrison School, the gardens, and a track and field. The roads and sidewalks were concrete. Moreover, the community around the campus was starting to develop. With the exception of two small towns, only empty prairie extended north to the Canadian border.

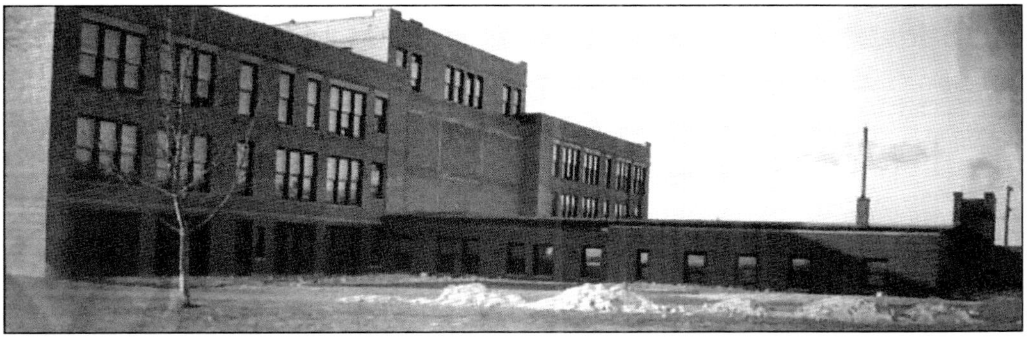

The campus gymnasium was located in the partially completed third wing of Old Main. The majority of the facility lay below ground. On March 5, 1925, appropriated funds were allocated for the remainder of the wing, which included an auditorium that was to be constructed over top of the gymnasium.

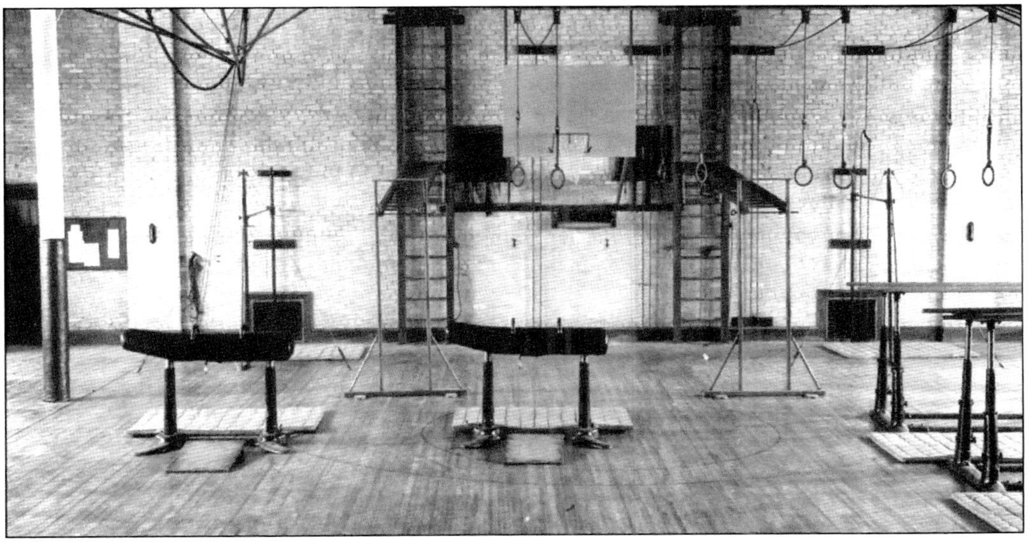

The equipment in the Old Main gymnasium supported the physical education program for both the normal and training schools. It was well equipped. It was used as a multipurpose facility until 1925 when the auditorium was constructed above it, which completed the original architectural design.

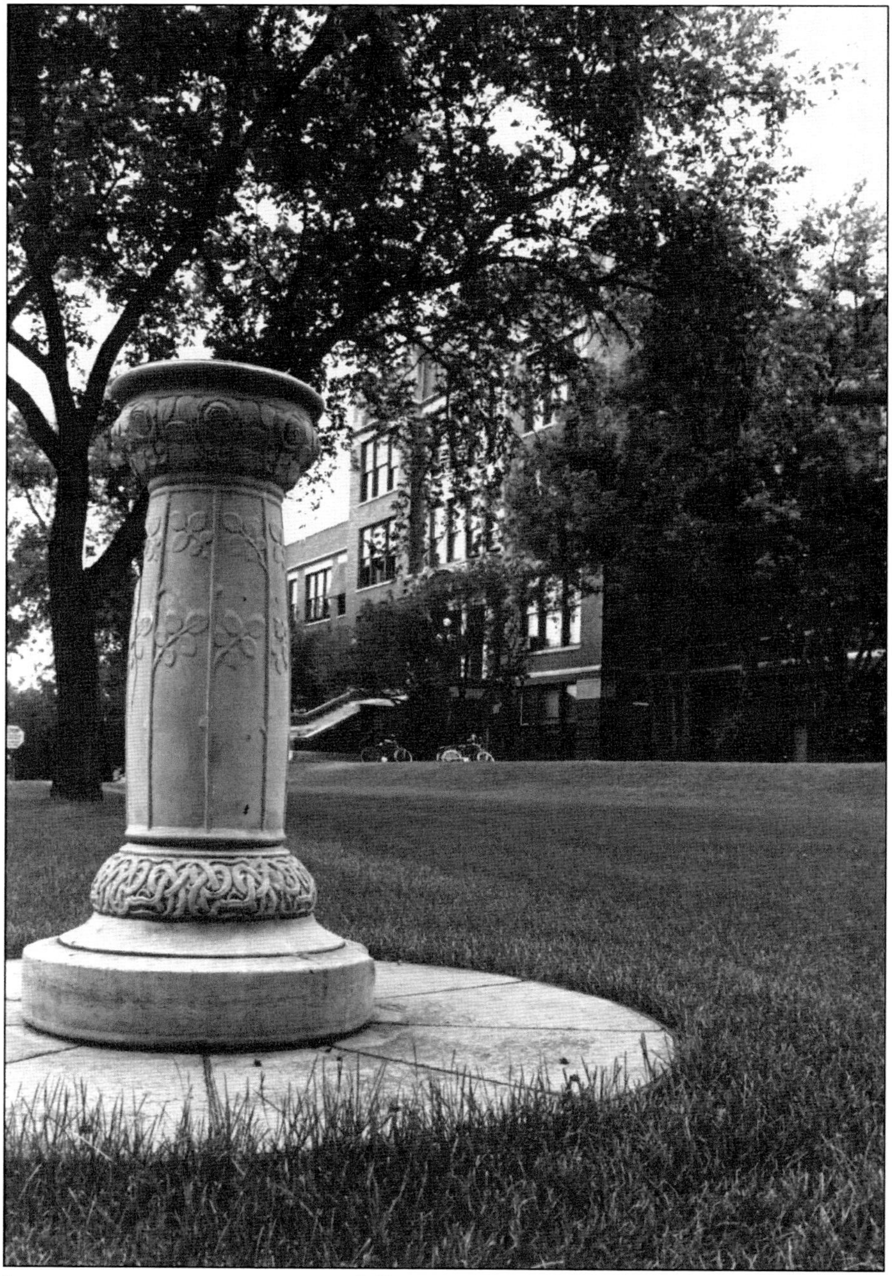

Over the past century, many trees and flowering plants have been added to the landscape in front of Old Main and around the campus. Once a barren, fenced pasture, the space now occupied by the campus has been transformed into an oasis on the north rim of the Mouse River Valley. Trees and plant life have become an intricate part of the campus, shading its facilities and occupants and providing a natural identity and sense of place to the campus. This early-1940s photograph captures the charm of the ellipse as the observer overlooks the entryway of Old Main. The sundial was a memorial gift to the campus from the class of 1934.

Two

THE COMMUNITY AND REGION

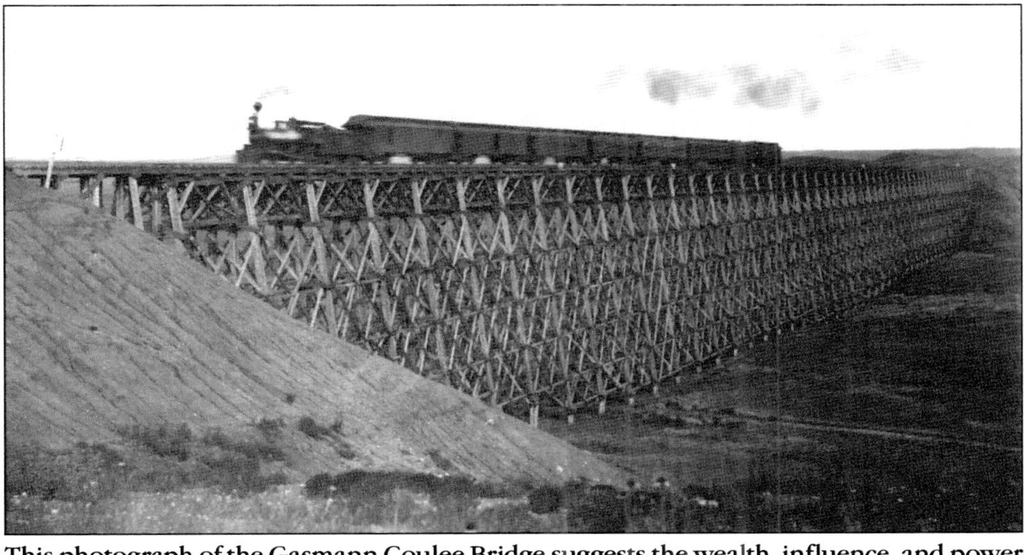

This photograph of the Gasmann Coulee Bridge suggests the wealth, influence, and power of the railroad on the Northern Great Plains at the dawn of the 20th century. Built by the Great Northern Railway just west of Minot during the winter of 1886–1887, the trestle took a direct hit from a tornado in 1898 and was destroyed. This photograph shows the original structure. By the second decade of the 20th century, the railroad was the primary employer in Minot. Facilities included a roundhouse, car house, and rail shops. By then, the SOO Line had arrived. Minot boasted two depots, and over a dozen trains arrived daily. The normal school's annual catalog recommended travel to the institution by train and offered transportation to and from the campus or nearby hotels.

13. LET US SUM UP

Expenses are low.

Minot is easily accessible.

More education means more money.

Happy social occasions are numerous.

The dormitory provides a fine student home.

The school is new and the equipment modern.

The students are serious and earnest of purpose.

Every graduate is sure of appointment.

The school encourages student Christian associations.

There is a democratic spirit. Simplicity of dress and manners is the rule.

At Minot, you may earn while you learn. A student can earn his way and remain on a par with those of means.

There is a large Model School where students secure apprentice teaching under normal conditions.

Students reserve individual help and enjoy close associations with instructors.

The Minot State Teachers College knows the need of the schools in northwestern North Dakota better than any other institution; therefore, it is better able to train teachers to meet the conditions of this section of the state.

"Why not Minot" State Teachers College

It was during this period that Minot, the Magic City, adopted the "Why Not Minot?" marketing and booster slogan. The logo adorned all the community's advertisements, brochures, maps, and business correspondence. In response, the State Normal School at Minot, like many businesses in the community, incorporated the slogan into its publications.

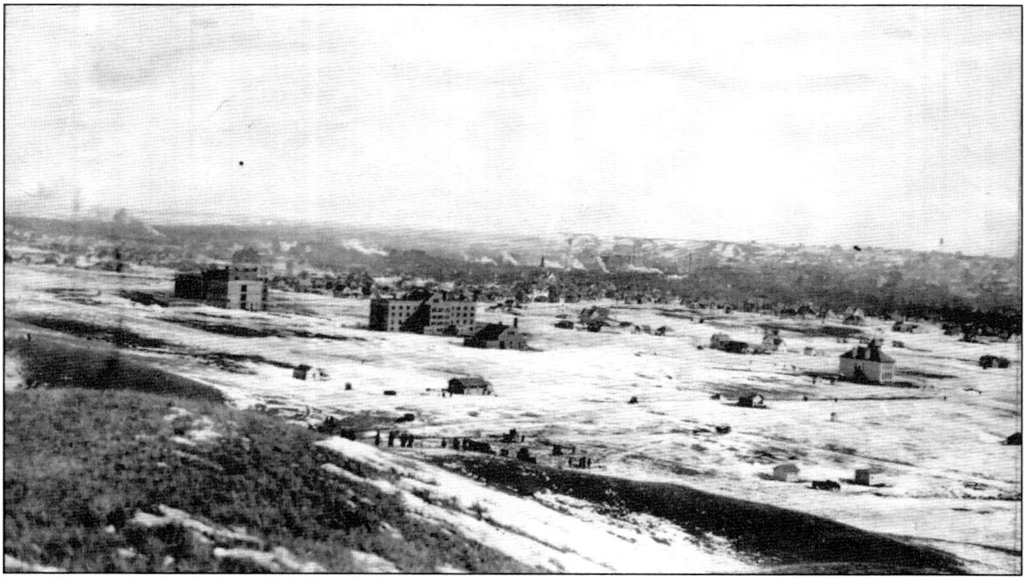

This 1916 photograph depicts the city of Minot, with its population of slightly more than 7,000 people, as situated in the Mouse River Valley. The campus buildings (center) were then located on the northwest edge of the city. In the distance, smoke rises from the community's coal- and wood-burning furnaces. In the foreground, people gather to talk and prepare for the climb up Normal Hill for a ski tournament.

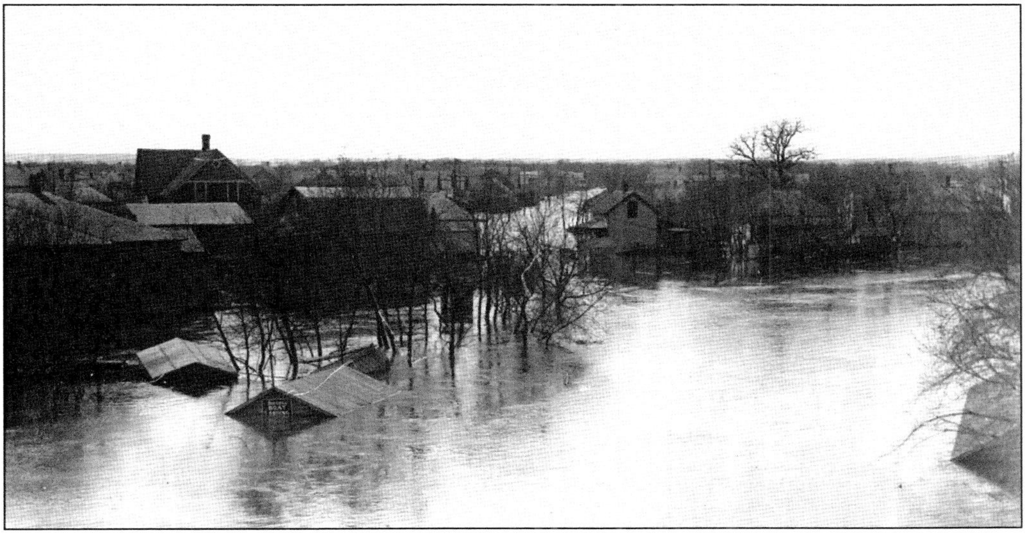

Mouse River floods have plagued the city of Minot from the beginning. In 1916, the river crested at 19.05 feet on the flood gauge on the Great Northern Railway roundhouse. The water did considerable damage to northeast and northwest Minot. Waters never reached the campus due to the gradual slope of North Hill. The river flooded again in 1923, 1925, 1927, and 1928.

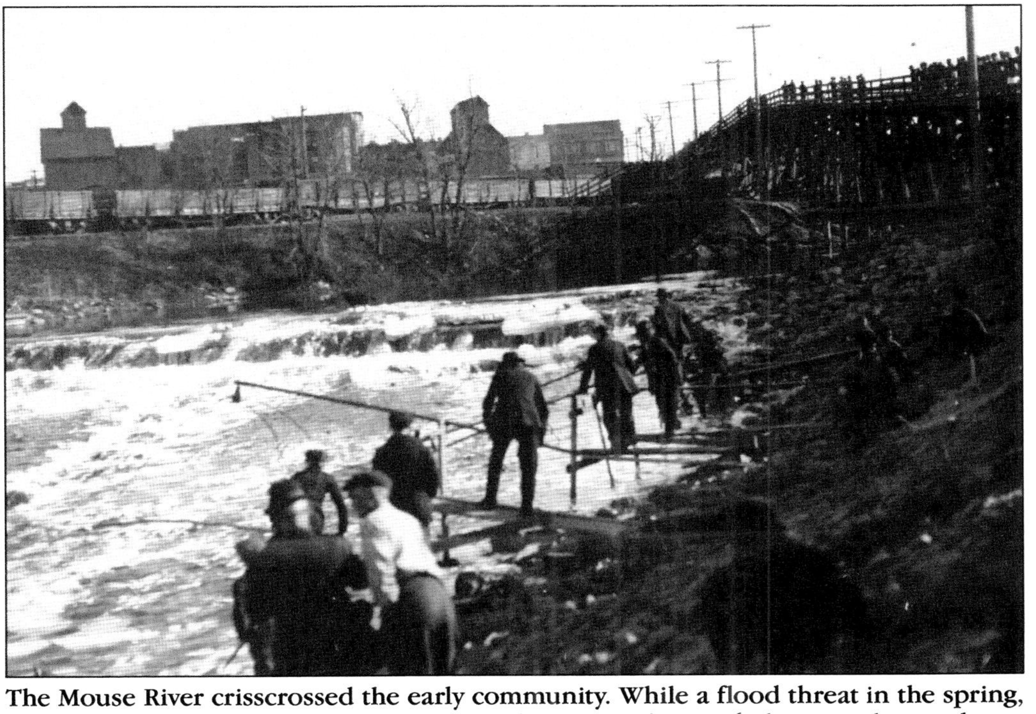

The Mouse River crisscrossed the early community. While a flood threat in the spring, it also provided the community with ice and sport. In this 1916 photograph, men brave cascading sheets of ice to fish the river beneath of the Ward Street viaduct (which was south of the campus). In the background, boxcars of the Great Northern Railway pass and the back side of Central Avenue stands out against the sky.

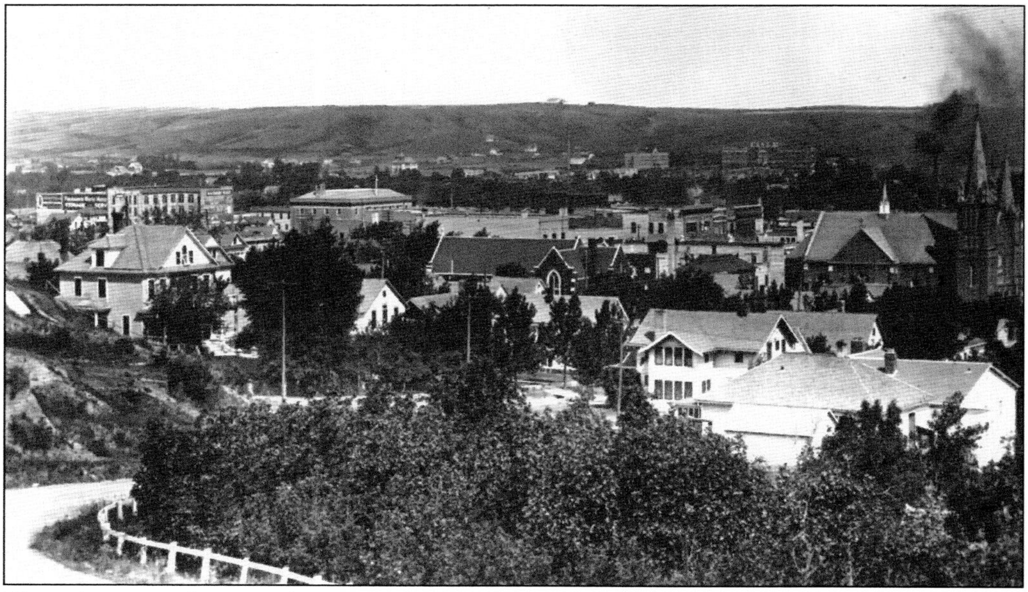

This photograph was taken on South Hill at the top of Ramstad Street looking north toward the campus. The west dormitory and Old Main are in the right background. In the far background, only a few buildings are visible on the otherwise barren sides and top of north hill. The wooded site on the hillside is one of the locations proposed for the institution during the communities' 1911–1912 debate.

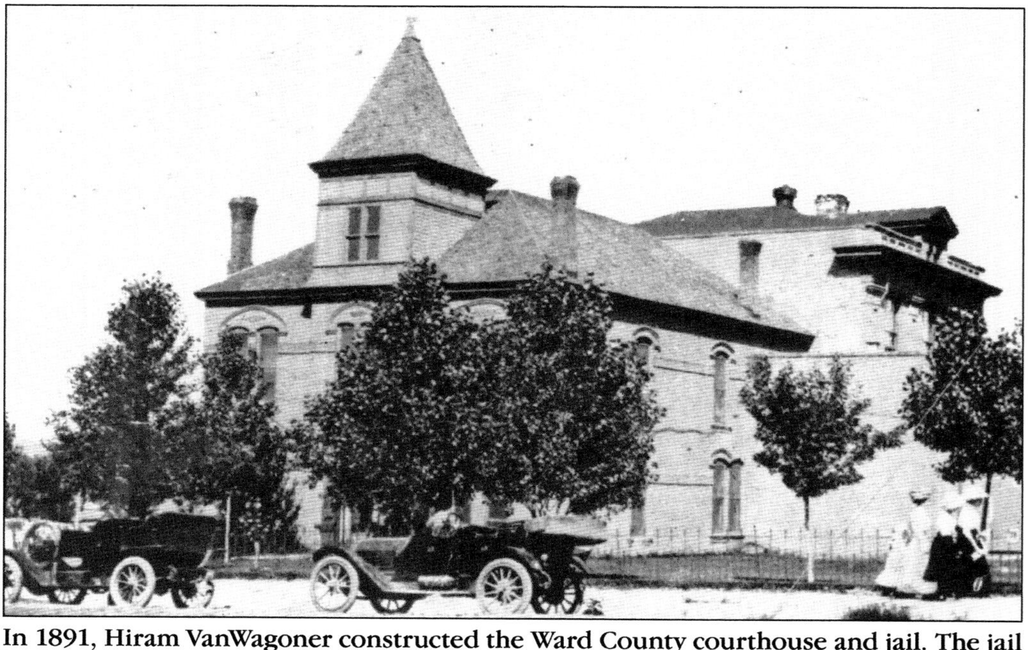

In 1891, Hiram VanWagoner constructed the Ward County courthouse and jail. The jail was enlarged in 1904. During the summer of 1913, the facility was the scene of continuous action. The contractor for Old Main and the west dormitory had become entangled in a labor dispute with transient Wobblies and the local Socialist Party. Authorities filled the jail to capacity with protestors that clogged Minot's downtown area.

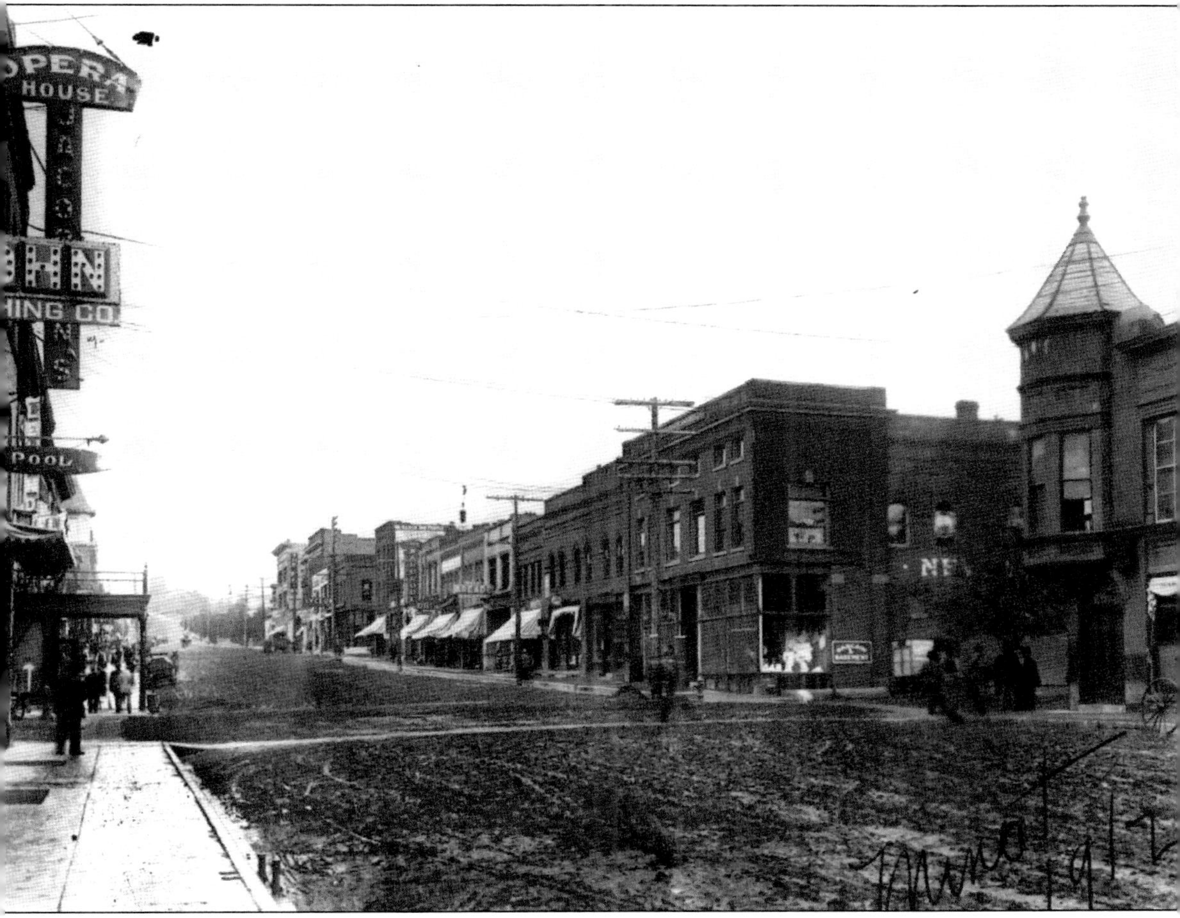

This 1912 photograph captures the heart of downtown Minot at the intersection of Main Street and Central Avenue. On the right is the Second National Bank, home of the Minot Socialist Local. Across Central Avenue to the south is the New York Store, the old Peter P. Lee Block. To the left is the Jacobson Hardware Store, opera house, Pioneer Store, Boston Store, and pool hall. In 1923, most of this block was destroyed by fire. The Leland Hotel was located across the street on the southeast corner and has the portico extended over the sidewalk. The street remained dirt until 1913 when contractor David Dinnie paved the surface with creosoted wood blocks. The project set off a labor dispute. During heavy rains, parts of the street often floated away. (State Historical Society of North Dakota.)

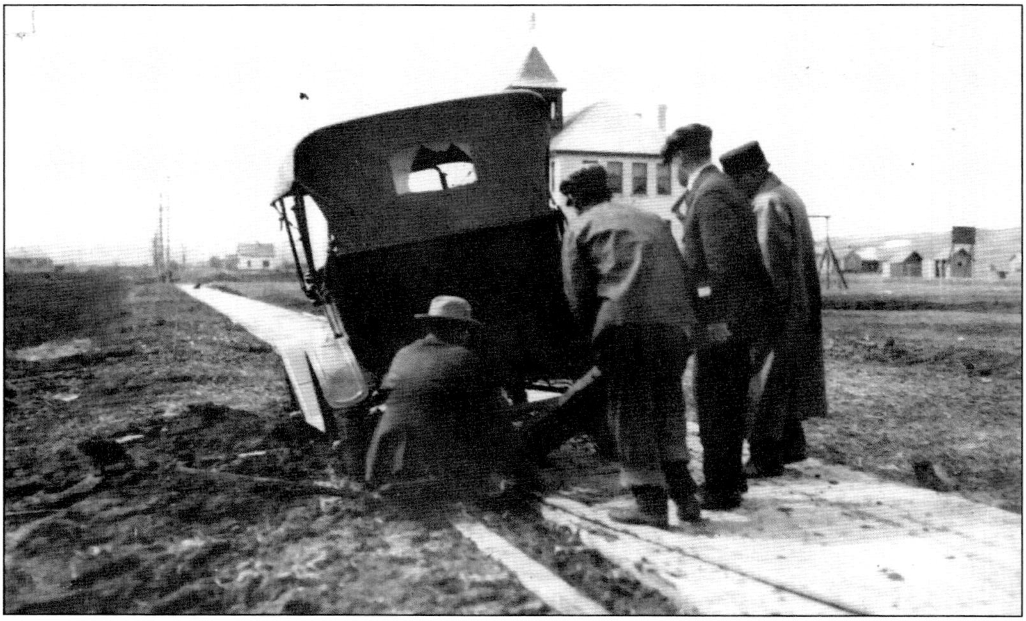

The roads around the campus remained unpaved throughout most of the 1920s. In his effort to avoid the muddy street, Minot's street commissioner tried to use the campus sidewalk as a roadway. As the photograph above shows, he failed.

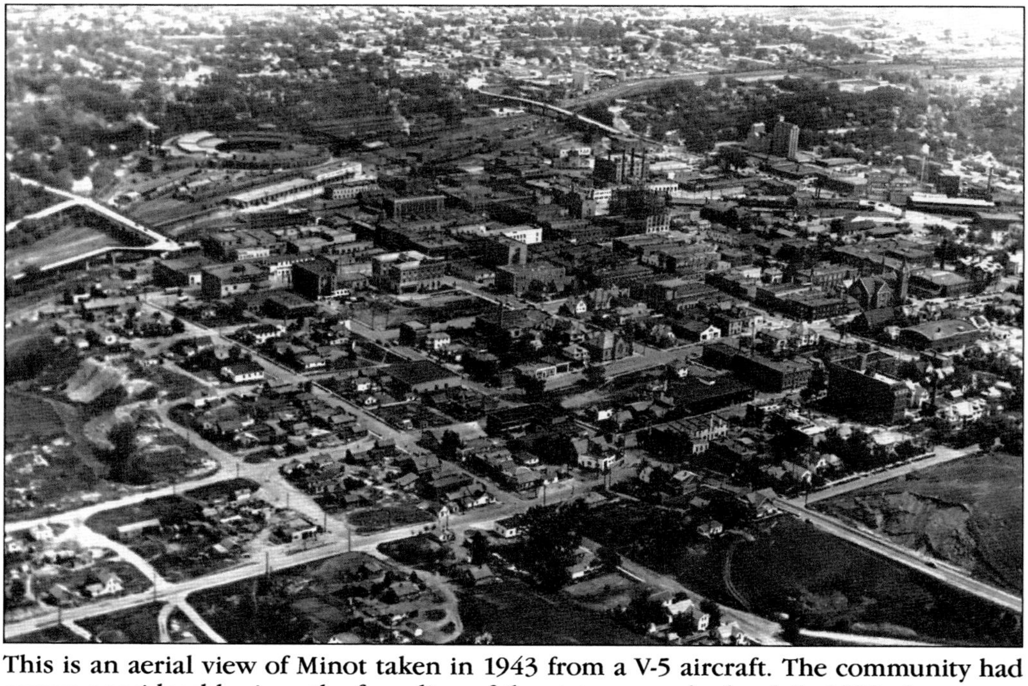

This is an aerial view of Minot taken in 1943 from a V-5 aircraft. The community had grown considerably since the founding of the state normal school. In 1913, downtown Minot contained a large number of hotels and railroad-associated business. The Great Northern Railway roundhouse and car house are in the left background. The campus is not visible in this photograph.

Three

Life at the Normal School

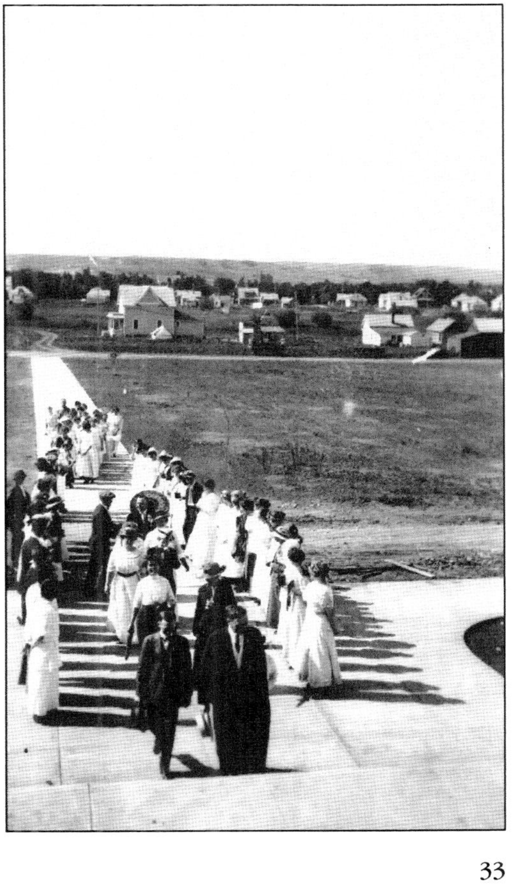

The school year ended on the last day of the spring term, Class Day, which was part of Commencement Week, with a processional that started on the ellipse. In this photograph, taken from the steps of Old Main on June 24, 1915, president Arthur Griswold Crane enters Old Main with the faculty, followed by the departing senior class. The lower classes entered last. Summer school commenced on July 1, 1915. The sidewalks had been poured recently; construction materials are still visible. The ellipse is still barren and has not been raked and seeded. The sparsely populated northwest corner of Minot, the tree-lined Mouse River, and South Hill are visible in the background.

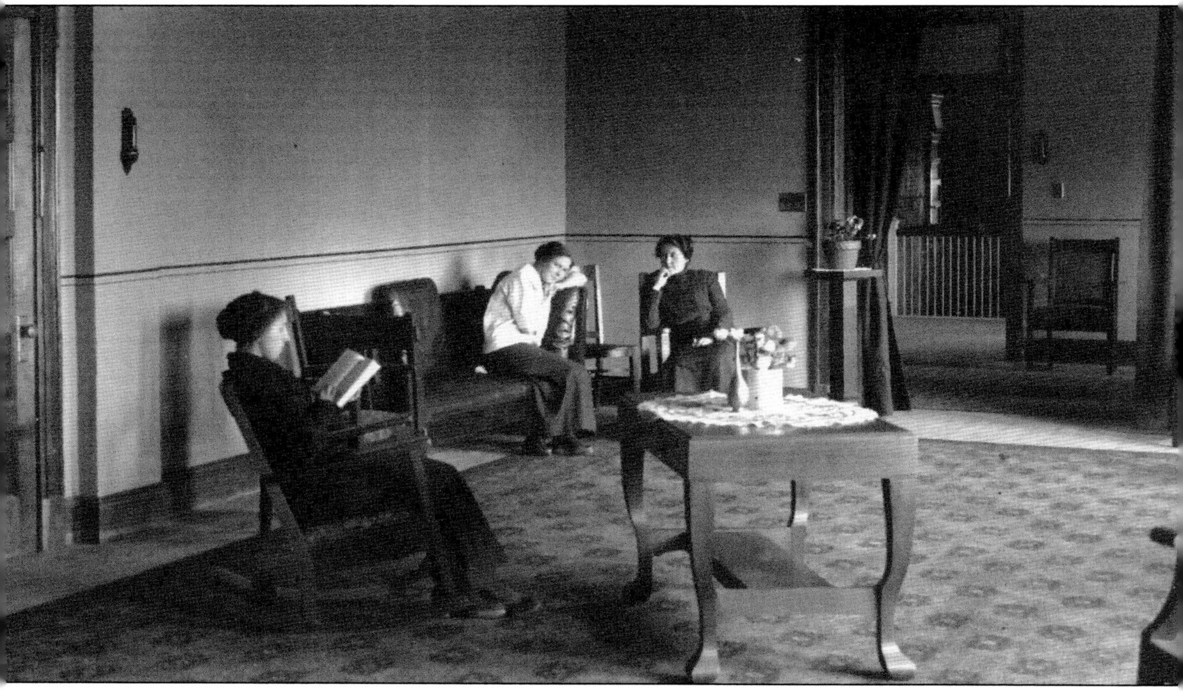

This photograph captures students engaged in conversation and reading in the west dormitory parlor, which was located on the first floor of the dormitory. The room was used as a gathering place where students congregated to talk, play piano, and sing songs. They were also popular for receptions and afternoon teas, which were usually chaperoned by the dormitory matron or club advisor. Reading rooms, which played an essential role in the lives of students, as television, computers, and radios did not exist, were located on the second and third floors. The wicker rockers, settees, and tables were hard oak. The dormitory matron maintained the rooms with assistance from the students. Flowers were a common sight in the dormitory. They came from the campus gardens, which were located behind the dormitory. Sliding doors and curtains were installed at the main entrances to the parlor and could be closed for privacy.

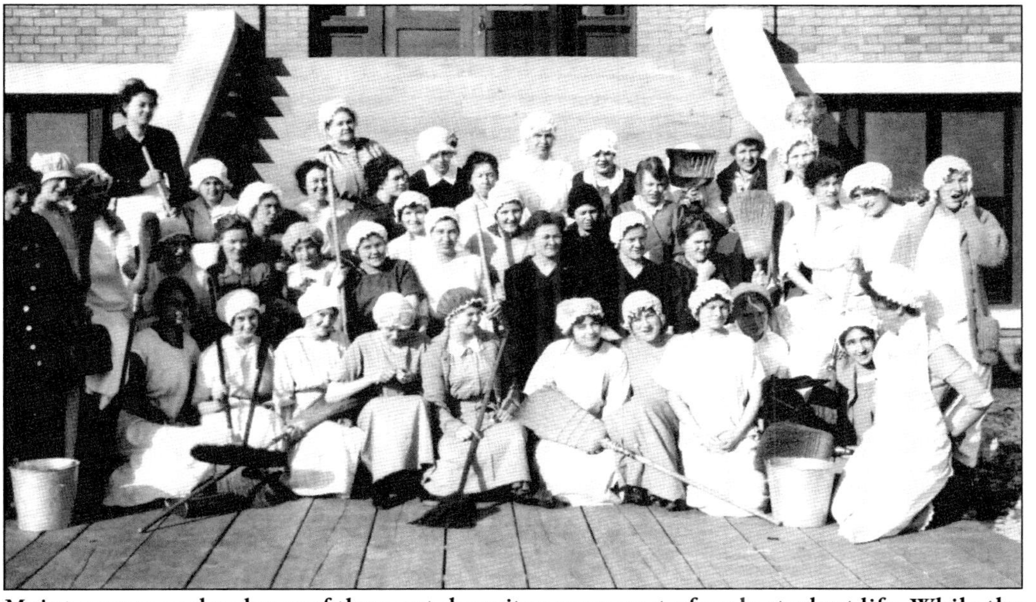

Maintenance and upkeep of the west dormitory was part of early student life. While the dormitory matron strove to make the dormitory homelike and sociable, occupants did much of the cleaning. Note the aprons, overalls, and dust caps. There were no modern appliances available, but buckets, mops, and brooms were plentiful. Female janitors were not hired until the early 1920s.

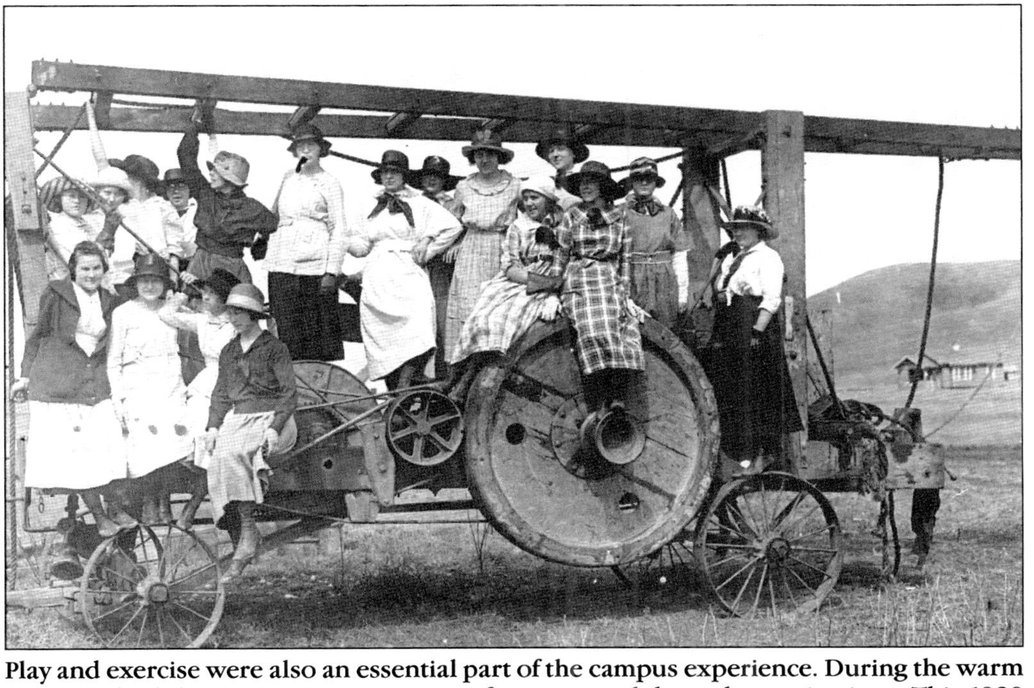

Play and exercise were also an essential part of the campus experience. During the warm months, day hikes were a common event for campus clubs and organizations. This 1920 photograph captures one of the girls' clubs on a field excursion on North Hill and the prairie beyond.

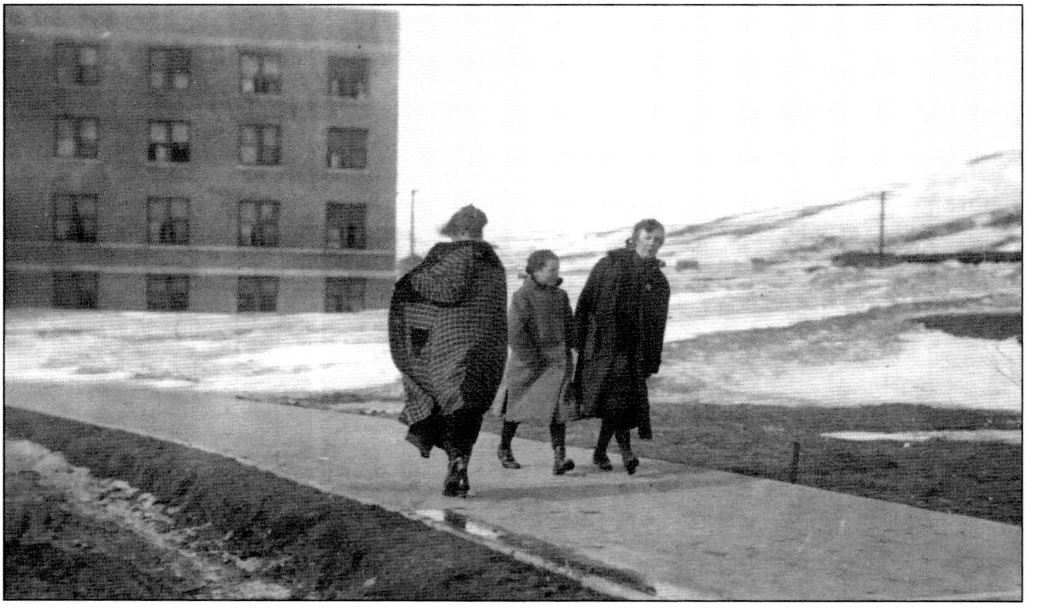

During the winter on the Northern Great Plains, it was not always a pleasant experience walking from building to building. This 1915 photograph captures students walking from the west dormitory to Old Main on a cloudy, overcast day. Beneath the raised walkway, a tunnel connected the buildings and was used to move people between the buildings in particularly inclement weather. It also housed the campus heating pipes and water system.

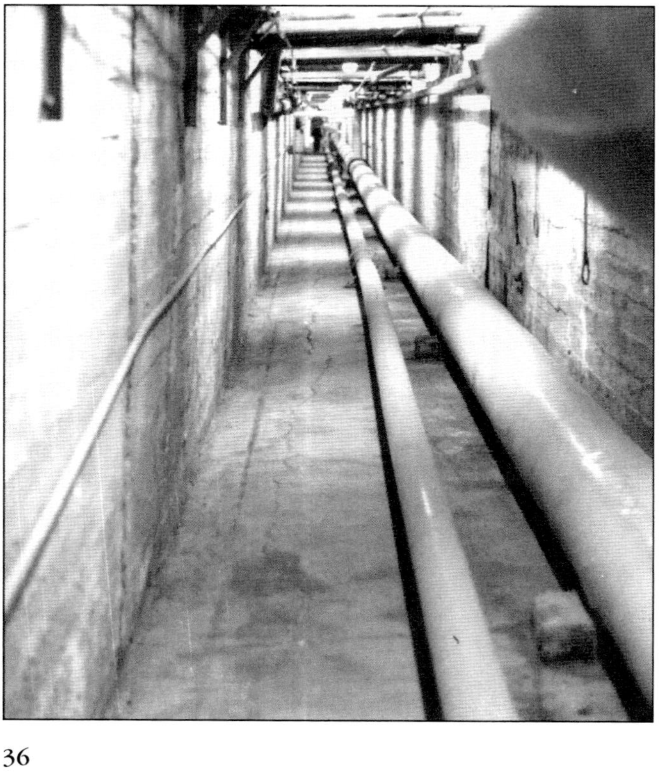

The tunnel that connected the buildings measured six feet wide and eight feet tall. To reduce the "closed in" feeling, the walls were painted a friendly green. The area was remarkably dry and warm compared to the weather aboveground during the winter months.

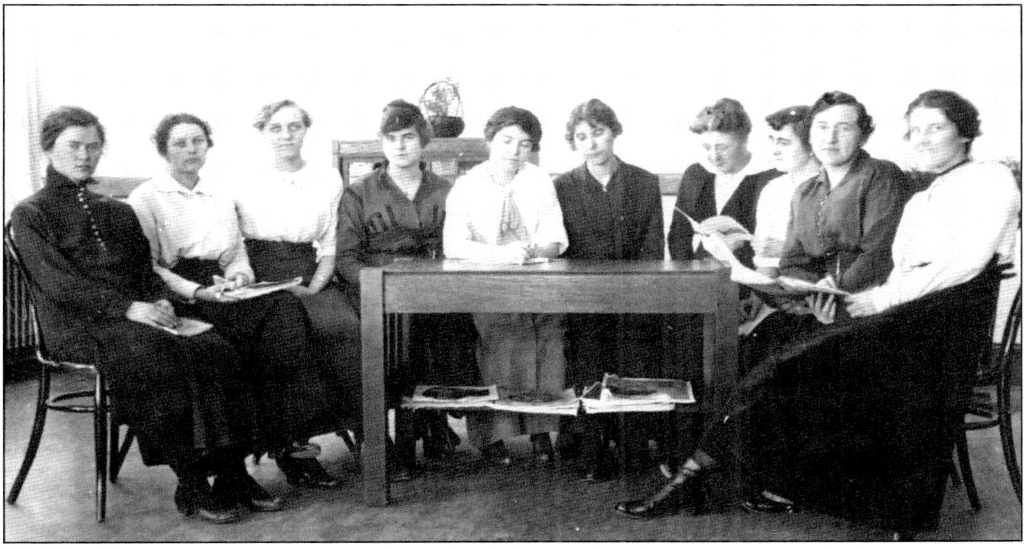

Student organizations and societies were an essential part of campus life. Evolving on campus to address the needs of students and the community, these organizations enhanced the educational programs. Above, one of the first organizations was the Young Women's Christian Association. Seated, from left to right, are president Inga Nordsletten, Florence Ducan, Bernice Southerly, Florence Franklin, Tena Kohrman, and their advisors Mrs. William Clarke, Huldah L. Winsted, Mary Agnes Cantell, Florence Perkett, and Laura May Crane. Other groups included the girls' and boys' Glee Clubs, Catholic Student Association, Vestalian Literary Society, and Webster Debating Club. Due to the low enrollment of men during the early years, the boys' Glee Club (below) accepted young men from the training school. Amy Simpson (center) was the advisor and director.

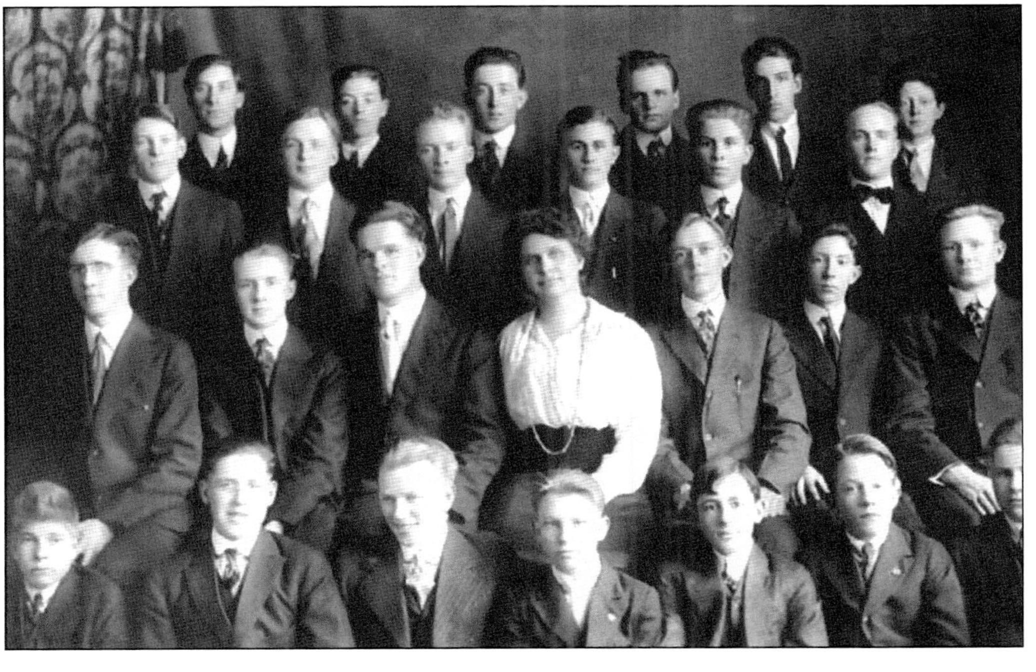

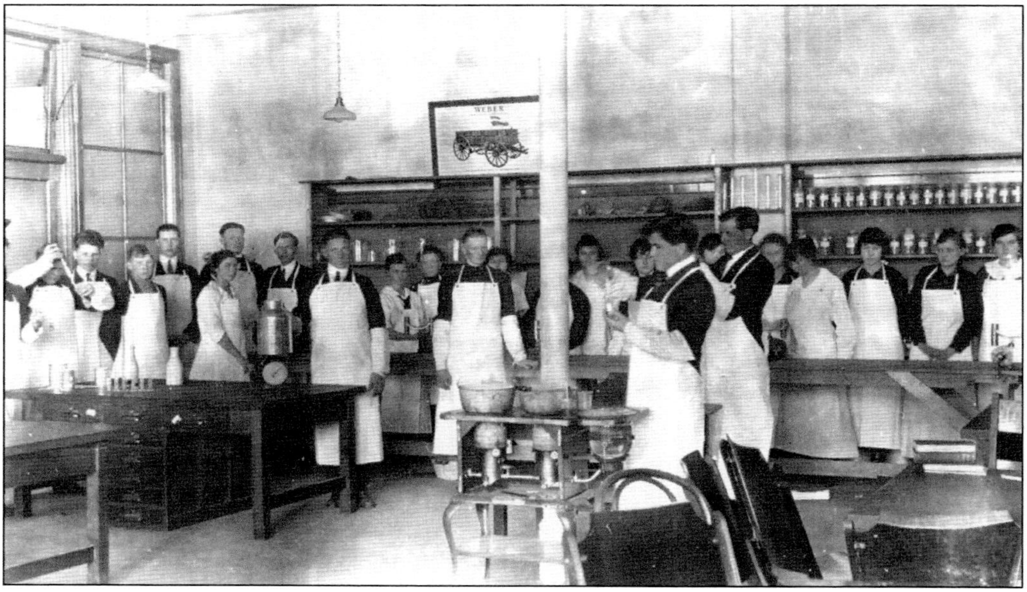

This 1917 photograph captures students conducting milk testing in the agricultural science laboratory of Old Main. At the time, the safety of milk for drinking was a concern. In an agricultural and ranching region, the knowledge of milk testing and testing skills fit the curriculum and proved useful for the communities.

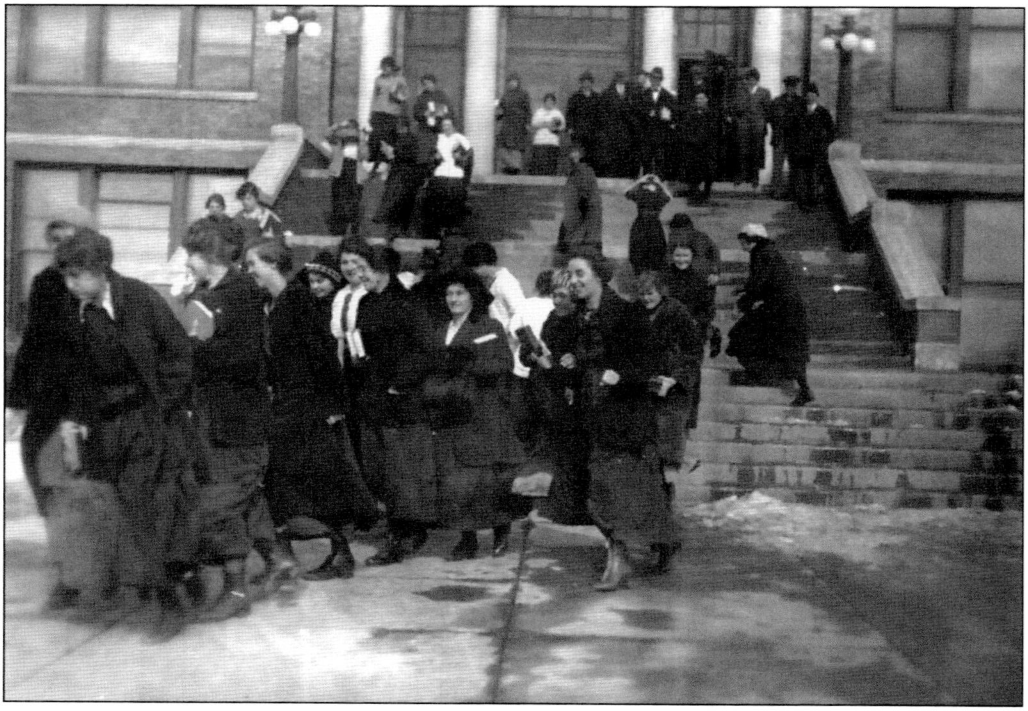

Much like today, students enjoyed the school day's end. This 1916 photograph reveals normal school students, faculty, and seniors from the training school leaving Old Main at the end of the school day.

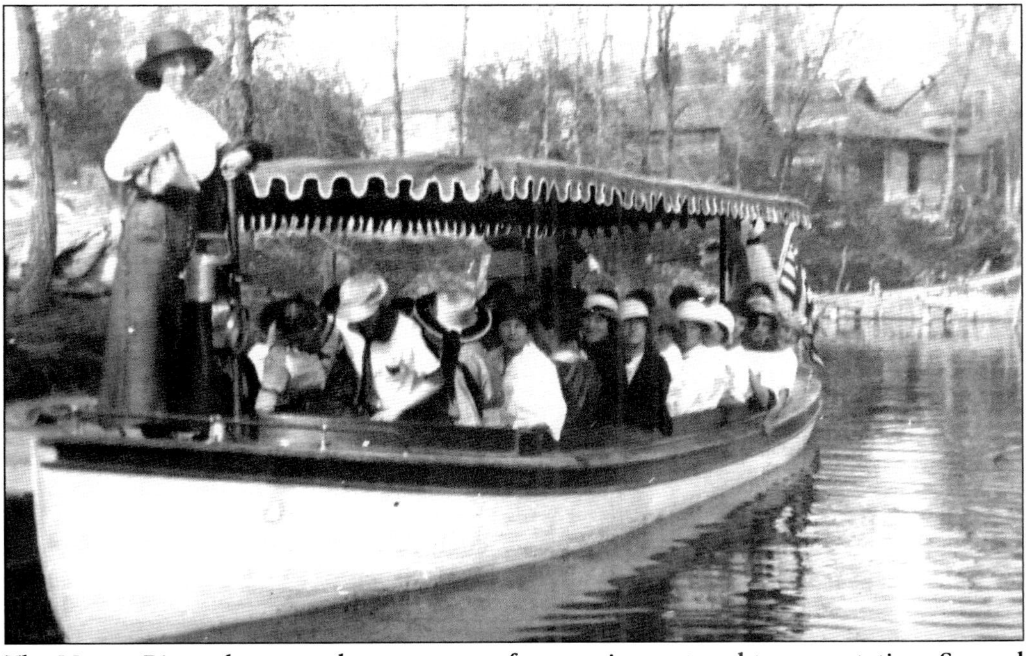

The Mouse River also served as a source of entertainment and transportation. Several motor-driven launches operated near the city parks and offered trips up and down the river for a small fee. In this photograph, members of the campus *Red and Green* newspaper took a launch for an afternoon trip.

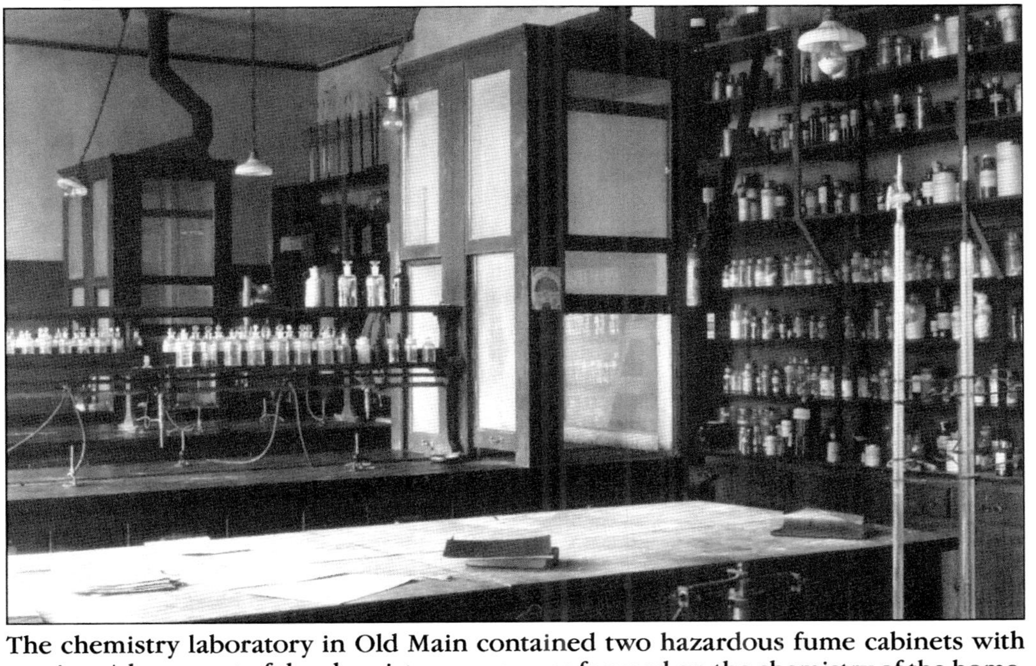

The chemistry laboratory in Old Main contained two hazardous fume cabinets with venting. A large part of the chemistry course was focused on the chemistry of the home. Students conducted careful laboratory study of soaps, cleaning compounds, dyes, drinking waters, fermentation, milk and dairy products, starch, and sugars.

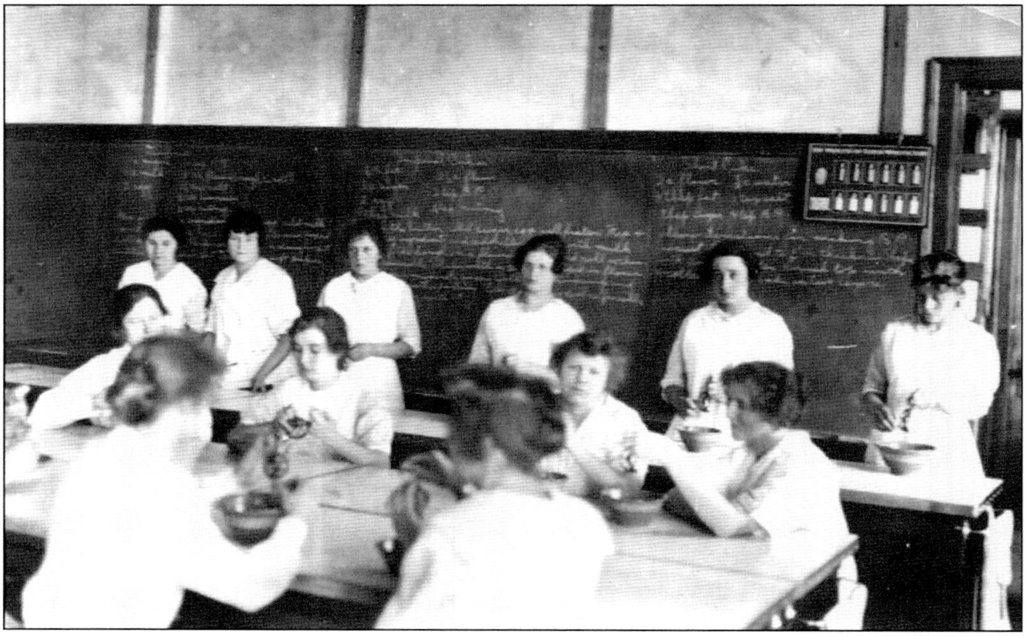

This May 1916 cooking class prepares one of the school cookie recipes written on the blackboard in the background. Note the students' aprons and equipment, which included a metal mixing bowl and hand mixer.

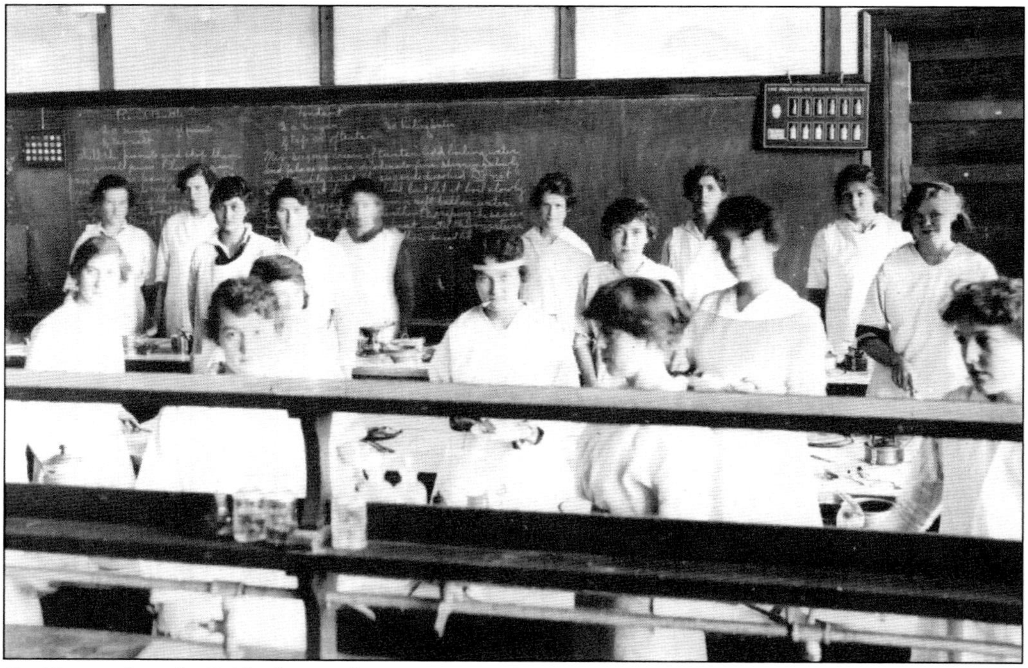

On December 4, 1916, the students prepared peanut brittle for the approaching holidays. The finished product made its way to the cafeteria, classrooms, and homes of the students. Note the samples of kitchen baking powders and spices in the mounted shadow boxes on the blackboard.

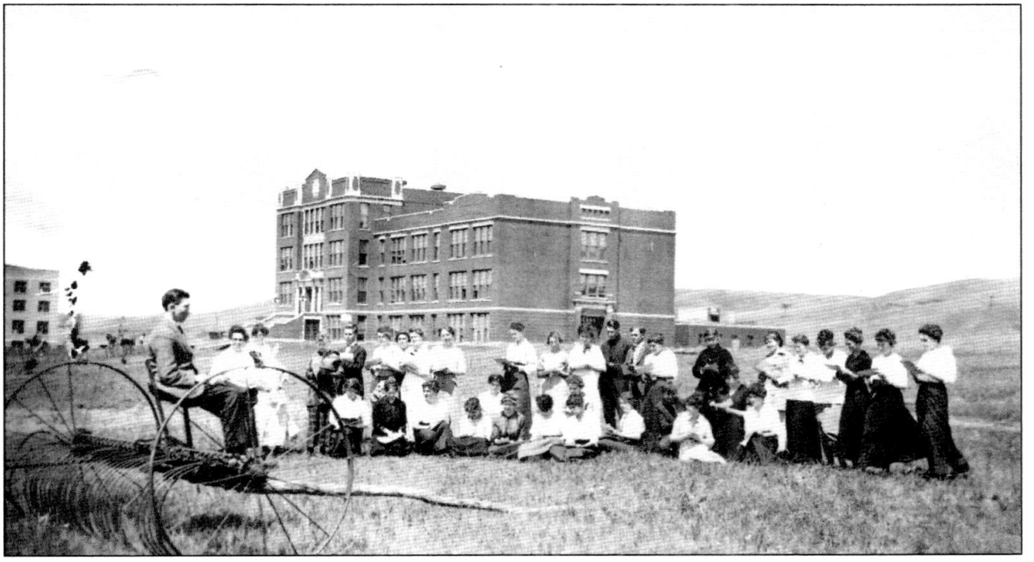

This art class prepared a portrait of the man setting on a piece of haying equipment, east of the ellipse and Old Main. The instructors used the prairie landscape and the equipment used to farm it as props and models for their students.

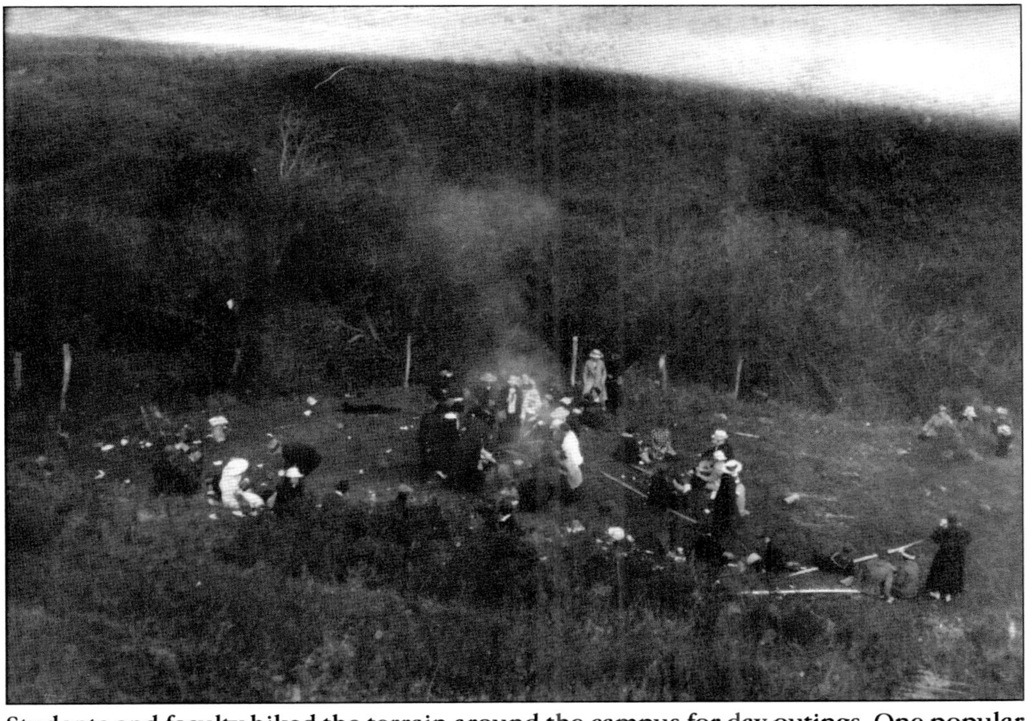

Students and faculty hiked the terrain around the campus for day outings. One popular location was the aquifer above the campus on North Hill. "The Springs" was the site for late-evening campfires, daytime hikes, and campfires for weenie cookouts. Students also used the local terrain in support of science projects, collecting plants and insects for their classes, or for use in the training school classrooms.

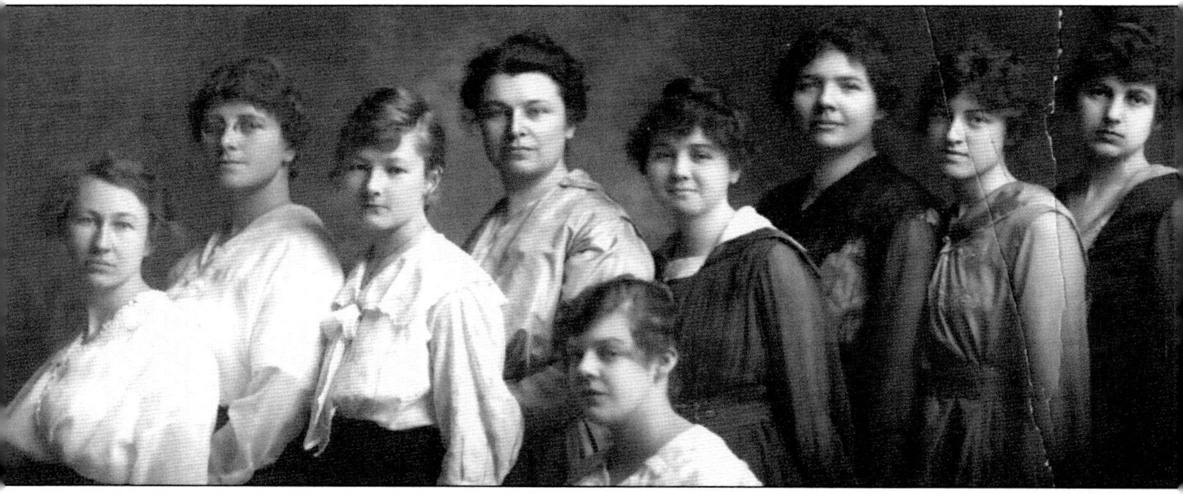

Students in the North Dakota normal school system were awarded an advanced teacher's certificate in two ways. Eighth-grade graduates completed the four-year teacher's course, and high school graduates completed the two-year advanced course. Advanced graduates were preferred by school superintendents because of their higher level of preparation compared to teachers with basic certification, but in rural North Dakota, they were a rare commodity. The students above graduated in 1917 with an advanced certificate. From left to right are Esther Gordon, Oda Young, Daphne Moehler, Florence Perkett (faculty advisor), Edith Ditwer, Ruth Regan, Edith Irow, Ruby Lambert, and Liddia Hrabe in front.

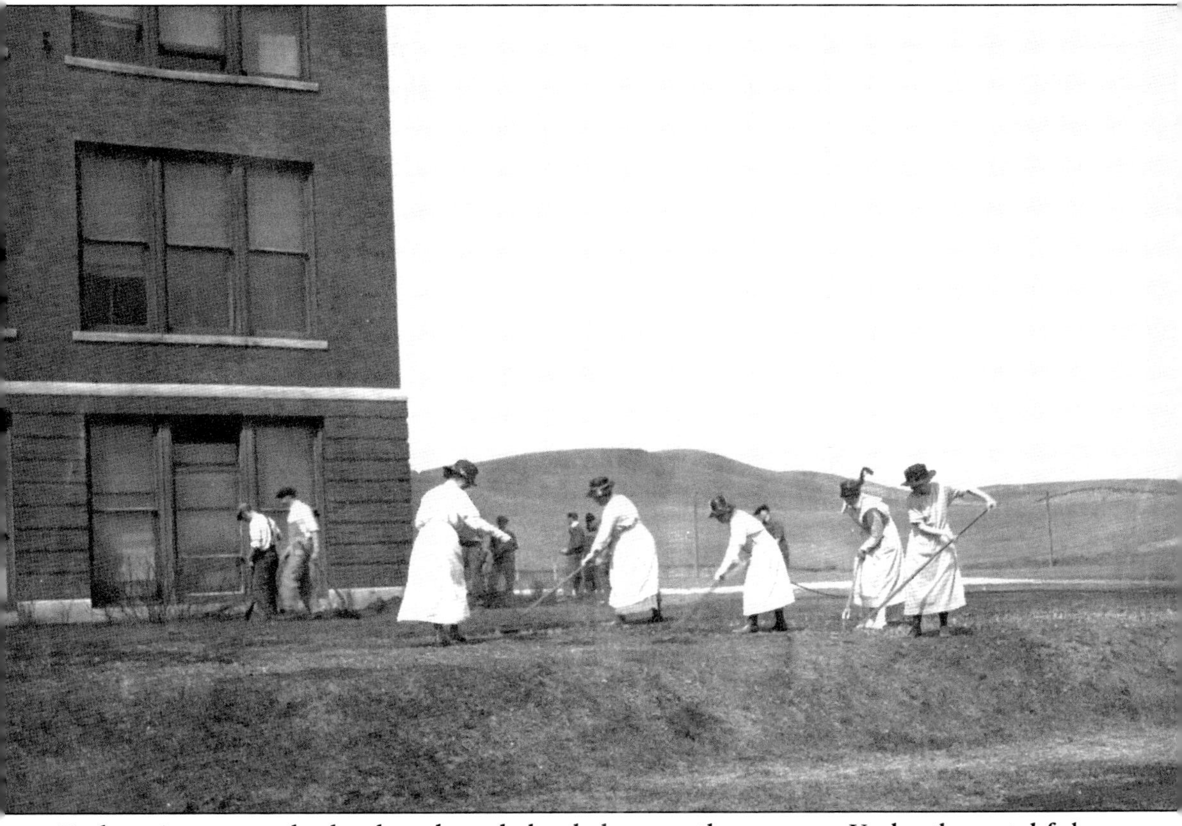

Each spring, normal school students helped clean up the campus. Under the watchful eye of a faculty member, each group was assigned a section to rake and, if necessary, sow grass seed. This group was responsible for the area in front of the east wing of Old Main. The campus grounds crew maintained the flowers and plants planted in front of Old Main. Note the barren landscape of North Hill in the background.

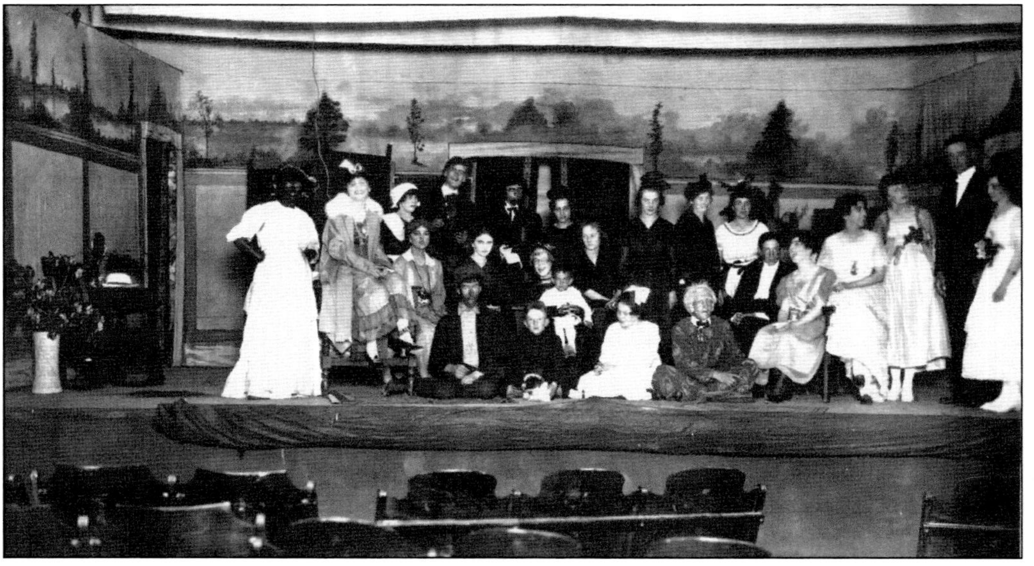

On campus, theater was an agent of entertainment and education. In the presentation of *Hoodoo*, a girl named Ann, who had been raised in an orphanage, was supposedly cursed until she married. As she grew up, she experienced tragedy, loneliness, and misery. Only after mistakenly thinking she has killed her neighbor does she find love. The play was adopted from the 1916 silent film *Hoodoo Ann*, written by D. W. Griffith.

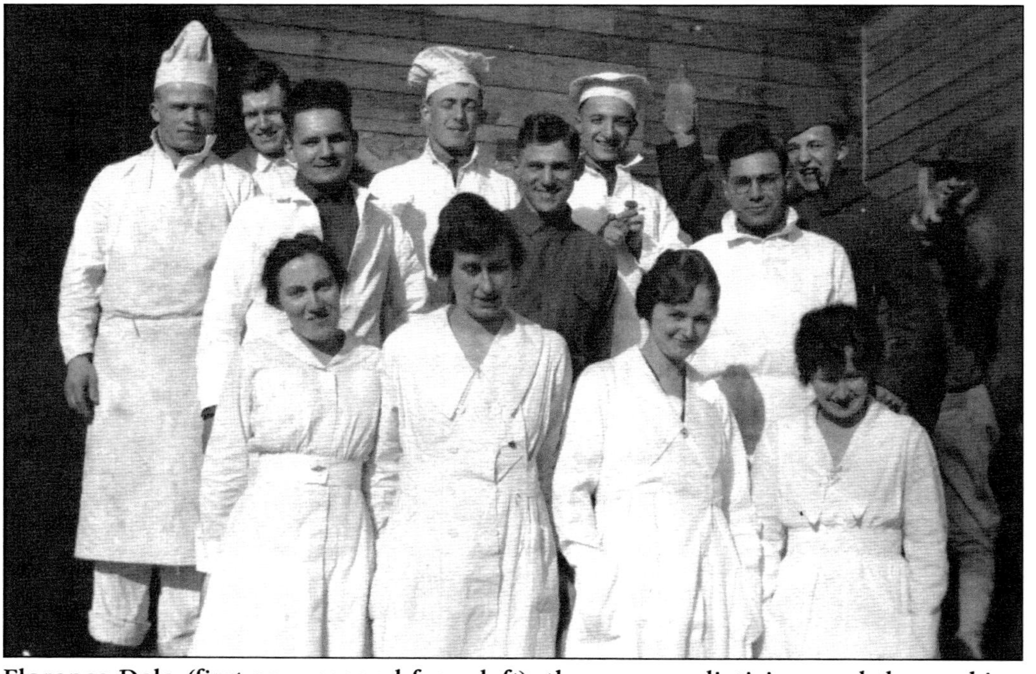

Florence Dale (first row, second from left), the campus dietician, and the cooking staff gather for a picture outside the kitchen. Dale planned daily meals for the campus kitchen.

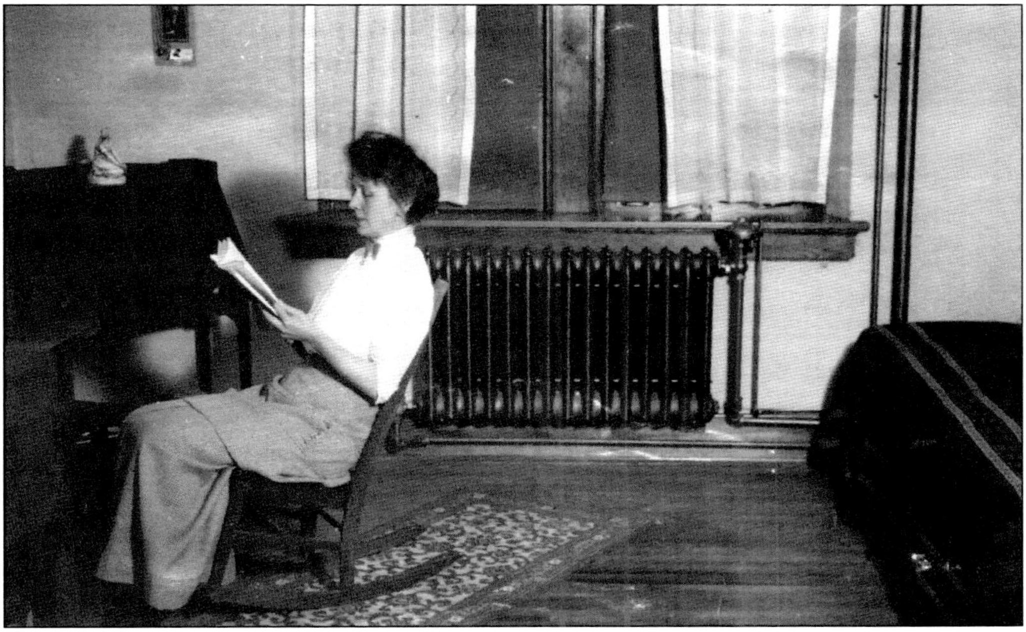

Some faculty resided in the campus dormitory. In this photograph, Julia McDonough, head of the Department of English, reviews papers in her room in the west dormitory. Note the steam radiator and small bed. Furniture was limited and spartan.

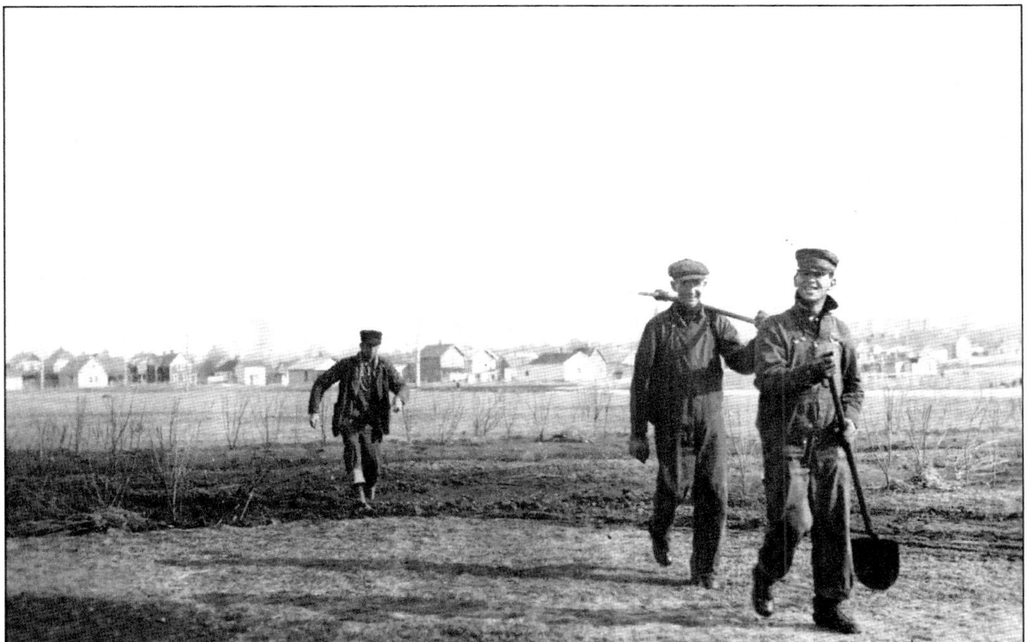

While faculty, staff, and students did a great deal of work on the campus grounds, most of the landscape maintenance was performed by the small farm staff, which included R. L. King, Miller Jenson, and Amos Brehmer.

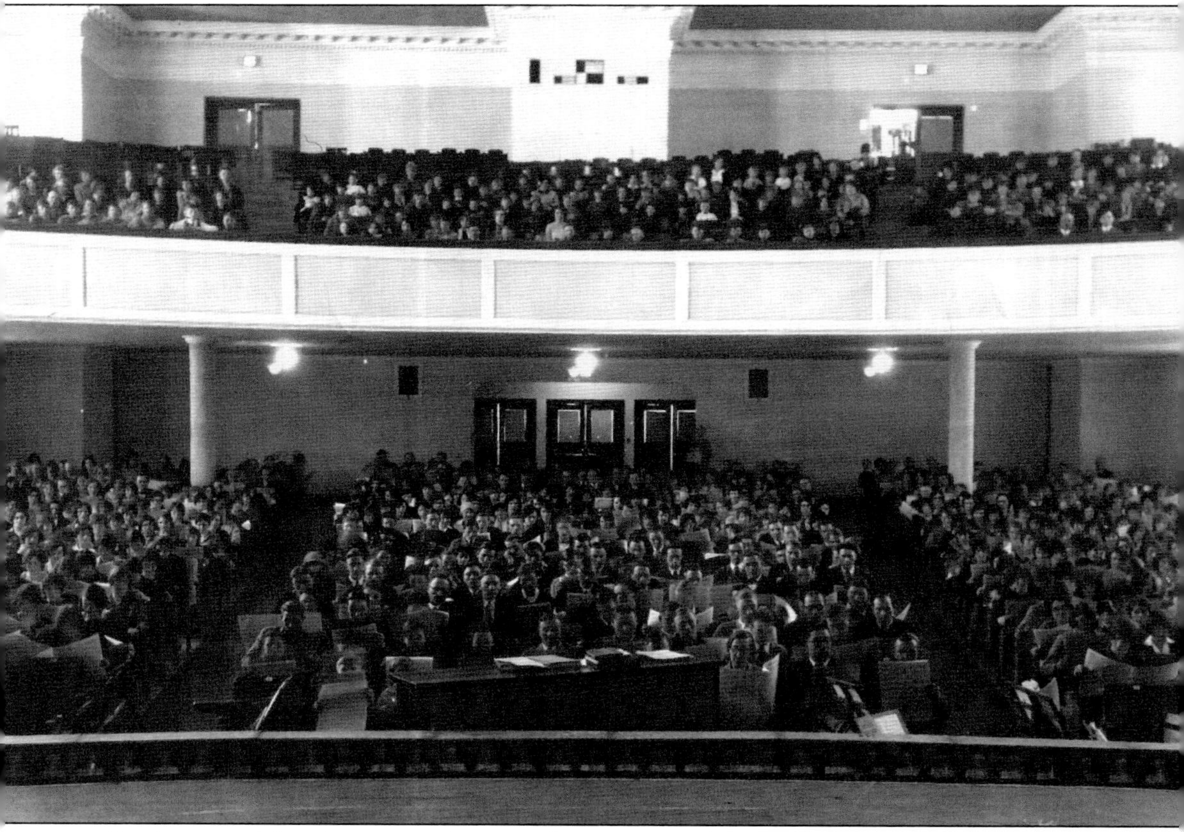

Students and faculty met twice a week at a general assembly. The program included a brief religious exercise, announcements, singing, short programs by students, addresses by prominent visitors, demonstrations of good teaching, short plays, and phonograph and radio entertainment. Students from the training school sat in the balcony. Students from the normal school occupied the auditorium's lower seating. The photograph above captures students reviewing the *Red and Green*.

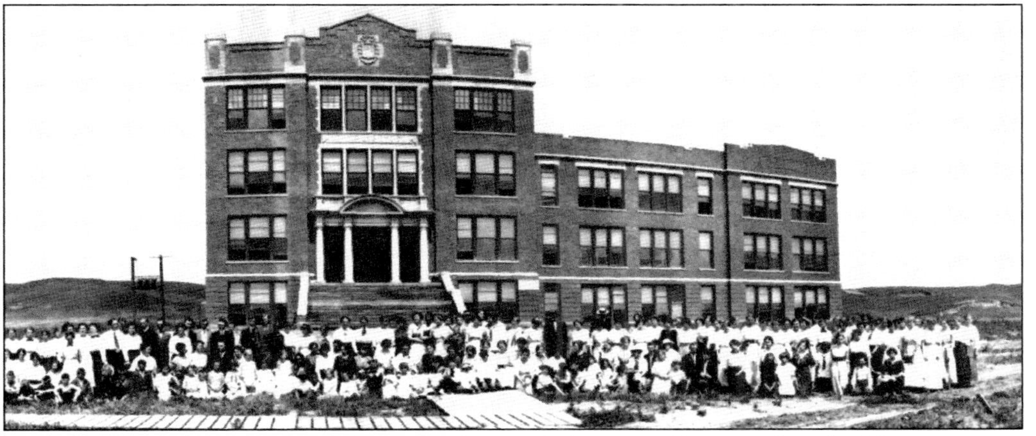

The summer session of 1914 poses in front of the partially completed Old Main. Note the wooden sidewalks, which were used until the summer of 1916.

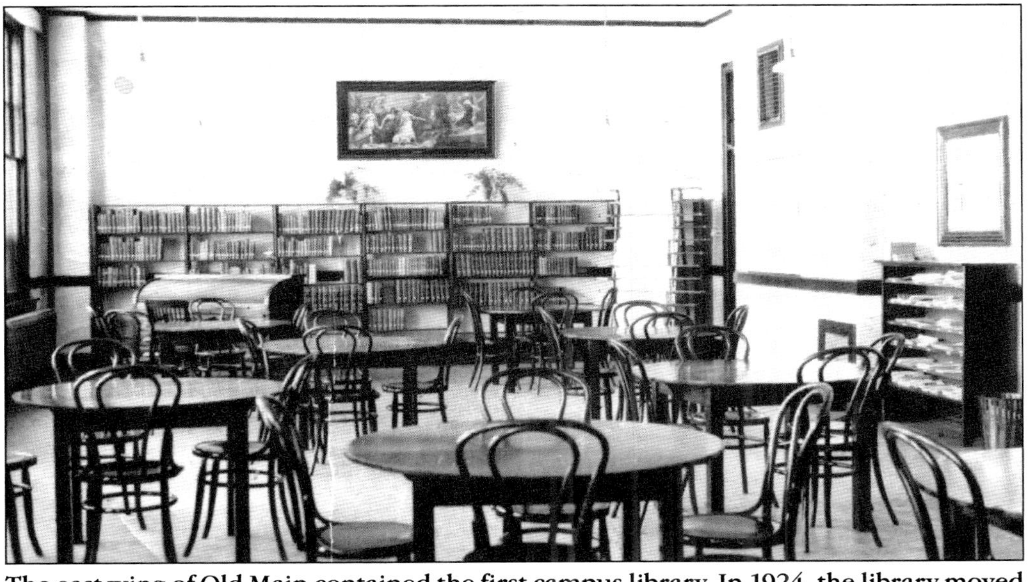

The east wing of Old Main contained the first campus library. In 1924, the library moved to the newly completed west wing, where it remained until 1957 when the Memorial Library was constructed. Inez Bager presented the painting on the library's wall, Guido Reni's *Aurora*, as a memorial gift from the class of 1914. At present, it hangs in the administrative building.

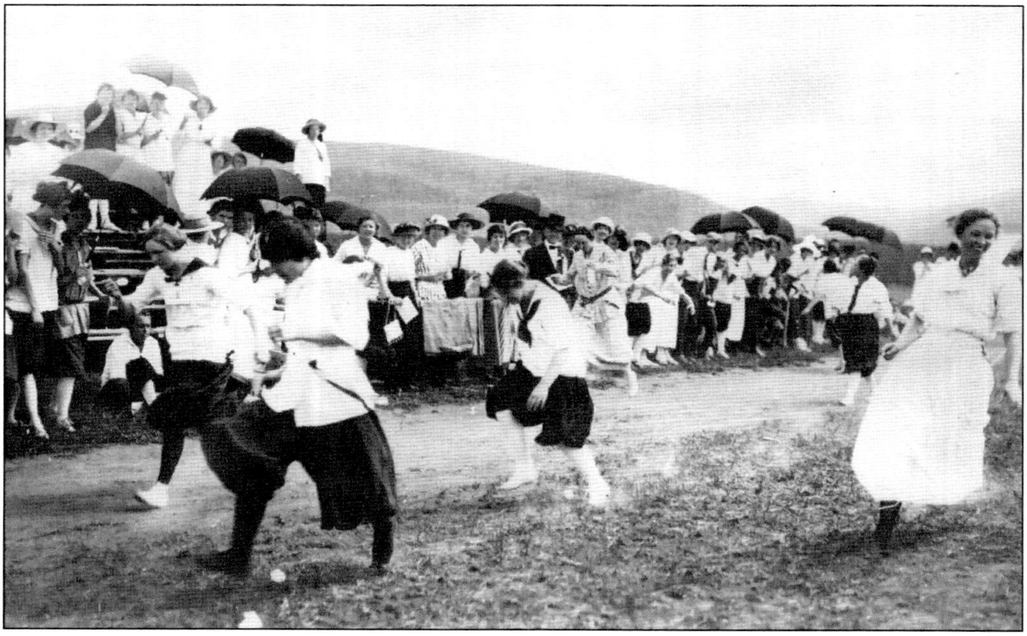

Summer school was not all work and no play, as evidenced by these photographs taken on July 22, 1916. Each summer the campus sponsored a field day for the normal and training school students who attended summer school. The 1916 event was held on the northwest corner of the campus where the campus football field was developed. Events included various track and field events, egg races, sack races, tugs-of-war, nail-hammering contests, and other events. The 1916 field day experienced a sprinkle of rain, but it apparently did not dampen the spirit of the participants.

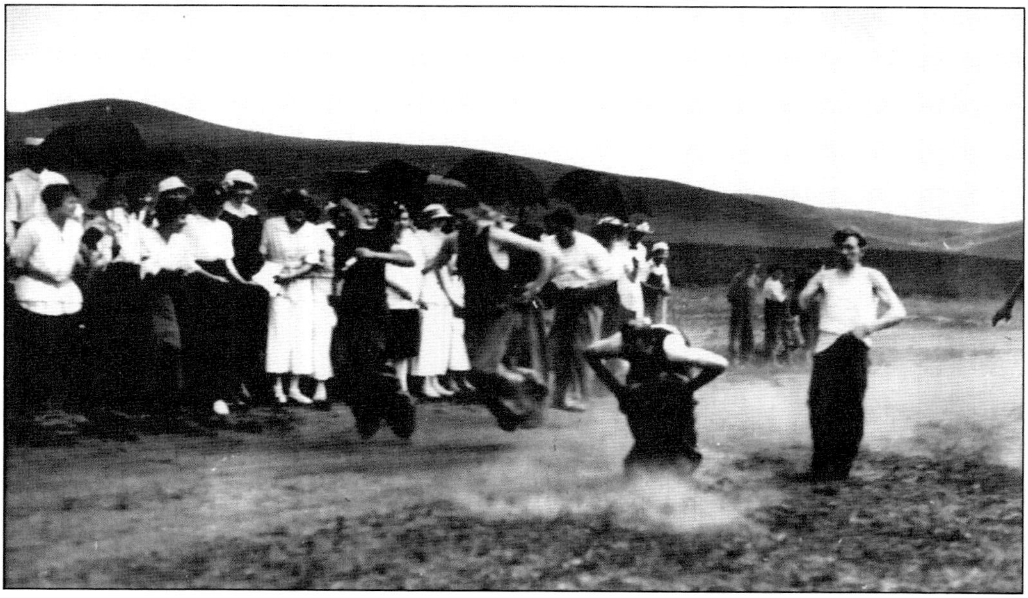

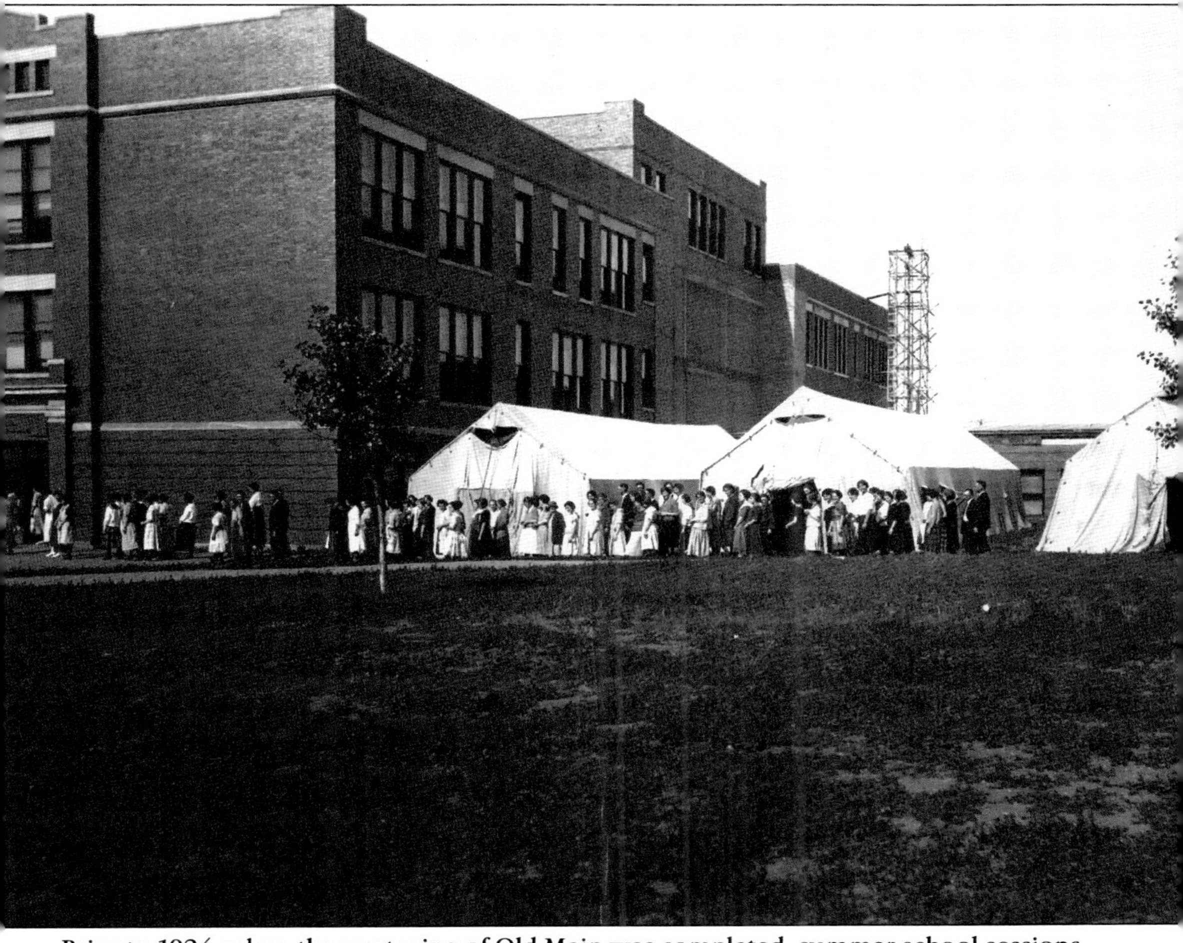

Prior to 1924, when the west wing of Old Main was completed, summer school sessions were very crowded. Numbers dropped significantly during World War I, but in the early 1920s, enrollments increased. The 1924 session had 661 summer enrollments, and tents were necessary to accommodate the large overflow of students seeking temporary teacher certification. The west wing of Old Main was under construction but was not completed in time for the summer session. Scaffolding for the bricklayers can be seen in the background. The third wing, which included the auditorium, was not funded until 1925. After 1924, tents were not necessary for summer sessions.

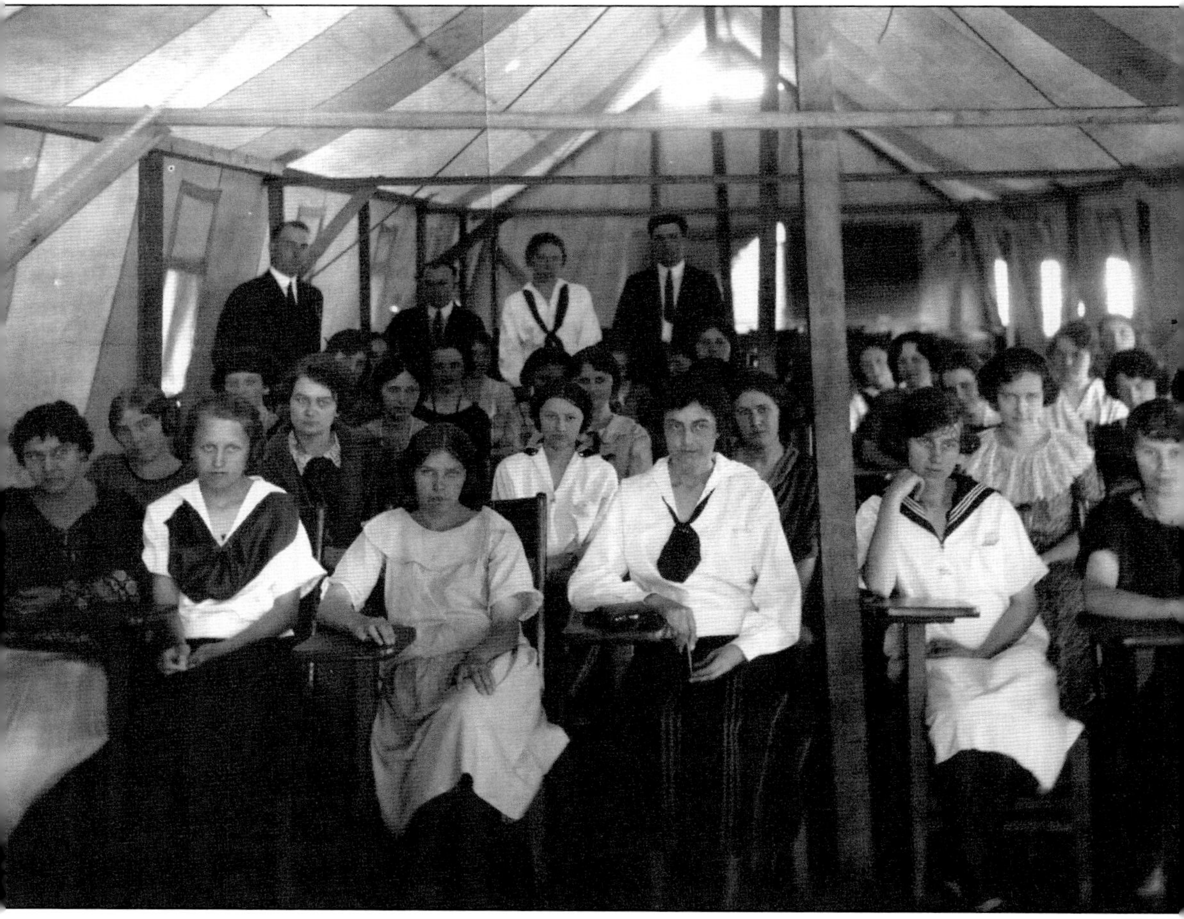

The crowded tents were hot despite the cross ventilation provided by the flap windows. To meet the instructional demand, the campus used ancillary teachers from community schools and other state institutions to augment the summer faculty. Although some normal school students attended, most summer students were returning educators from the state's rural schools seeking additional hours or extensions of their certifications. As shown in this photograph, the tents had two rooms and supported two sessions simultaneously. Desks were brought in from the campus training school to accommodate the students.

Four

Life at the Training School

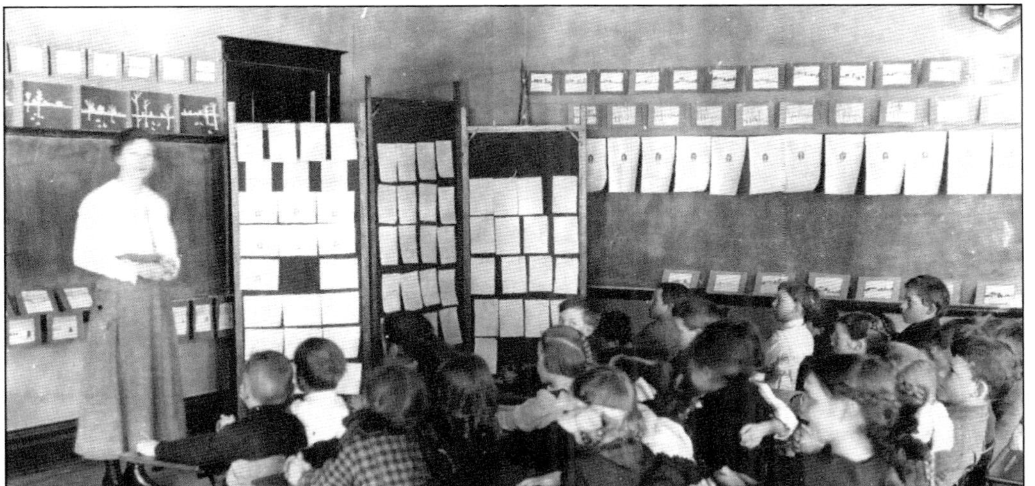

In the training school, the heart of the normal school, senior students or cadet teachers learned and practiced the art of teaching. The training school operated with a principal and instructors known as critics. Critics sought to keep conditions as normal as possible for the primary students. Critics oversaw the primary students' education, availability of resources, and extracurricular activities. These activities included sports, theater, scouting, and other activities. During classroom instructions, critics supervised each cadet student working in the classroom. Critics reviewed each lesson prior to the cadet's engagement with the primary students.

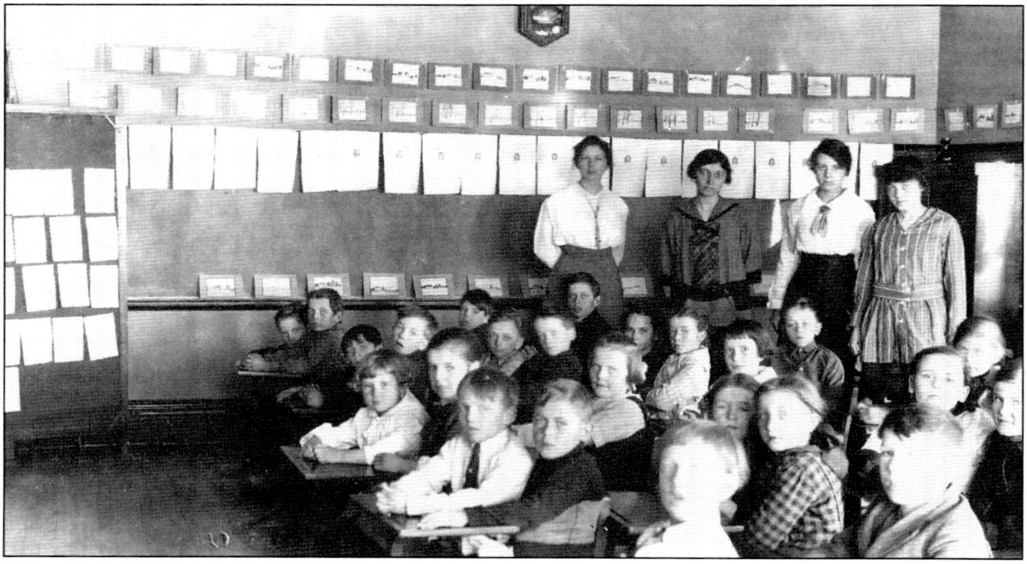

Students received a great deal of individual attention in the training school. The constant presence of a cadet provided the opportunity for one-on-one instruction. For teachers in rural schools this was often impossible unless it involved working after school hours.

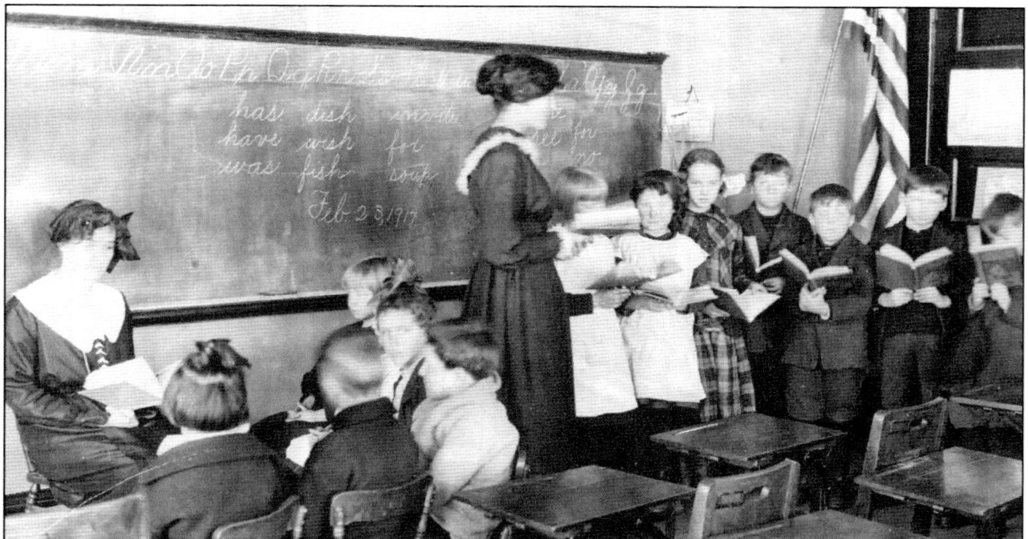

The constant presence of cadets also permitted the use of small groups for specialized, focused instruction. Unlike teachers in many of the state's rural schools, critics had years of experience and training. This provided a much richer learning experience for the students. Moreover, it provided the cadets access to methods and devices they otherwise would not have experienced.

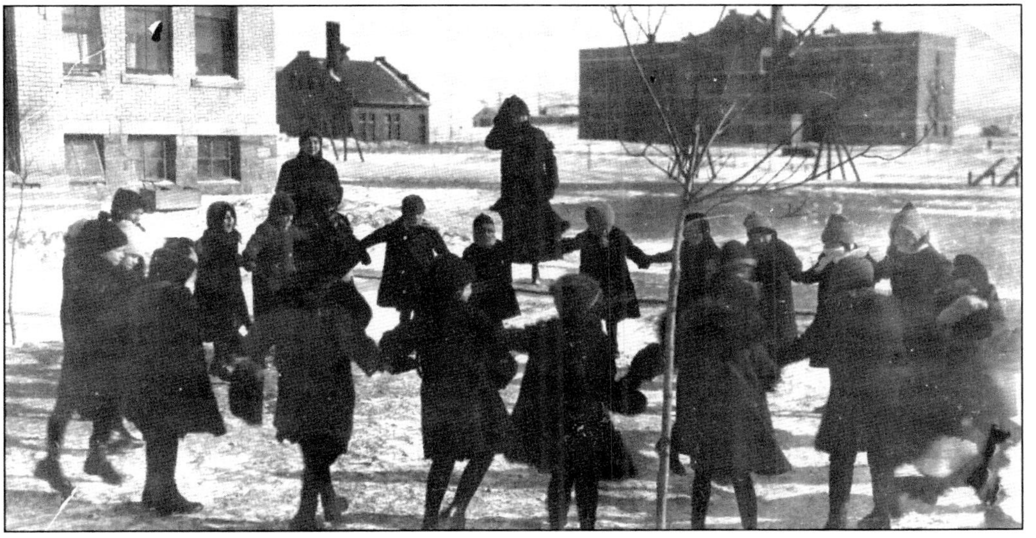

Play was an important part of the training school day, even on cold winter days. In this photograph taken in February 1917, students play "rat and cat" under the observation of their student teacher and class critic.

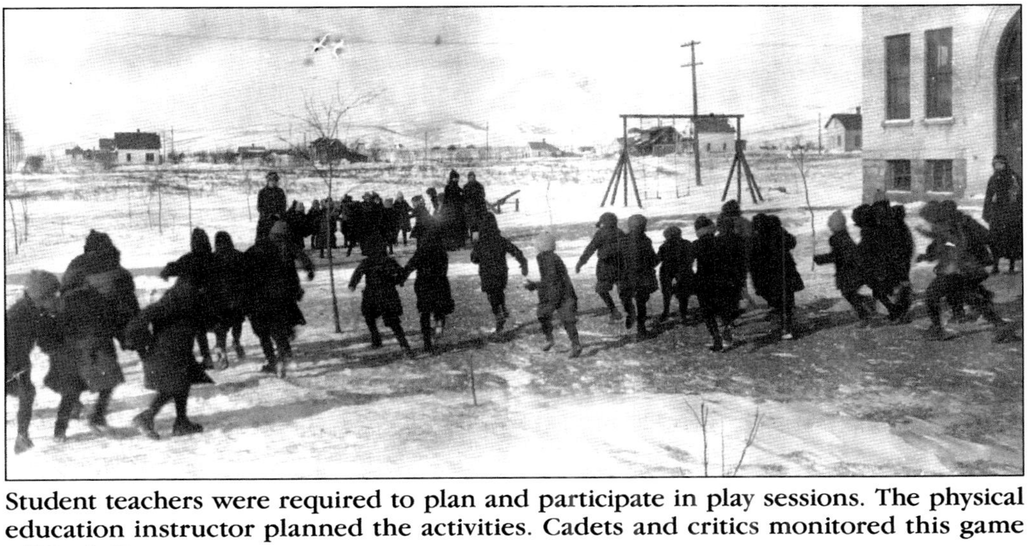

Student teachers were required to plan and participate in play sessions. The physical education instructor planned the activities. Cadets and critics monitored this game of Pinch-O.

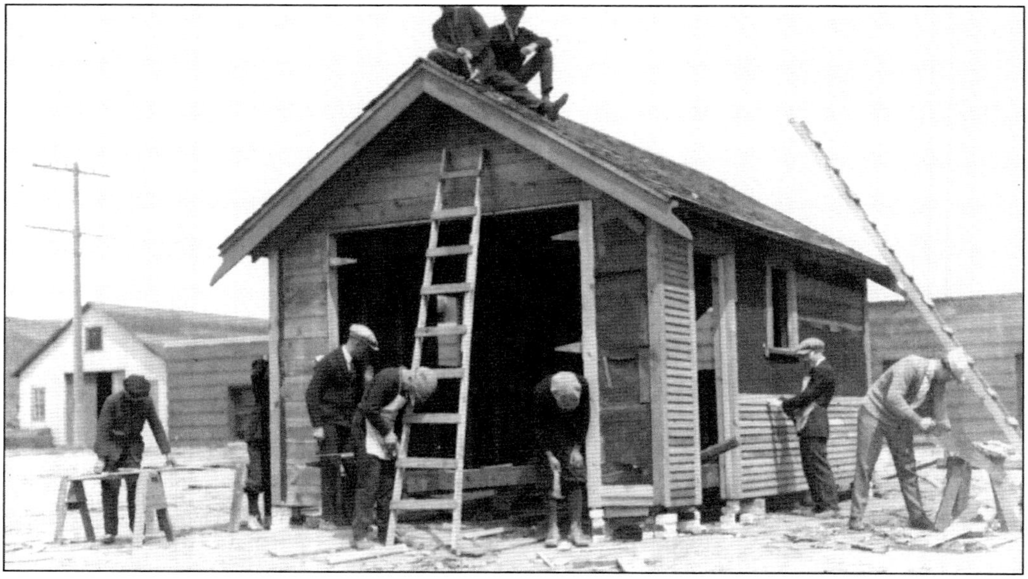

Normal school curriculum added manual training in 1916. This curriculum provided a variety of programs to prepare young men for life, one being a course in practical carpentry. Eleven young men in the training school participated. They constructed a 12-by-18-foot garage on the grounds. The building was sold at cost to a family in the community. The funds earned were then directed to another project.

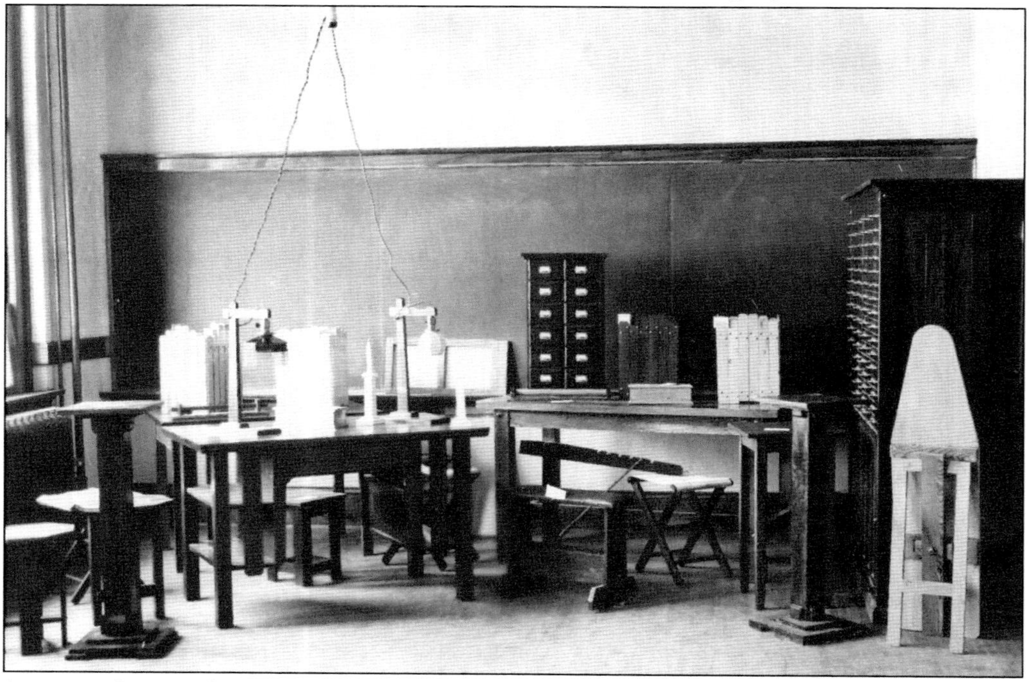

As part of manual training, the boys received instruction in basic woodworking. They learned to create chairs, stools, tables, stands, ironing boards, and other products for use around the home.

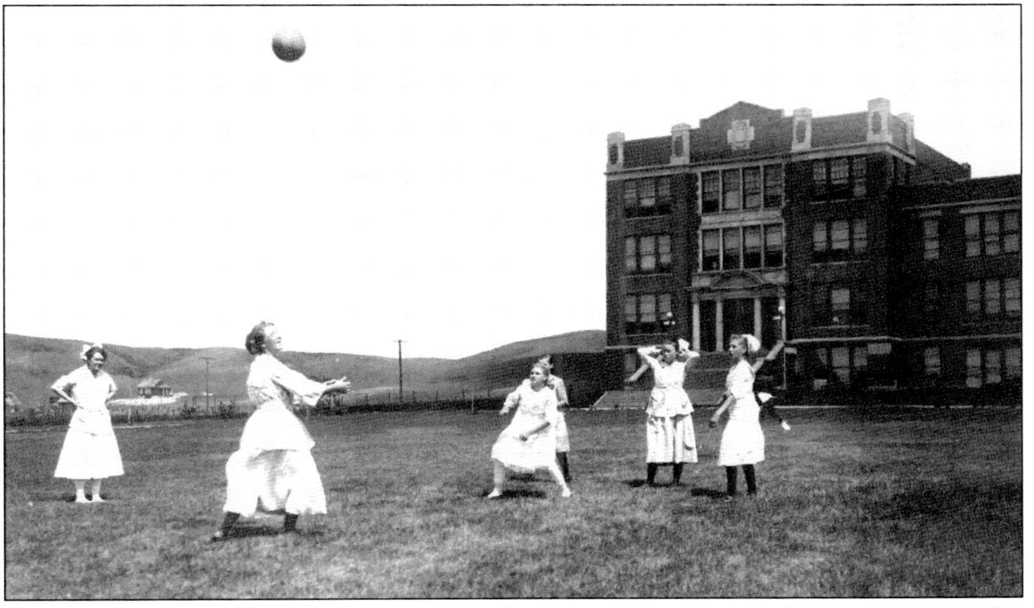

In 1917, young women from the training school used the ellipse in front of Old Main for volleyball practice. The area was more suited to such activities than the rough grounds around the training school.

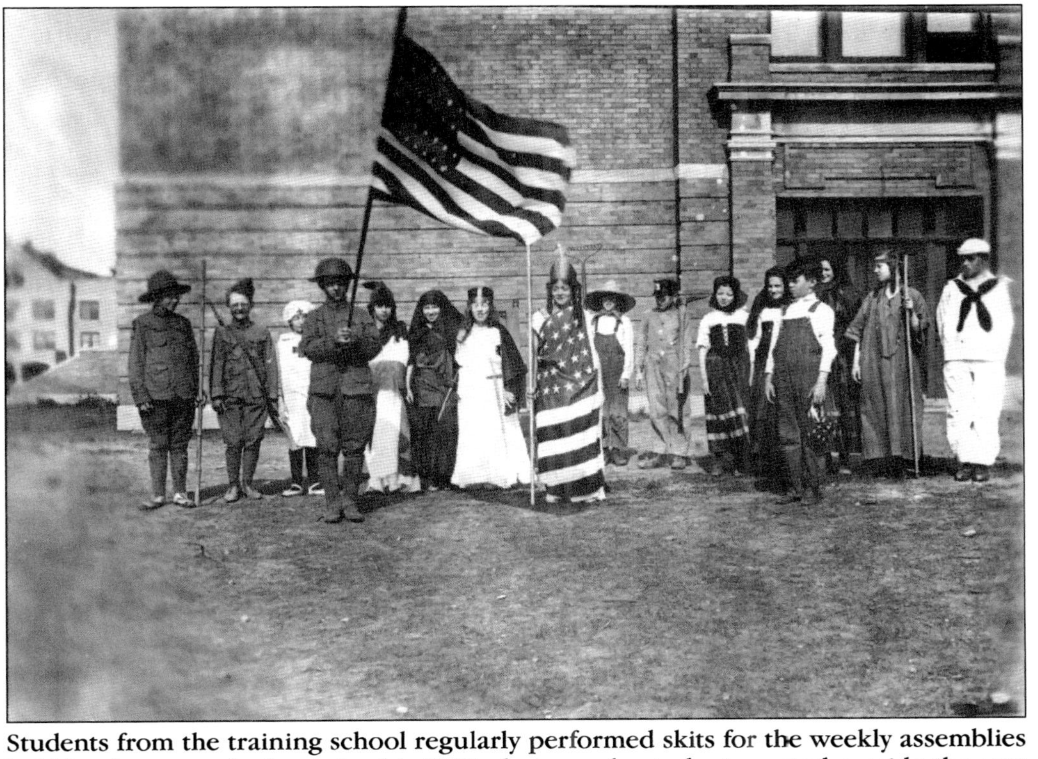

Students from the training school regularly performed skits for the weekly assemblies held by the normal school. In this 1917 photograph, students waited outside the east doors of Old Main to be ushered into the gymnasium.

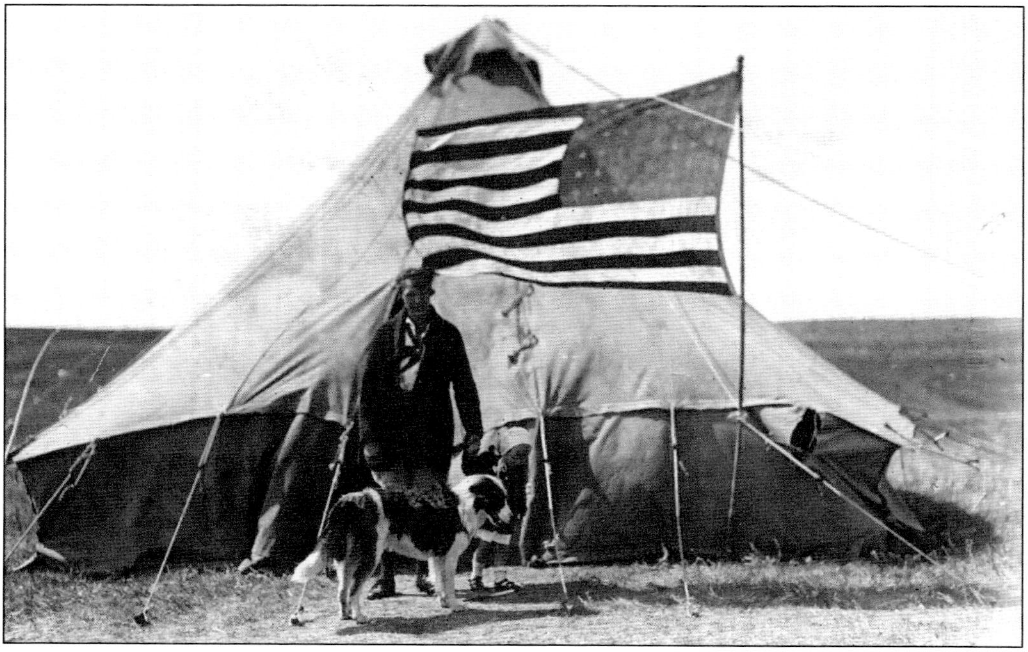

Starting in 1920, the Boy Scouts of America became part of the training school program. George Mueller (physical education instructor) was the first scoutmaster for Troop 5, and Mrs. Mueller (above) served as the scout mother. They spent a great deal of time at nearby Rice Lake where they camped on the open prairie.

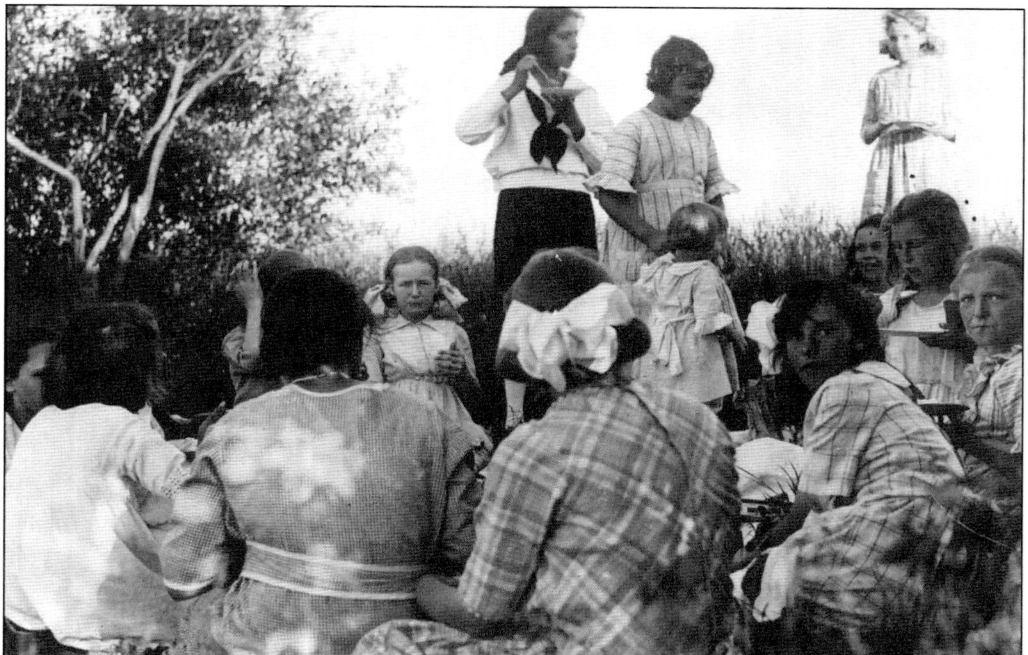

As shown above, the girls at the training school mirrored many of the boys' activities at Rice Lake. However, the two groups remained physically separated.

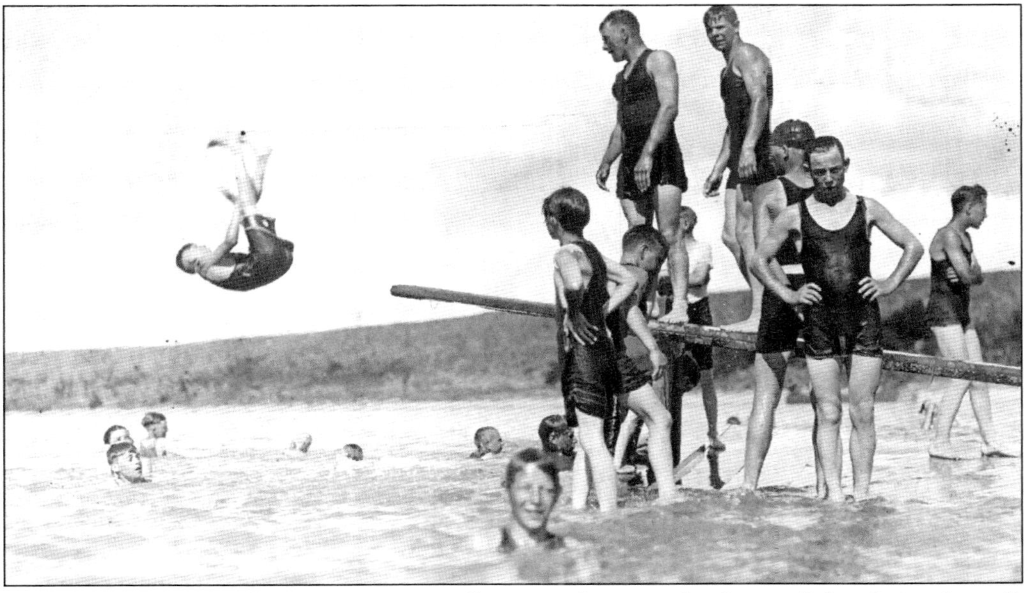

From the diving platform, George Mueller (standing on the front of the diving board) supervised swimming at Lake Rice. He was famous for his diving antics. A township within Ward County, with a population of 16 people, Rice Lake covered approximately 1.8 square miles; it was a popular site for outings.

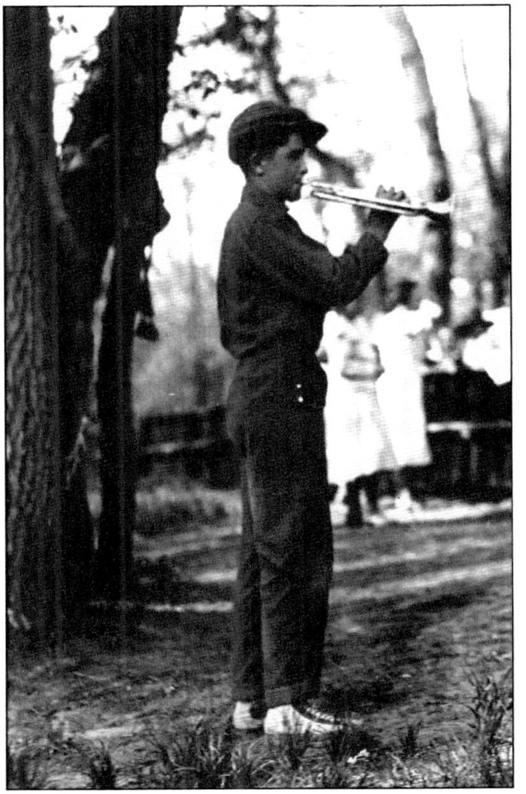

Each year, the normal school faculty and cadet teachers held a picnic for the training school students. In this June 1920 photograph, student Gordon Davy sounds "mess call" for the seventh- and eighth-grade classes in Oak Park, one of Minot's city parks. The campus used the parks extensively.

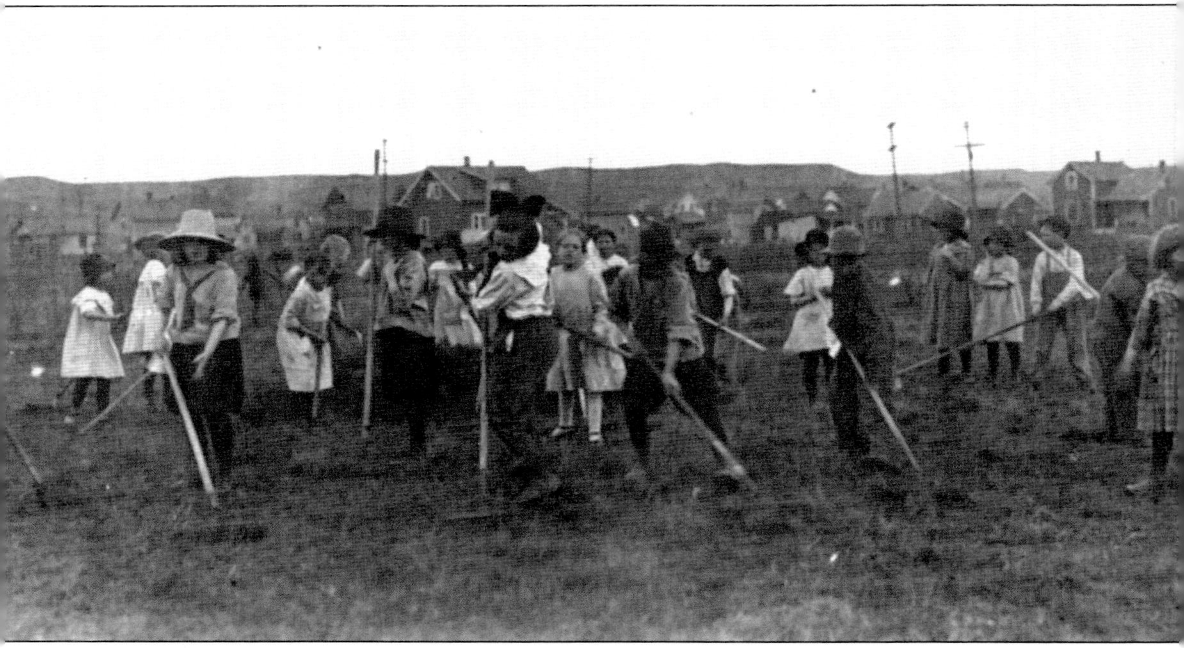

Each spring students from the training school helped the faculty and staff prepare the training school grounds and playground. In this photograph, students rake the dead grass and debris into a pile, which was then hauled away. The rakes are longer than most of the students are tall. Older students, faculty, and staff followed behind with planting projects. Note how almost every student is equipped with a hat.

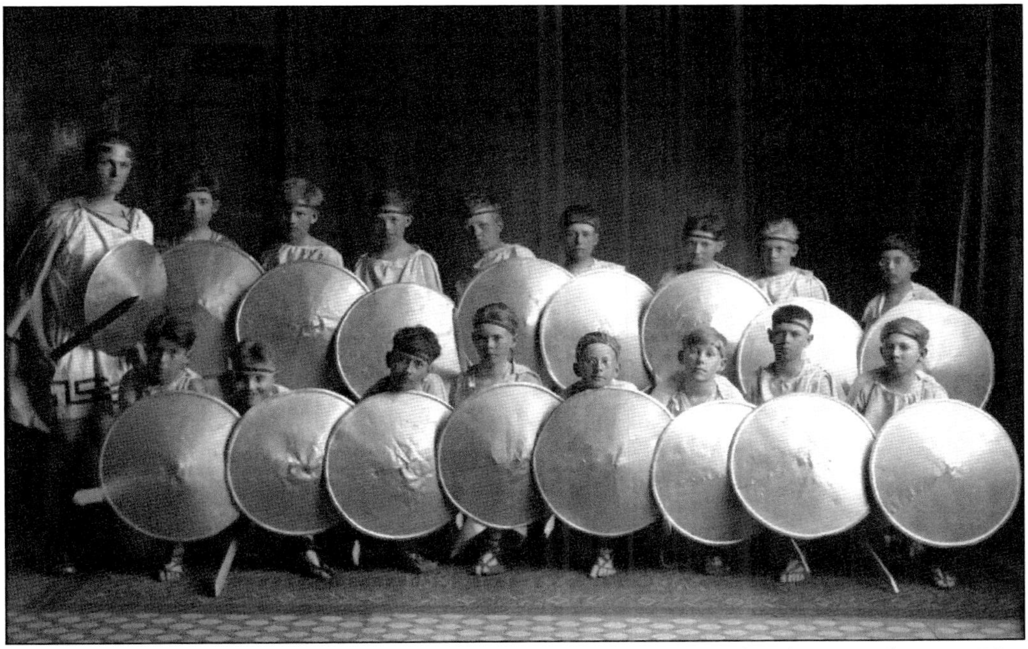

Theater played an important role in the normal and training school curriculum. In May 1921, the campus produced an educational play entitled *The Light*. In the photograph above, the young men of the training school perform skits on the origins of Greek and western culture.

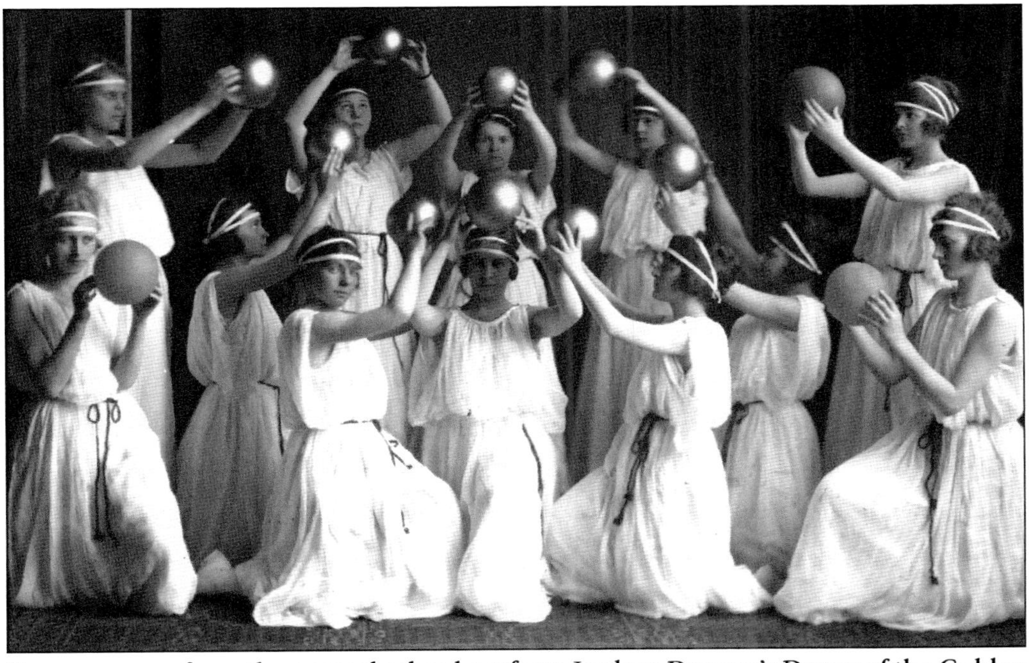

Young women from the normal school perform Isadora Duncan's Dance of the Golden Ball. Extremely popular in the early 20th century, Duncan was considered by many to be the mother of modern dance.

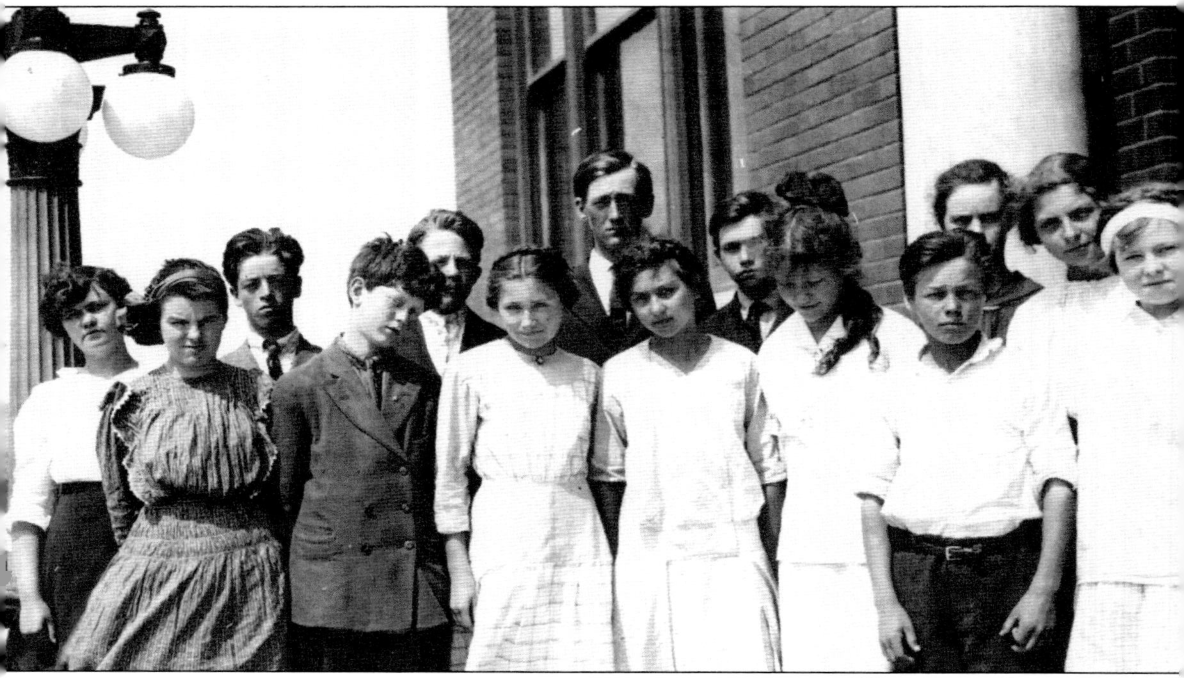

William F. Clarke, superintendent of the training school, poses with the eighth-grade graduating class of 1915 on the steps of Old Main. Training school graduation was celebrated during the week of normal school commencement exercises. Included are Myrtha Wilber, Rachel Allee, Edward Malone, Claude Holcomb, Herbert Green, Bertha Renz, Charles Hanson, Lucille Ring, Charles Wilber, Hilda Abrahamson, Alfred Hanson, Anira Lantz, Ivyl Holcomb, and Rose Gilmore. The electrolier in the left background, one of two, was presented to the institution by Gladys Mumford, class president for the normal school class of 1915.

Five

WORKING IN THE TRAINING SCHOOL GARDENS

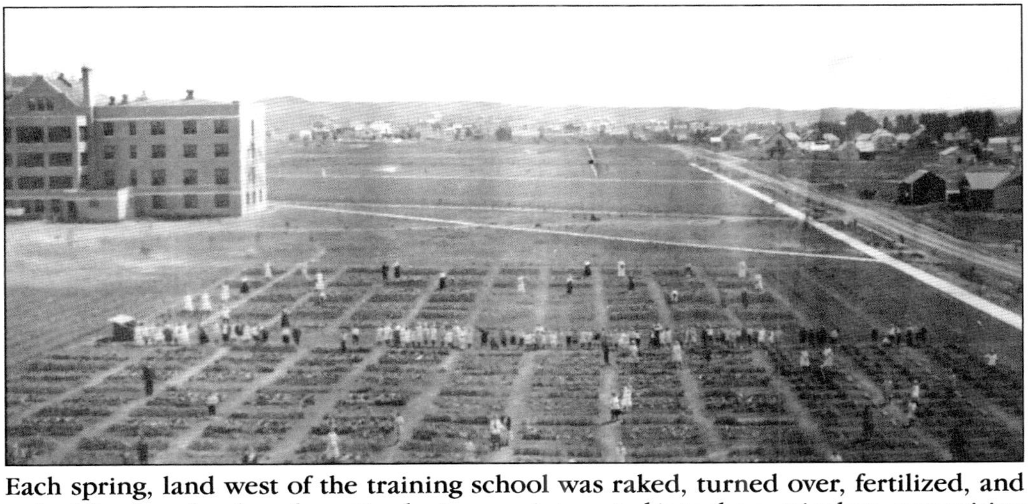

Each spring, land west of the training school was raked, turned over, fertilized, and staked for the school gardens. Gardening was integrated into the curriculum, comprising manual and industrial education for the students and reflecting the agricultural nature of the region. Superintendent William F. Clarke noted that garden work contributed to "moral growth of the child." Clarke believed that the work developed the "ability to cooperate with others and to respect the rights of others" and served as an "efficient means of nature study" and a means to "cultivate the child's capacity for appreciating the element of beauty." During the 1920s and 1930s, the gardens played an essential role in meeting the economic and dietary needs of the campus.

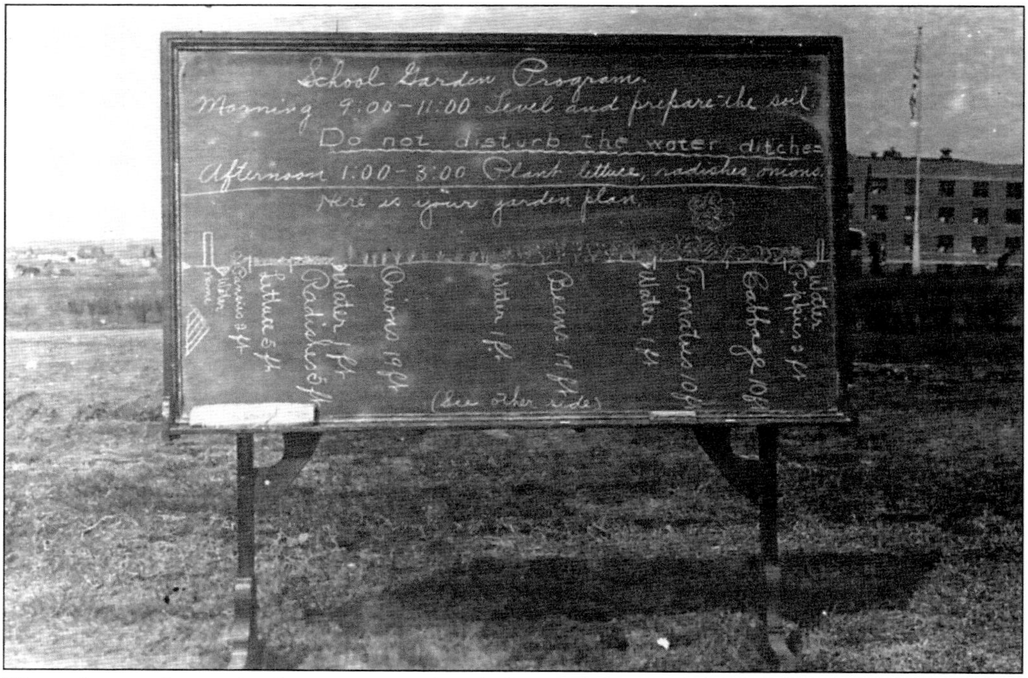

The primary classes in the training school planned their garden plots with the assistance of the agricultural instructor, their instructors, and critics. The normal school's agricultural instructor, James McArthur used a blackboard to outline the garden layout so students could visualize the project. The size of the garden was determined by the number of students.

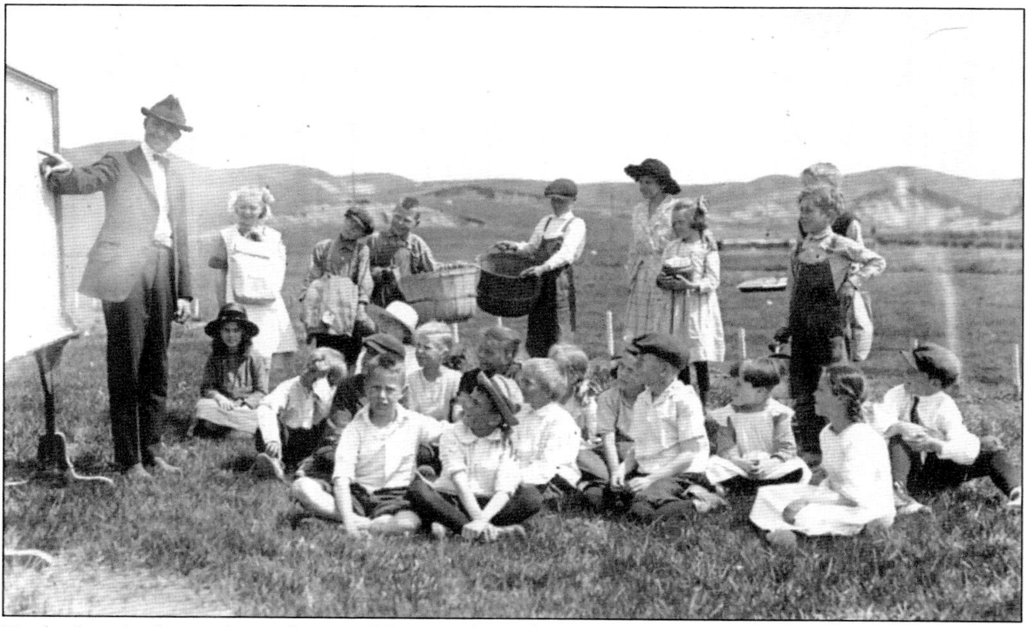

Each class had a variety of vegetables seeds and received instruction in planting them. The 1915 plan included poppies, cabbage, tomatoes, beans, onions, radishes, and lettuce.

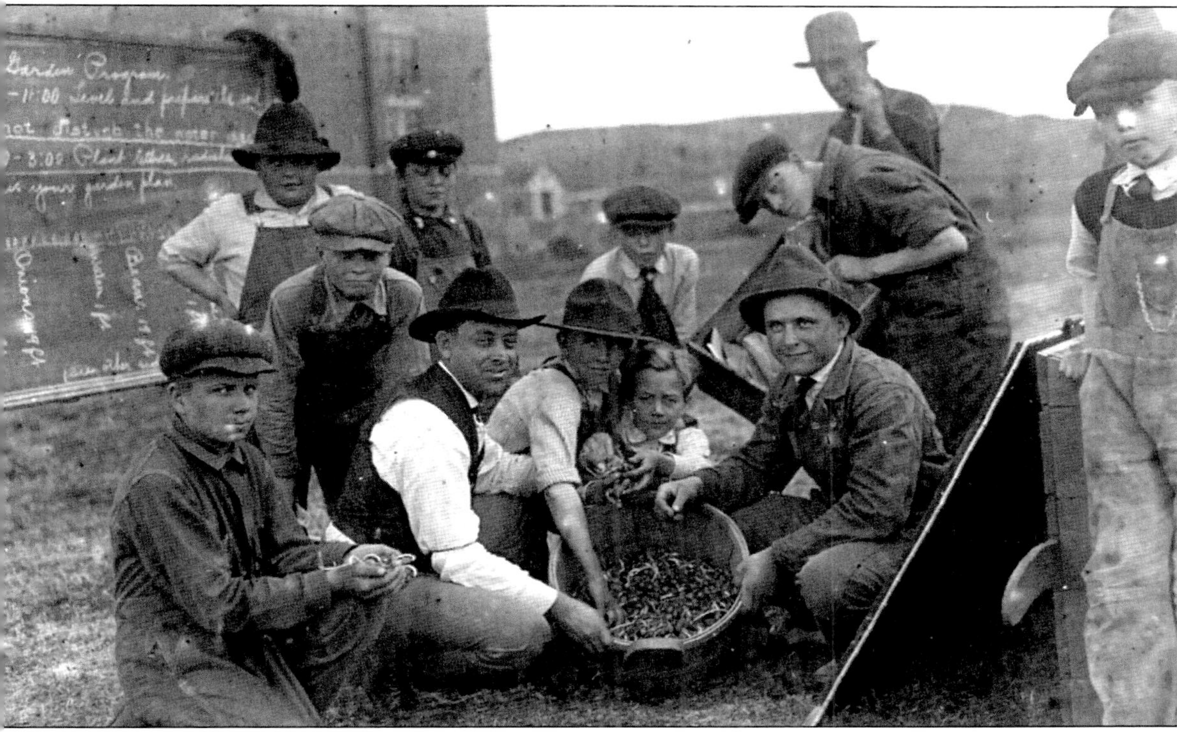

Here students show off their seeds before planting. James McArthur, agriculture and botany instructor (knelling at the right), and the campus grounds crew provided leadership and direction. McArthur selected flowers and plants that proved themselves hardy and successful in the Minot area. Some of the main crops included tomatoes, cabbage, carrots, peas, parsnips, radishes, turnips, lettuce, and beets. Flowers included nasturtiums, snapdragons, verbenas, poppies, pinks, stocks, phlox, pansies, zinnias, petunias, forget-me-nots, and candytuft.

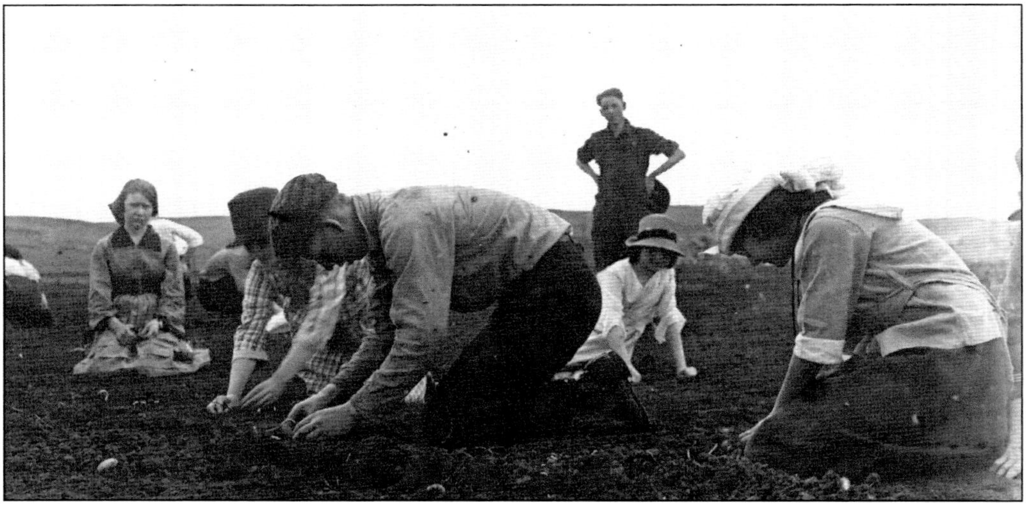

Students carefully planted onion sets. The gardens were not just an experiment. They provided the school and some families with food. As a result, garden work was taken seriously.

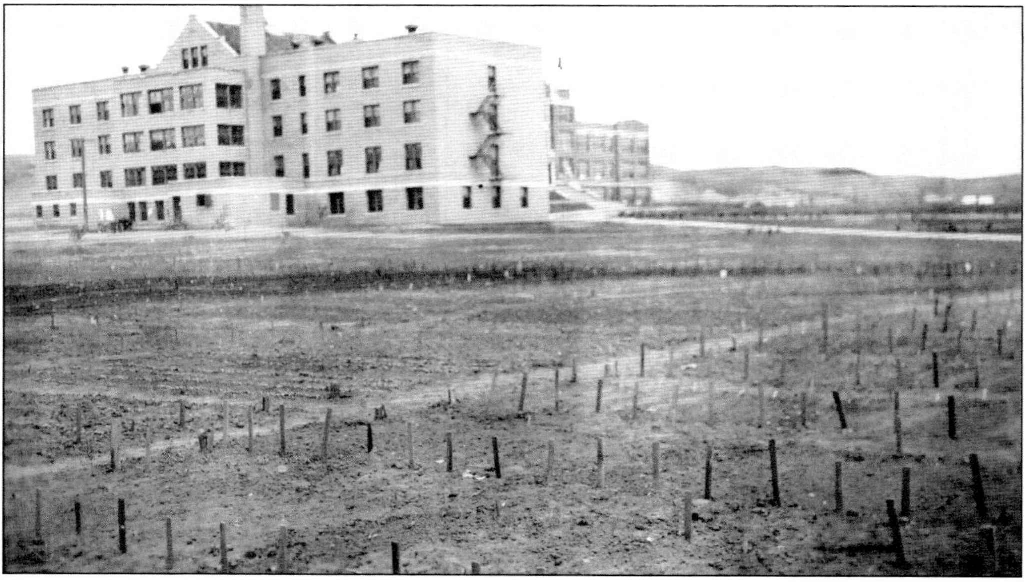

Each class participated in preparing the garden plot. In this 1916 photograph, the field has been prepared and planted. Rows averaged 75 feet long. Each plat was five feet long and separated by paths three feet wide. This accommodated students and visitors. Stakes marked each student's plat.

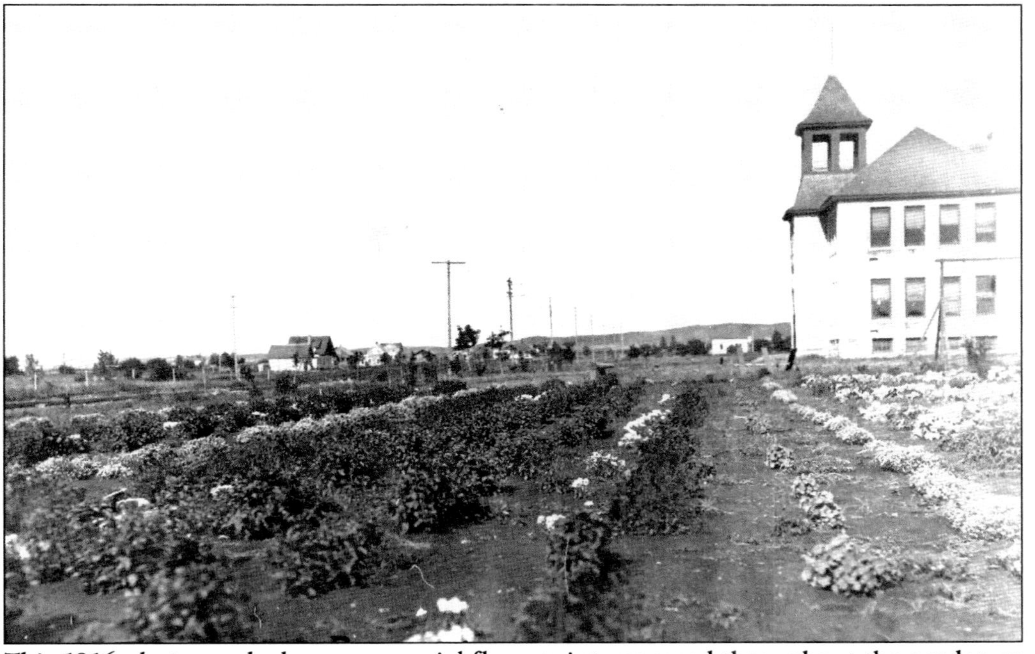

This 1916 photograph shows perennial flowers interspersed throughout the garden as borders and screens. Taller flowering plants were used in the center for a decorative touch and cutting. The campus used the Minneapolis garden plan.

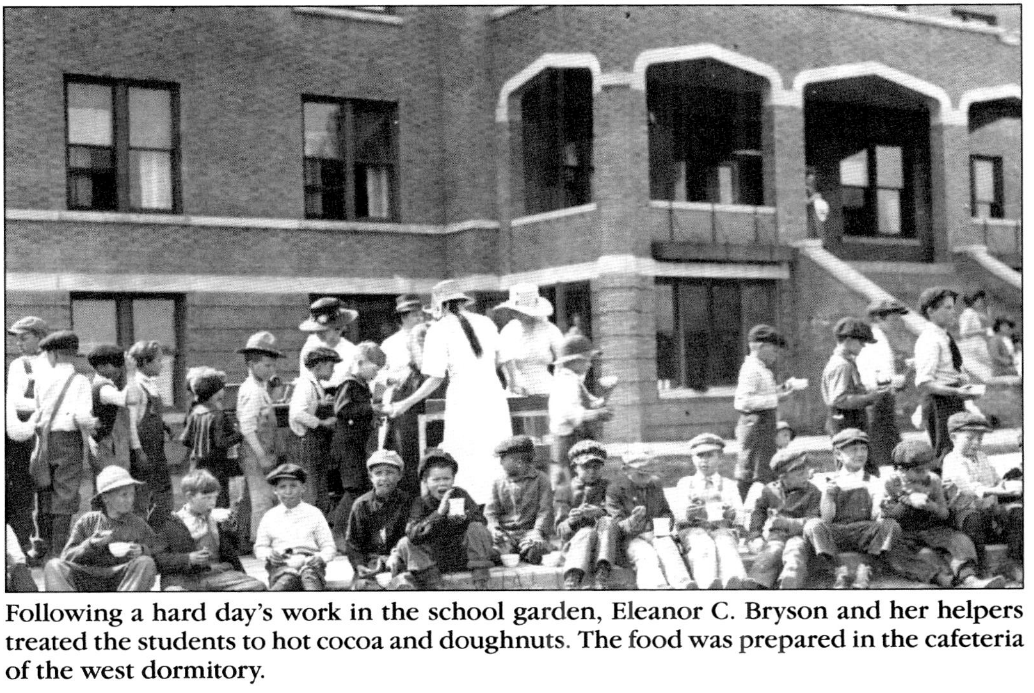

Following a hard day's work in the school garden, Eleanor C. Bryson and her helpers treated the students to hot cocoa and doughnuts. The food was prepared in the cafeteria of the west dormitory.

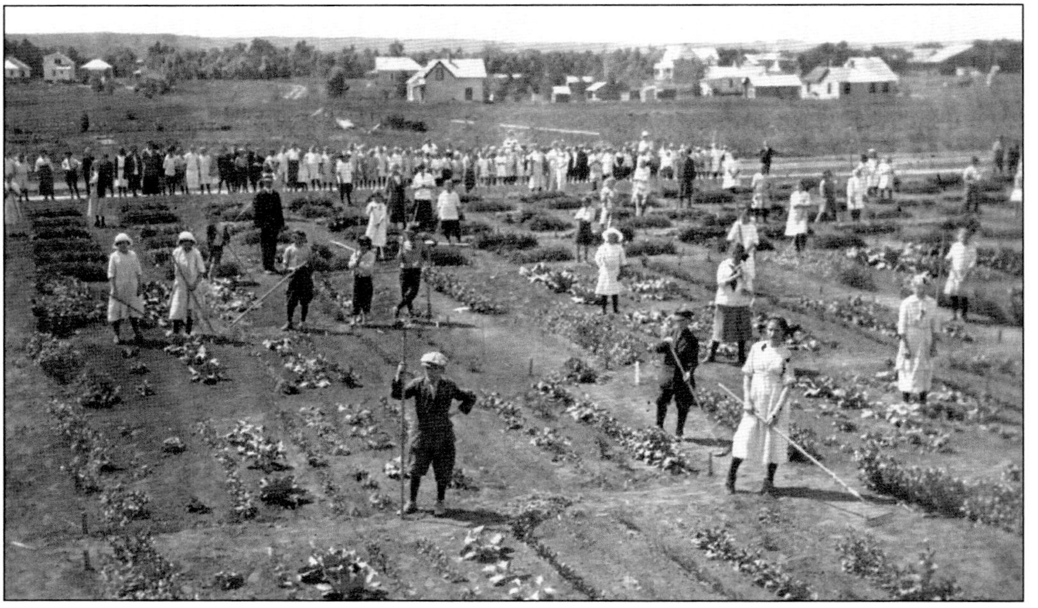

Students worked in the garden a minimum of one hour per week throughout the growing season and harvest. In this 1915 photograph, a class waits its turn to rotate in the field.

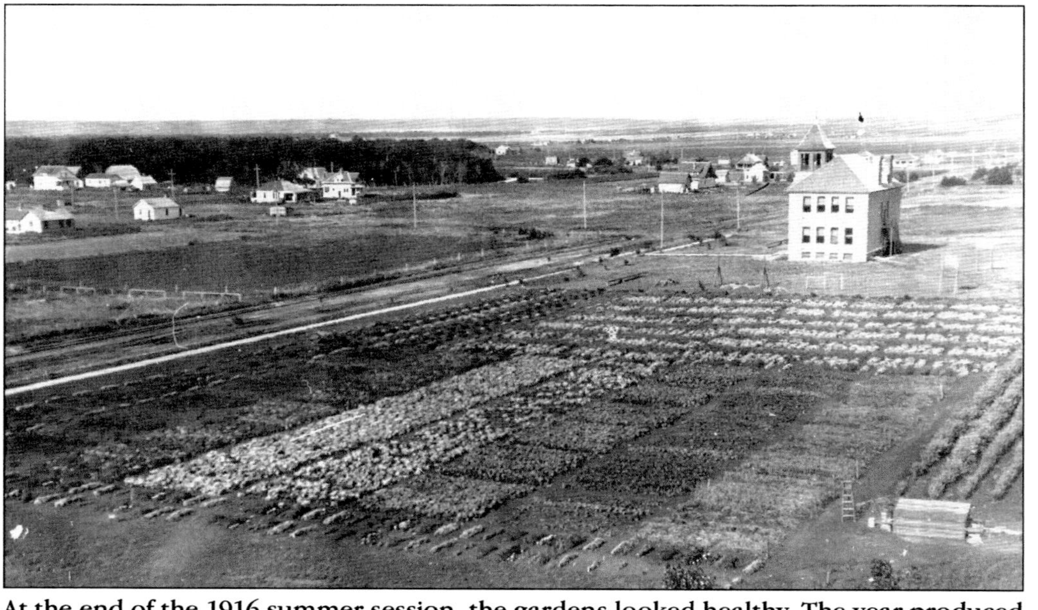

At the end of the 1916 summer session, the gardens looked healthy. The year produced sufficient rainfall and a record flood. The Mouse River can be seen in the background as it meanders north toward the Canadian border. The open prairie is still visible west of the training school.

Six

Celebrations and Holidays on the Northern Plains

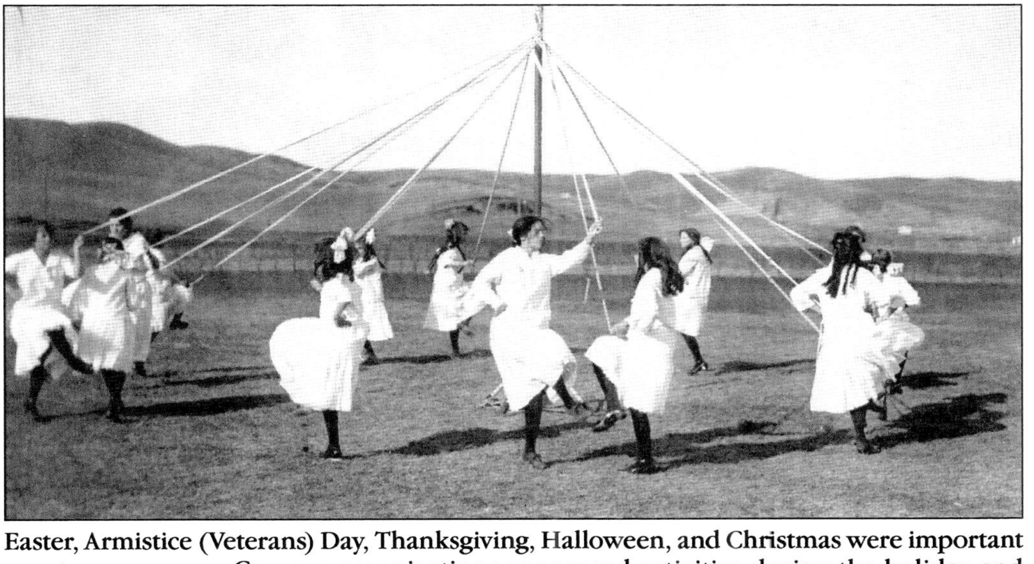

Easter, Armistice (Veterans) Day, Thanksgiving, Halloween, and Christmas were important events on campus. Campus organizations sponsored activities during the holiday and around-campus activities such as commencement. The normal school performed the May Fete, the crowning event of the academic year. In conjunction, the training school performed the Festival of Spring. The maypole dance (shown), Schottiche, and Highland Fling were among the most popular performances. The girls with the "best general record in the Physical Education Department throughout the year performed the dances."

Annual May Fete
"The Return of Spring"

The Campus
Monday evening, June eleventh, seven-thirty o'clock

SYNOPSIS AND PROGRAM

Winter and his forces are in power in the world. Spring enters preceded by her Heralds and accompanied by her attendants, the Pasque Flowers. Winter disputes her approach and the forces of Winter and Spring contend for the throne. Spring is victorious and takes the throne. The West Wind and Sun enter and waken the flowers. Cornflowers, Violets, Iris, Poppies, Roses, Rose Buds, Buttercups, Tulips, Lilies, Daffodils and Forest Trees spring into bloom. The Clouds bring the warm spring rain and the Rainbow accompanies them. The Fire Flies and The Fairies follow the flowers.

THE DANCES

Mondanet Majanek - - - - - - - - - - - Snow Flakes
Troika - - - - - - - - - - - - - - Heralds
Spring Song - - - - - - - - - - - - Pasque Flowers
Directoire Gavotte
Violette - - - - - - - - - - - - - - Spring
Pastorale - - - - - - - - - - - Sun and West Wind
Norwegian Mountain March - - - - - - - - - - Rosebuds
Danish Dance of Greeting - - - - - - - - - Corn Flowers
Ace of Diamonds - - - - - - - - - - - Buttercups
Kinder Polka - - - - - - - - - - - - - Iris
Hop Mother Annika - - - - - - - - - - - Lilies
Bleking - - - - - - - - - - - - - - Violets
Tantoli - - - - - - - - - - - - - - Roses
Swedish Klap Dans - - - - - - - - - - - Tulips
Poppies - - - - - - - - - - - - - Poppies
Gustaf's Skael - - - - - - - - - - - Wood Nymphs
Scotch Harvester - - - - - - - - - - - - Clouds
White Rose Mazurka - - - - - - - - - - - Rainbow
Minuet - - - - - - - - - - - - - - Fairies
Spanish Dance - - - - - - - - - - - - Fire Flies
May Pole Dance - - - - - - - - - - - - Daffodils
Sunbeam Schottische - - - - - - - - - - - Honor Girls

Assembling of All Dancers for the Harvest Dance, Reap the Flax

The annual May Fete program was a dynamic affair and required a great deal of preparation and coordination between the training and normal schools. As shown by the 1923 program, the synopsis reflected a recognition and deep respect for the seasons and their impact on the Northern Great Plains. Many of the program's characters could be found in the training school garden or on the normal school ellipse.

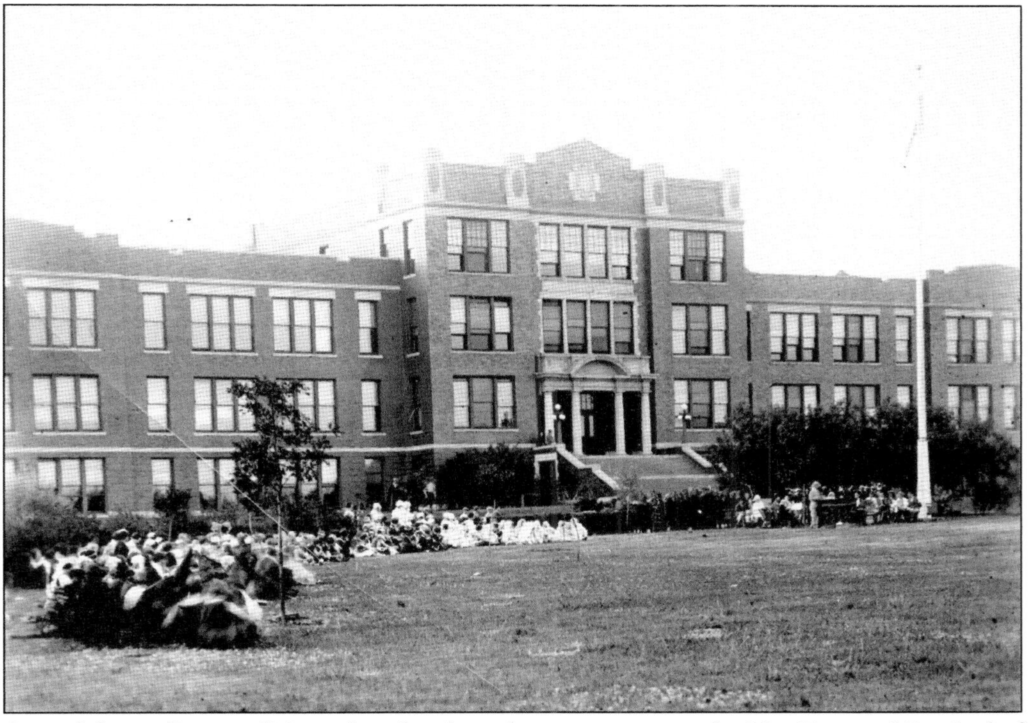

One of the earliest traditions that developed on campus was the May Fete and Festival of Spring. The events were performed on the lawn of Old Main. They were the culmination of the physical education activities for girls in the normal and training school. It was also a way to recognize the relationship between the schools. The theme and size of the event varied from year to year. The photograph above shows dancers waiting for their time to perform. Below is a photograph of the audience on the ellipse in front of Old Main.

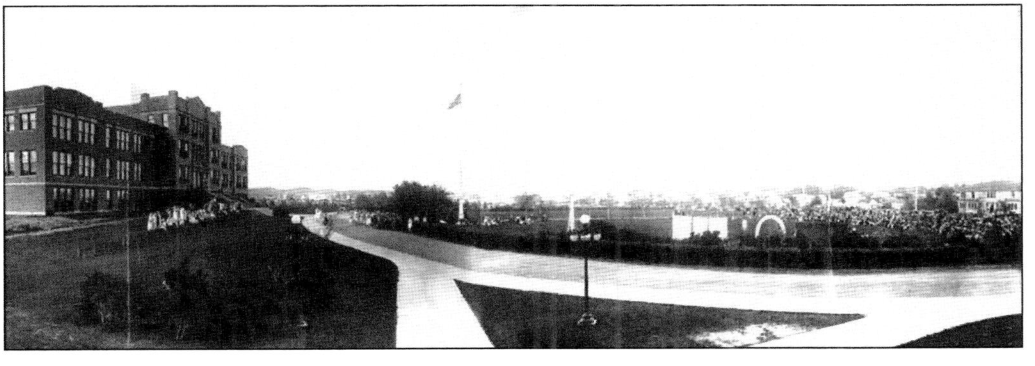

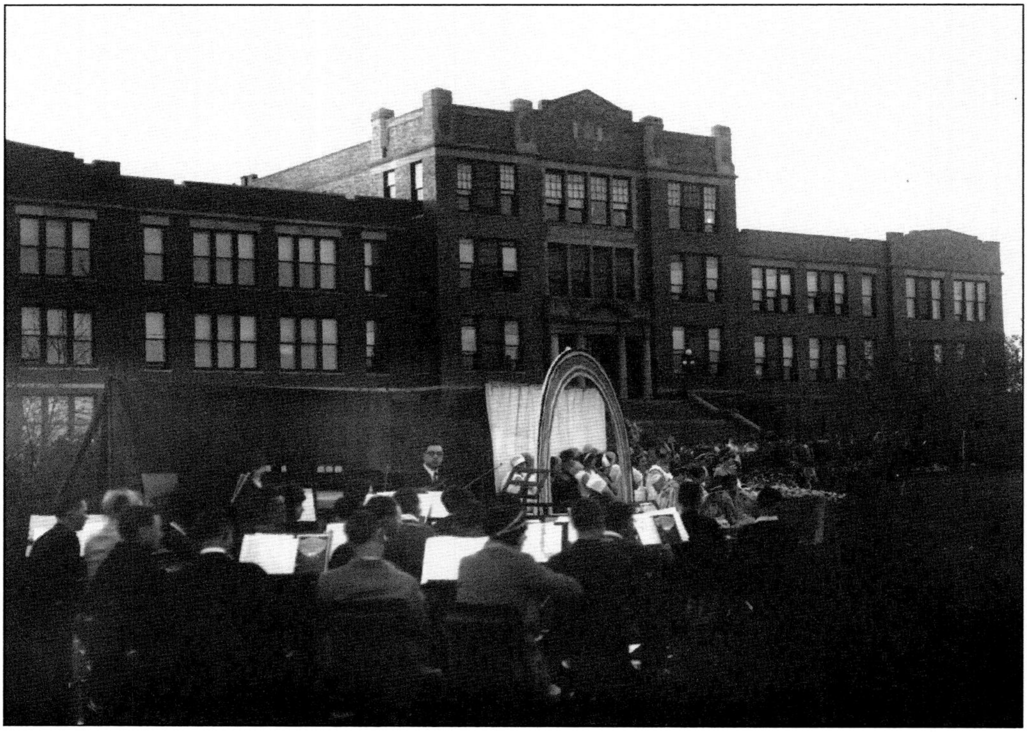

The Minot State Teachers College orchestra prepares to play under the direction of musical director Dr. Arturo Petrucci. Dancers entered the ellipse for their performances through the archway adjacent to the band. Notice the performers in the background along the north side of the ellipse.

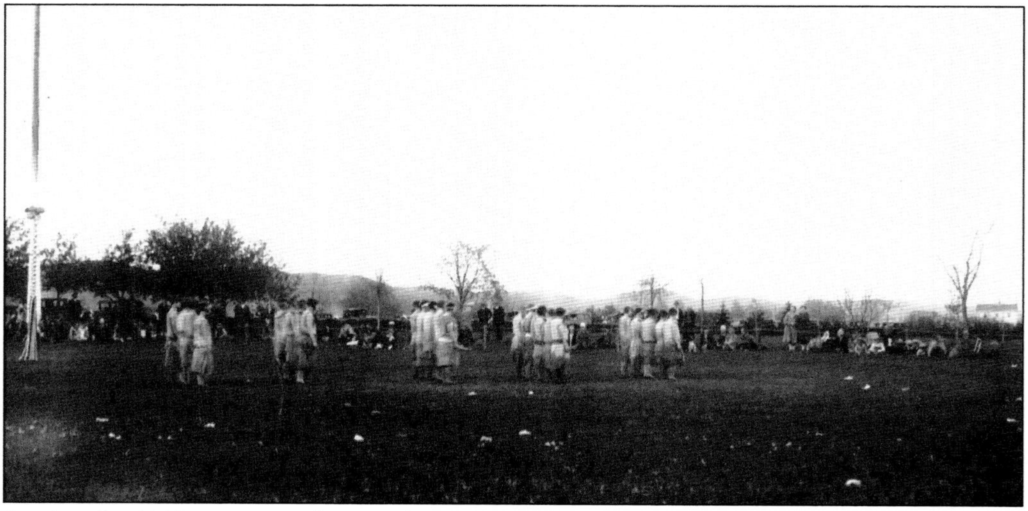

During the 1923 May Fete, dancers from the normal school lined up for their presentation. The band was located to the right, adjacent to Old Main. The audience formed along the entire front (south side) of the ellipse and usually numbered several thousand. The presentation was a major event in early Minot, which boasted a population in 1923 of slightly over 10,000 people.

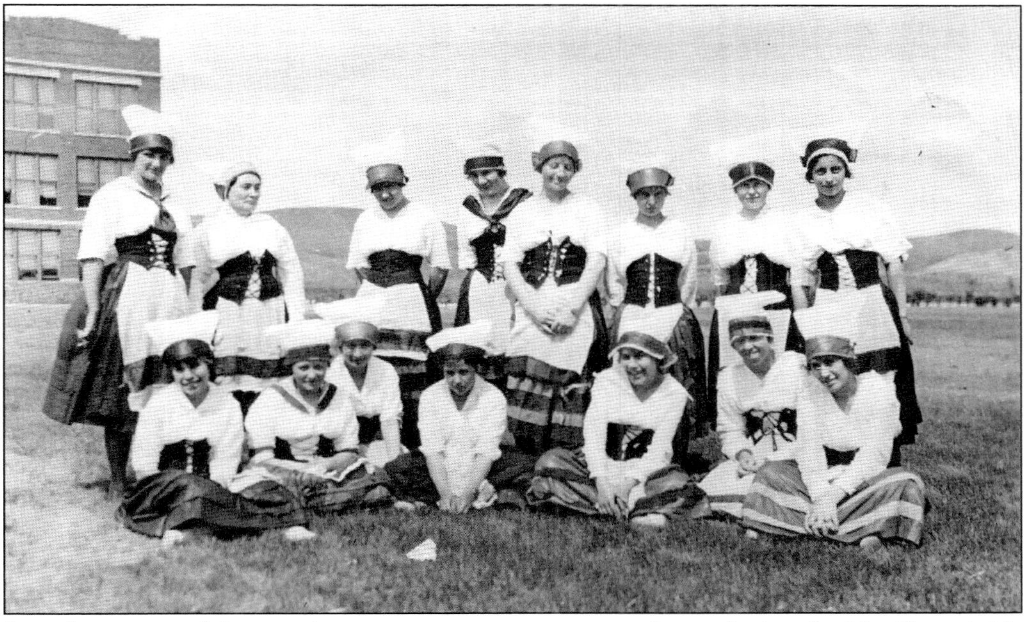

Scandinavian and Germanic costumes were a common theme during the May Fete. Aside from being a celebration of the new academic year, graduation, and the arrival of spring, it was viewed as a celebration of customs, heritage, and life.

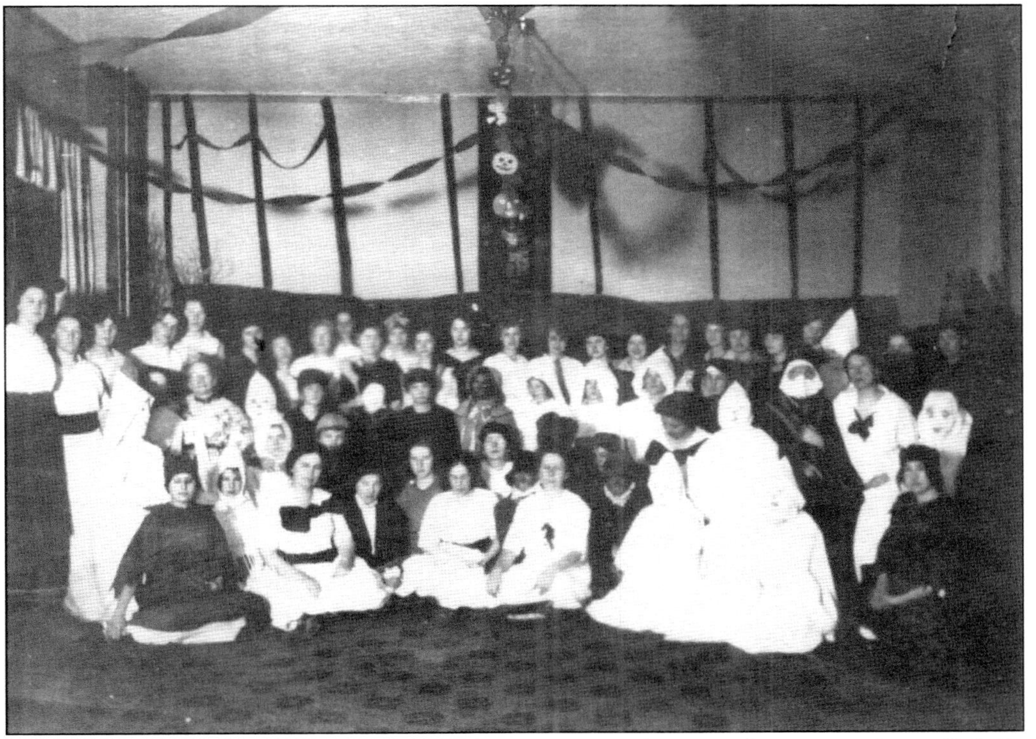

In 1914, the campus held its first Halloween party in the west dormitory. A candlelight meal followed with cocoa, apples, and Halloween treats.

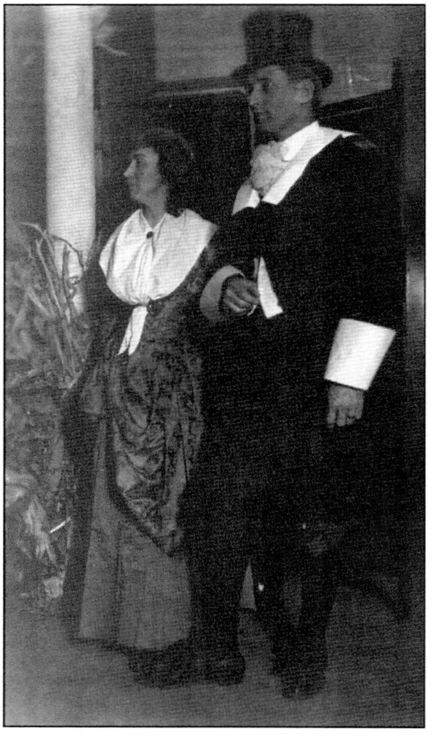

In 1914, the campus held its first Thanksgiving party. President Arthur Griswold Crane and his wife attended the event in costume. The campus provided a splendid meal and an evening of music. The event was held in the Old Main gymnasium. It was the only place suitable for large gatherings during this period.

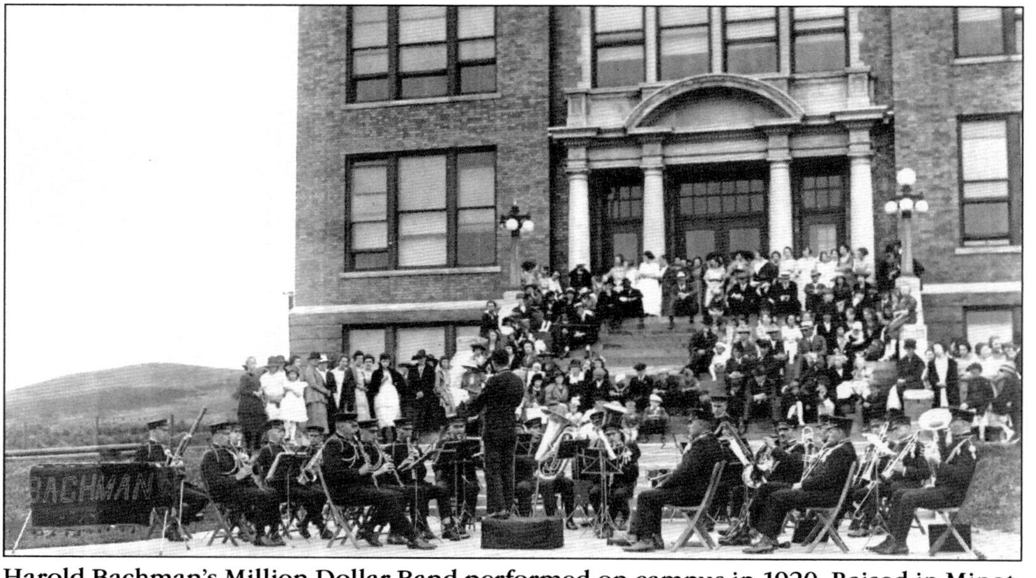

Harold Bachman's Million Dollar Band performed on campus in 1920. Raised in Minot, Bachman volunteered for the North Dakota National Guard and established the Second Infantry Band. His group entertained the doughboys across Europe. At a concert in St. Nazaire, Gen. Hunter Liggett commented that "the band was worth a million dollars to the United States Army," hence the name. Following the war, he was the director of bands at the University of Chicago from 1935 to 1942 and Marching Gator Band at the University of Florida from 1948 to 1958.

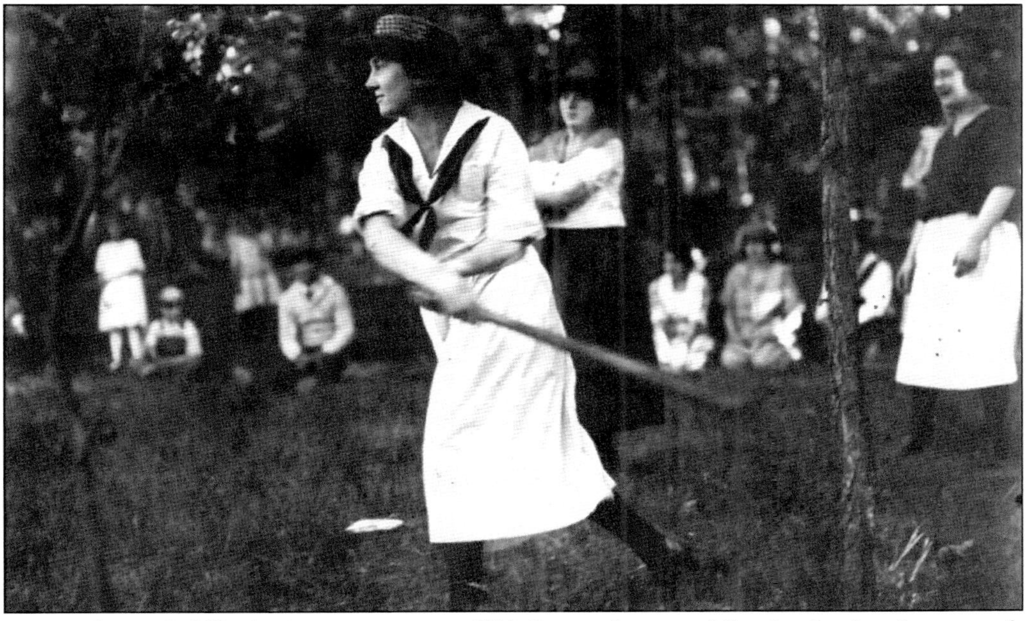

Spring through fall, picnics were a part of life for students and faculty. In the photograph above, students from the 1921 junior and senior classes joined for a day of fun in Oak Park, which was a short distance from the campus.

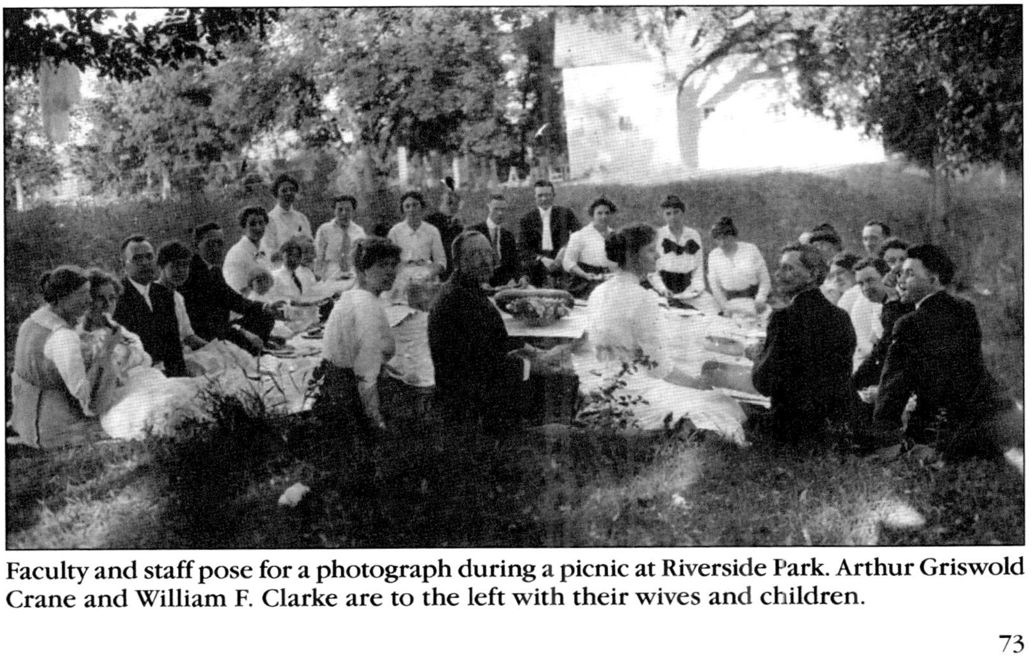

Faculty and staff pose for a photograph during a picnic at Riverside Park. Arthur Griswold Crane and William F. Clarke are to the left with their wives and children.

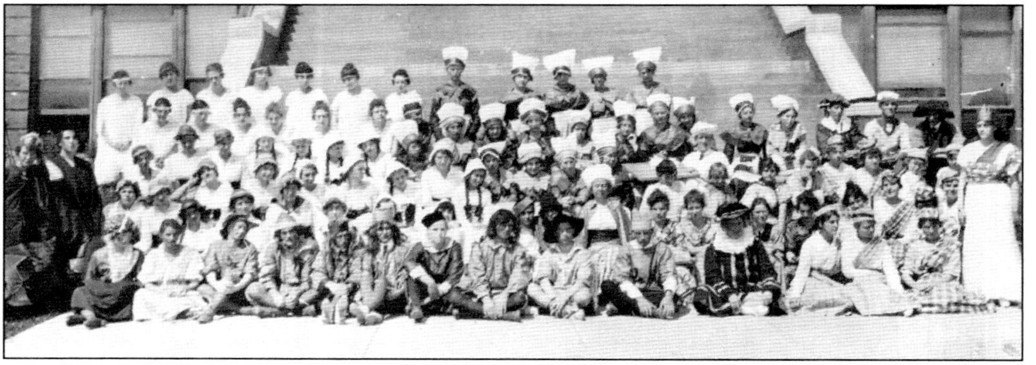

In 1916, the Shakespeare Festival was a splendid affair with indoor theater, choral presentations, and an outdoor presentation at Lincoln Lake. Above is the entire cast of the festival in front of Old Main.

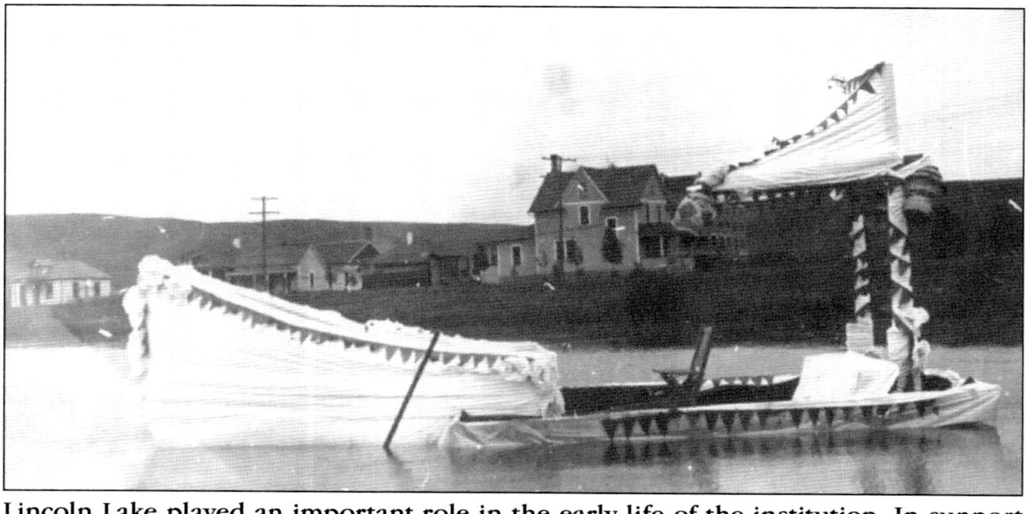

Lincoln Lake played an important role in the early life of the institution. In support of the Shakespeare Festival a floating stage was constructed on the lake. A small boat ferried actors to the platform.

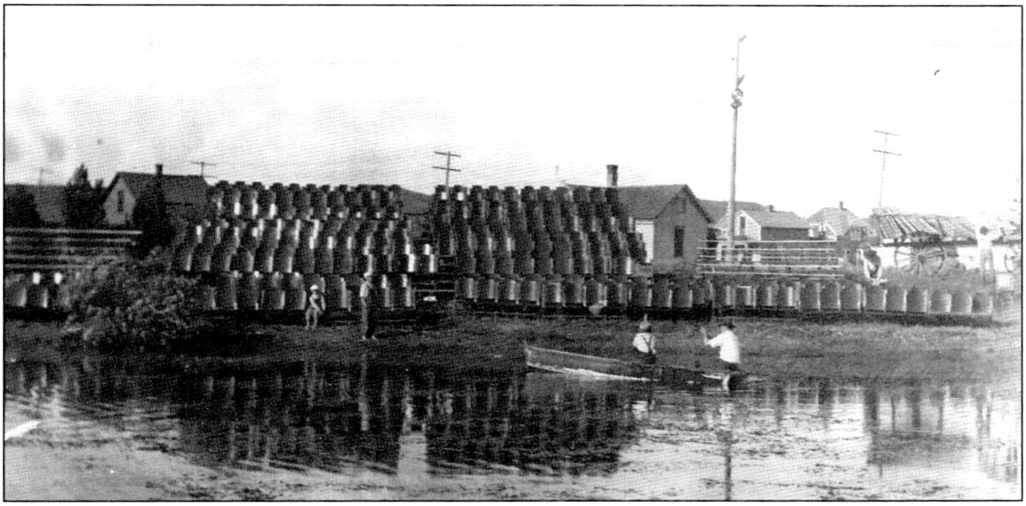
Bleachers from the campus field and seats from the Old Main gymnasium were wrapped around the north side of Lincoln Lake and Park for the Shakespeare Festival.

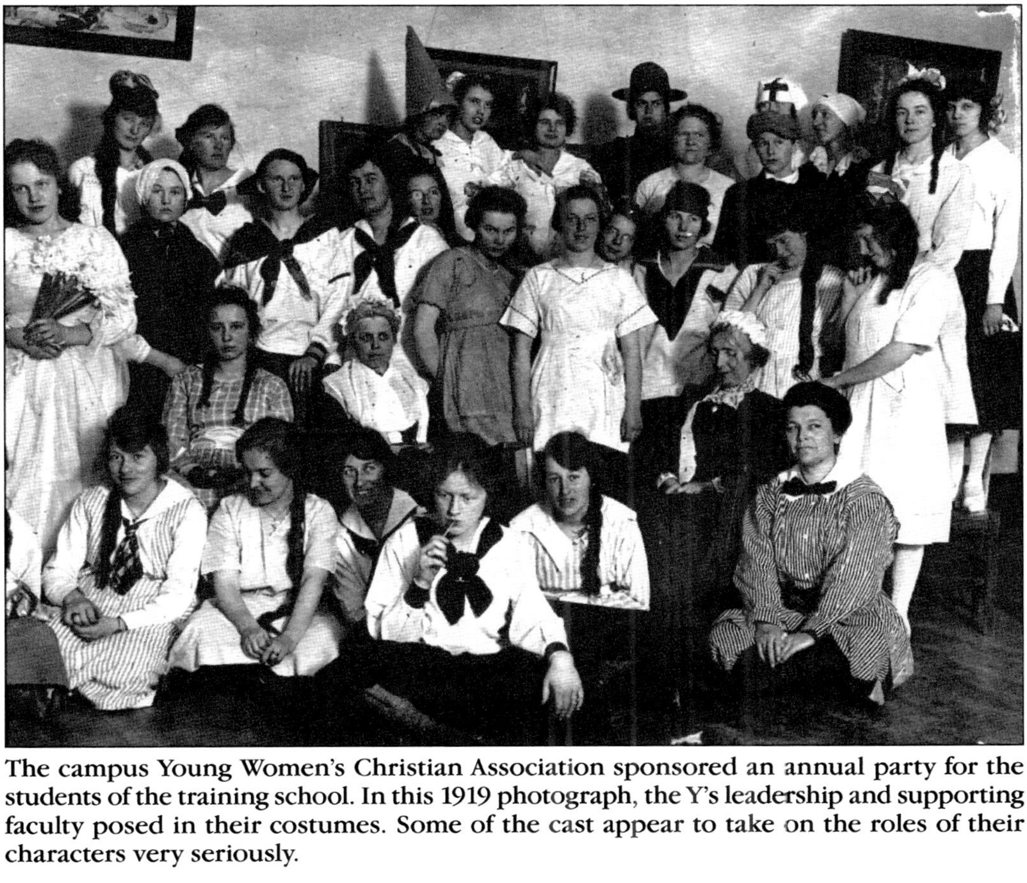
The campus Young Women's Christian Association sponsored an annual party for the students of the training school. In this 1919 photograph, the Y's leadership and supporting faculty posed in their costumes. Some of the cast appear to take on the roles of their characters very seriously.

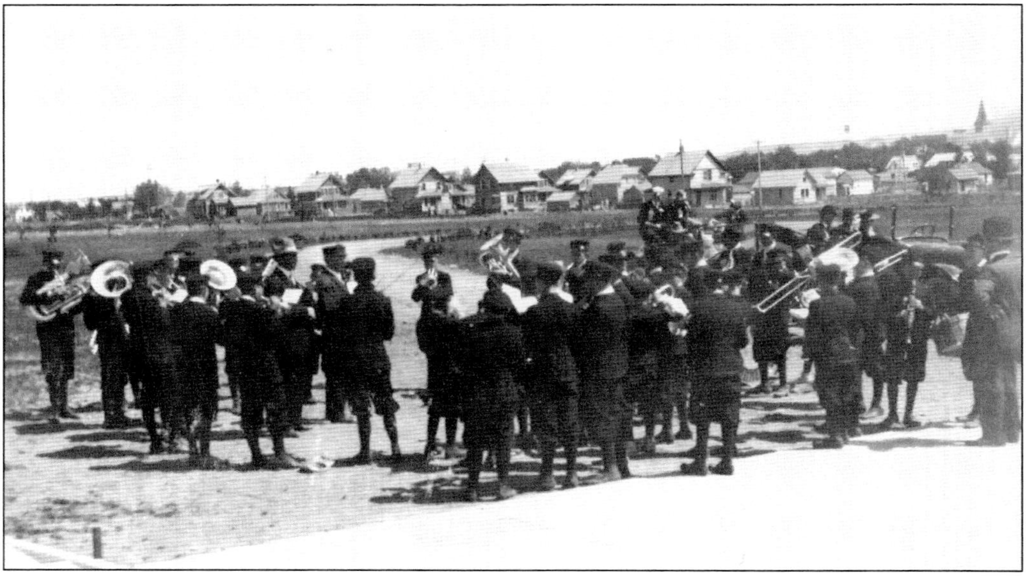

On June 8, 1916, the Minneapolis Working Boy's Band played on the steps of Old Main for the campus and community. The group was organized in 1897 and was incorporated in 1913. The group had two objectives. First, the group's sponsors wanted to provide musical training to boys, but more importantly, at the same time they wanted to provide an environment in which the boys could develop character, ideals, and respect for law and order. By the 1940s, more than 5,000 boys had played in its ranks. (*The Story of a Big Band of Little Men*, Special Collections, Minneapolis Central Library.)

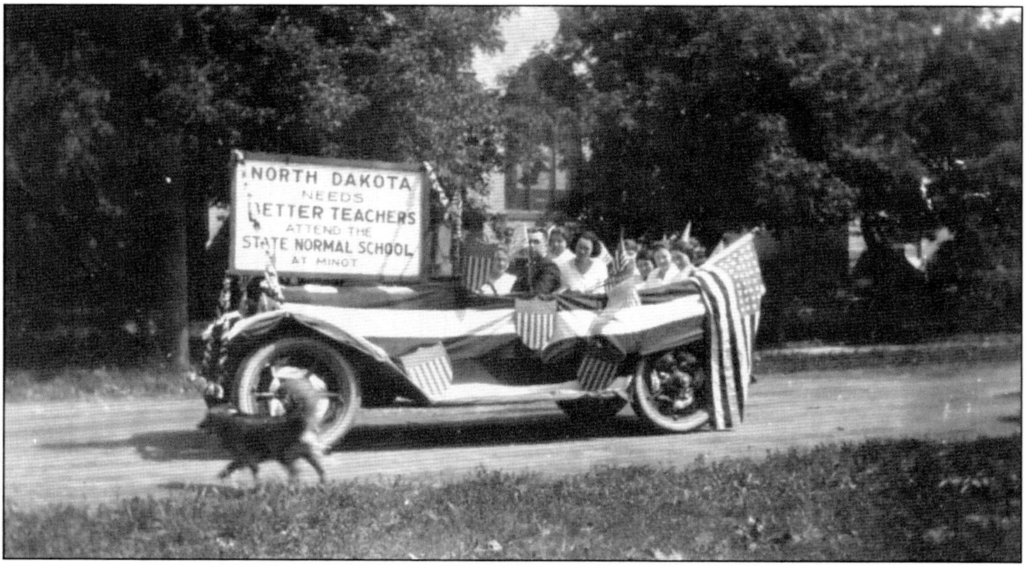

In early Minot, Independence Day was celebrated with a parade, complete with marching bands and floats. During the July 4, 1923, celebration, the normal school participated with a vehicle decorated with flags and red, white, and blue banners. Note the marketing sign for teachers.

Seven

Early Sports on the Northern Plains

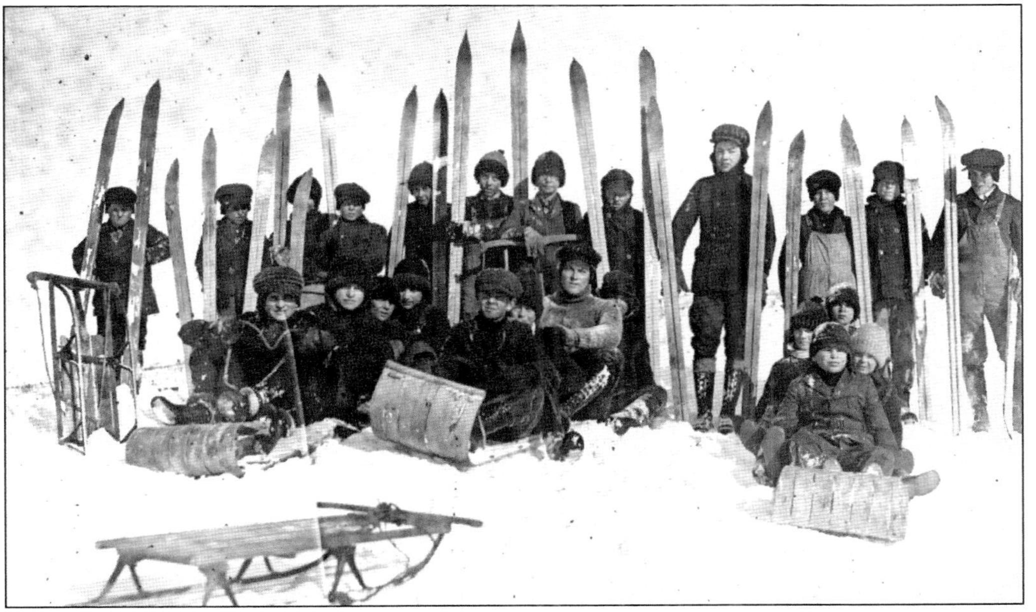

Sports on campus were far from dull. Normal Hill, a part of North Hill, was located behind the campus field. It provided an ideal location for sledding, tobogganing, and skiing. One block south of campus, an oxbow in the Mouse River provided a convenient place for swimming and relaxation. Even on the semiarid Northern Great Plains, the Mouse River Valley terrain provided sufficient diversity to meet the campus's needs. In this 1916 photograph, one of the physical education classes from the training school poses for a picture atop Normal Hill. The school provided the toboggans and skis. George J. Altmann, the physical education instructor, is seated on the middle toboggan.

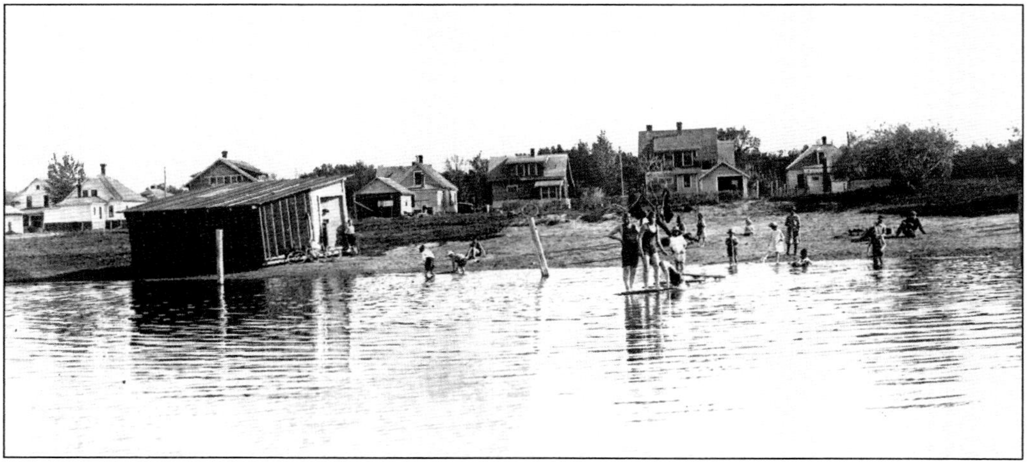

Lincoln Lake and Park, located directly south, one block from campus, was formed around an oxbow of the meandering Mouse River. The lake was popular with the students from the normal and training schools. Under an arrangement with the Minot Park Board, the normal school had control over improvements and care of the park and lake. The 15-acre park boasted a bathing beach, tarpaper-covered bathhouse, and lifeguard. The Minot Rotary Club, park board, and normal school financed the facility.

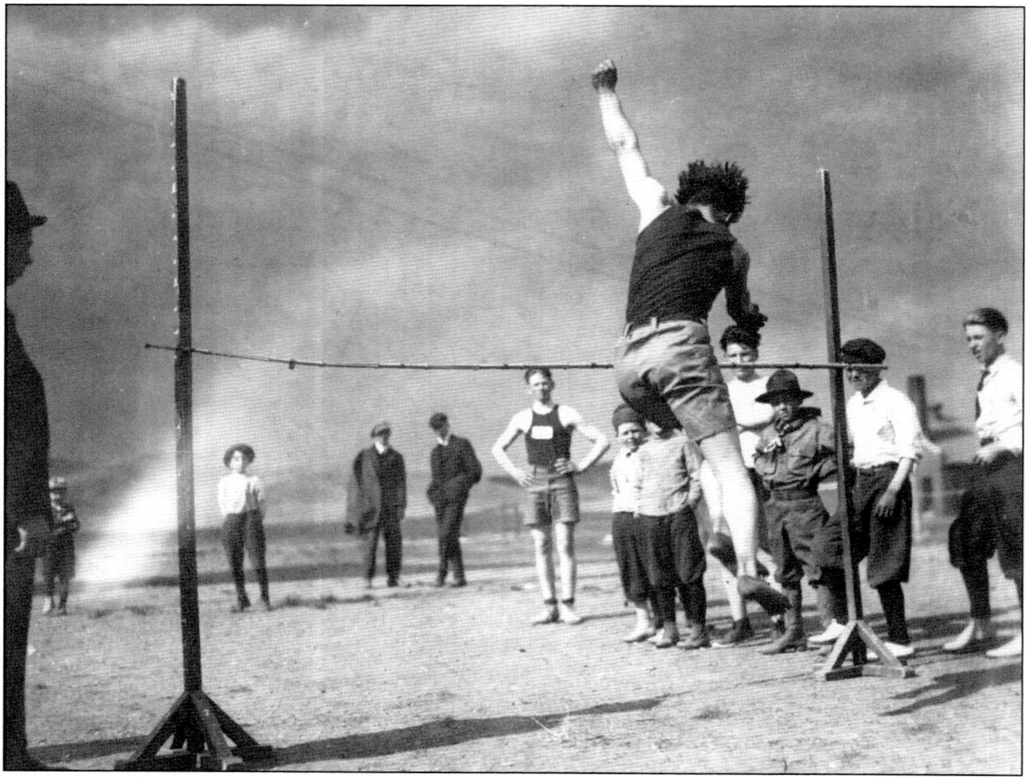

In this 1916 photograph, a student from the training school high school attempts the running high jump during a school activity. The field and track were located at the rear of the training school on the northwest corner of the campus property.

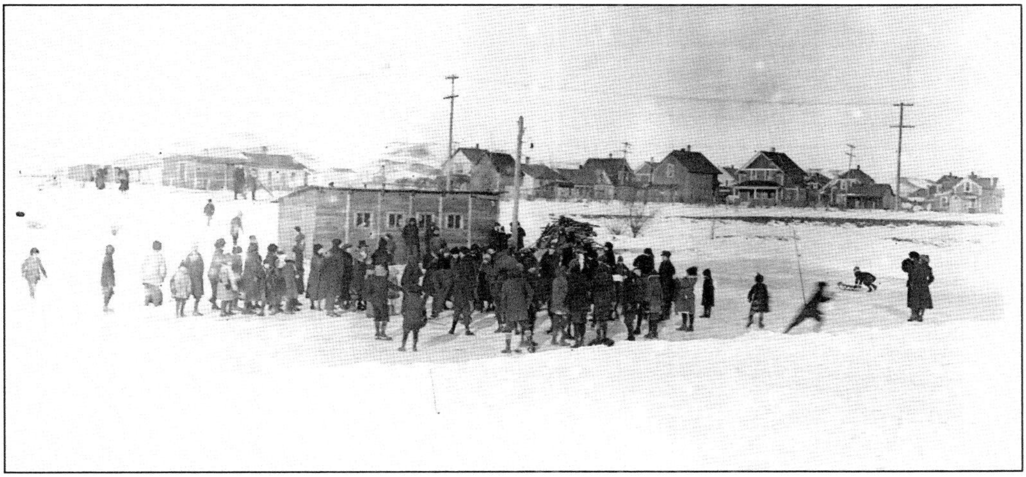

Lincoln Lake was transformed into a skating rink during the winter months. To keep the snow from drifting across the ice, snow fences were installed. The area was lit for nighttime use. The toboggan slides were installed nearby, and the bathhouse was converted into a warming cabin. Skating and tobogganing were part of the training school curriculum. Spring Lake, northeast of the campus, was also popular for winter sports.

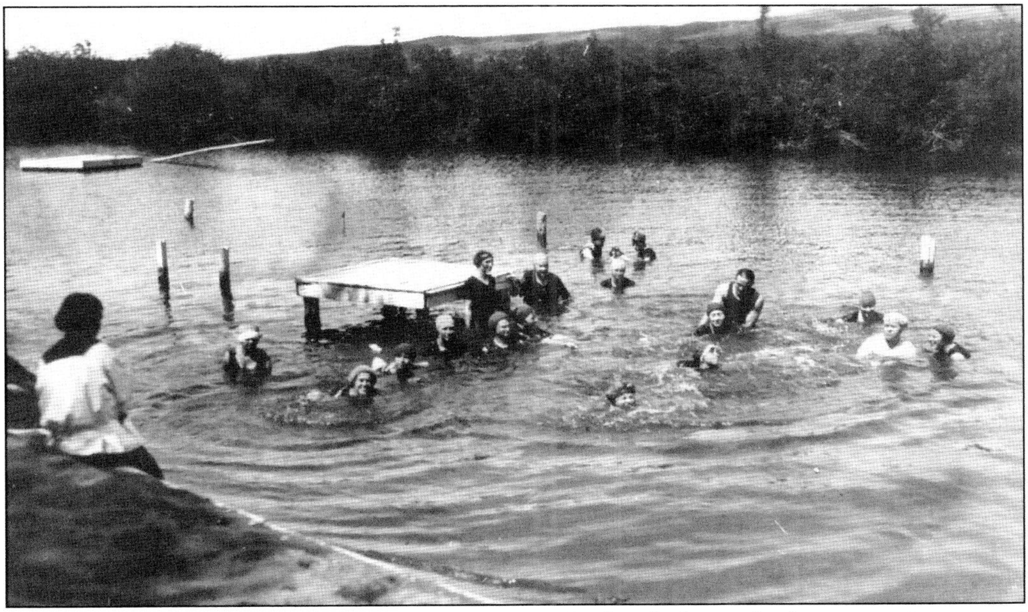

Swimming lessons were provided to the normal school physical education classes and training school students at Riverside Park (Roosevelt Park). The park had a modern bathhouse, beaches, slide, and picnic ground. Most of the students in this class appear to have been adult learners, which was not uncommon in a community on the Great Plains.

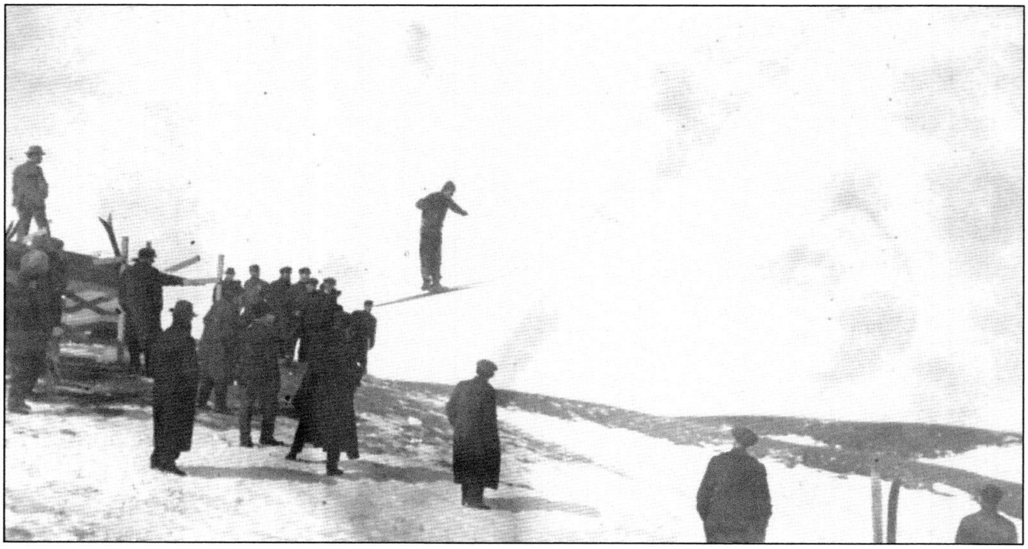

Ski tournaments were held on North Hill behind the campus. The area sported a downhill run and a ski jump. In this February 1917 photograph, a jumper takes the leap off the ski jump.

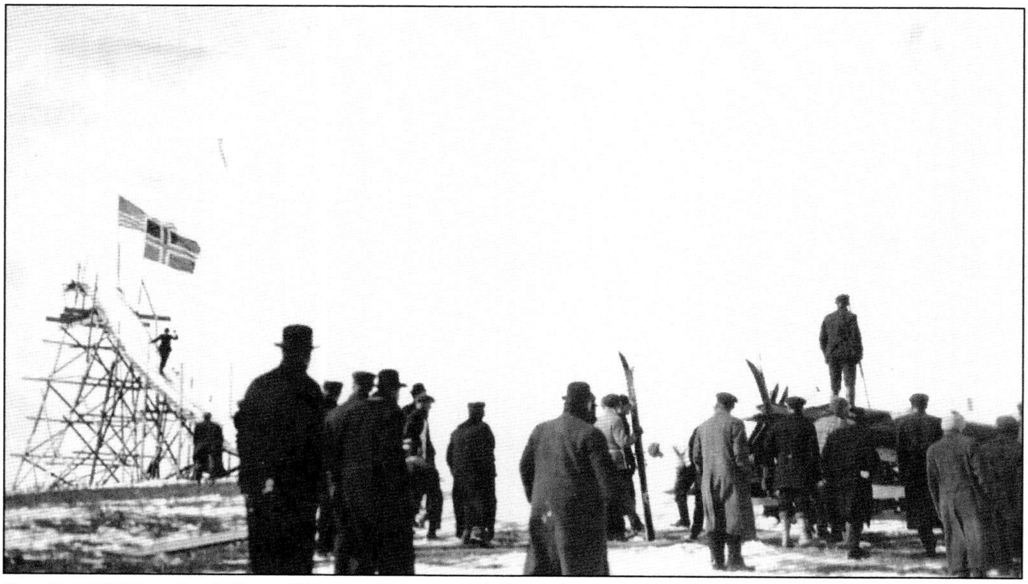

By the 1930s, the Minot Winter Sports Club had built a 225-foot-long jump on the site. The 1932 Olympian skiers Casper Oimoen, Guttorm Paulsen of Chicago, and Pedar Falstad of Devil's Lake used it.

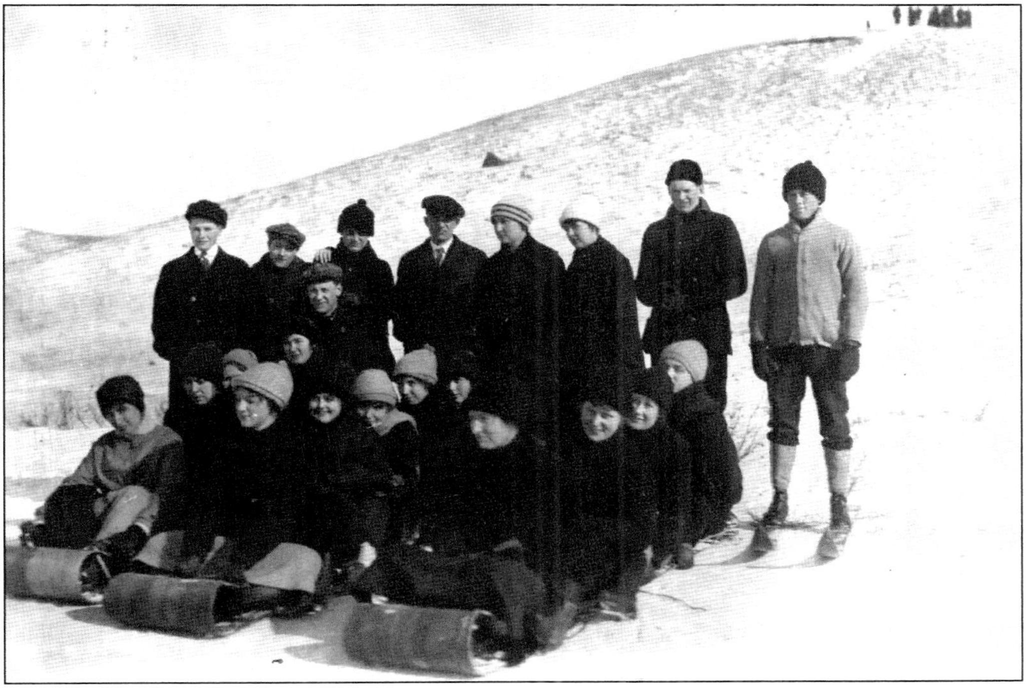

Tobogganing was a very popular sport in early Minot and part of the training school physical education curriculum. Most of the runs occurred off the slopes behind the campus on Normal Hill. Note in this photograph that toboggan rides were segregated. Only girls are on the bobs, and the young men on the hilltop wait their turn.

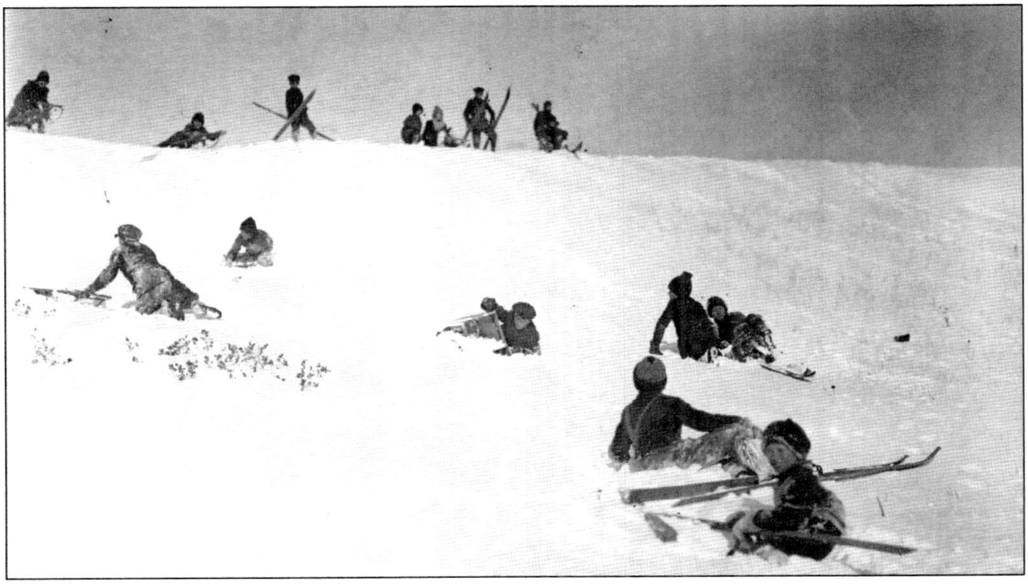

Students from the training school tried to master skiing while others attempted the steep slope on their "flyers." As seen, not many made it down the Normal Hill. Yet spirits seemed high, and despite the accumulation of snowbound failures, others continued to challenge the hill.

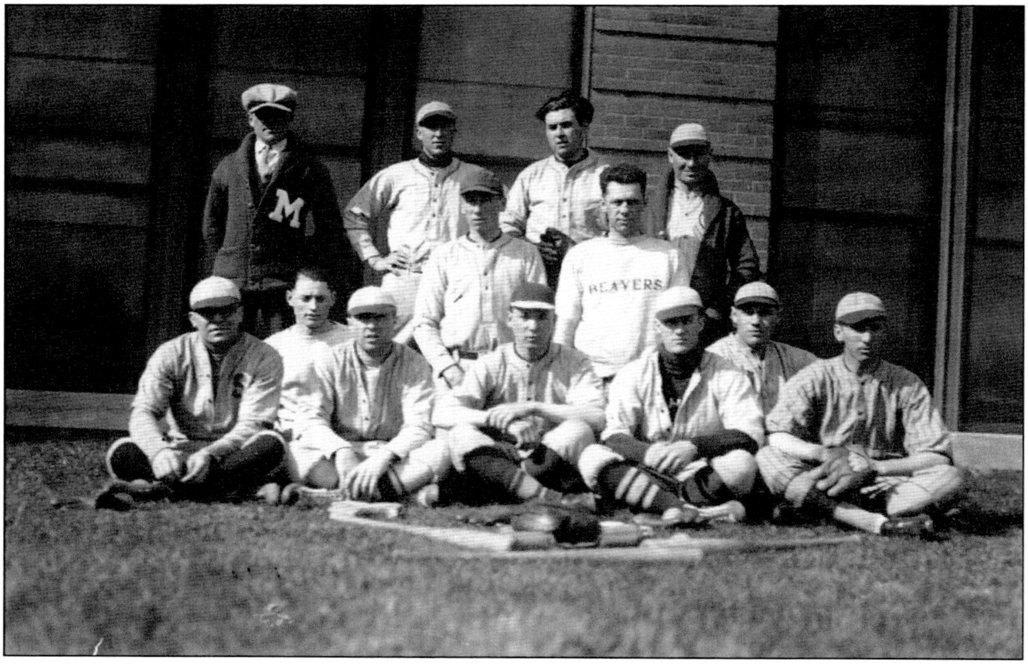

Coach Carl E. Bublitz is seen with the 1925 Beavers baseball team. One team member's jersey (right, second row) bears the name of the school's newly appointed mascot: Beavers. It is the earliest known photograph of a sport team using the beaver logo.

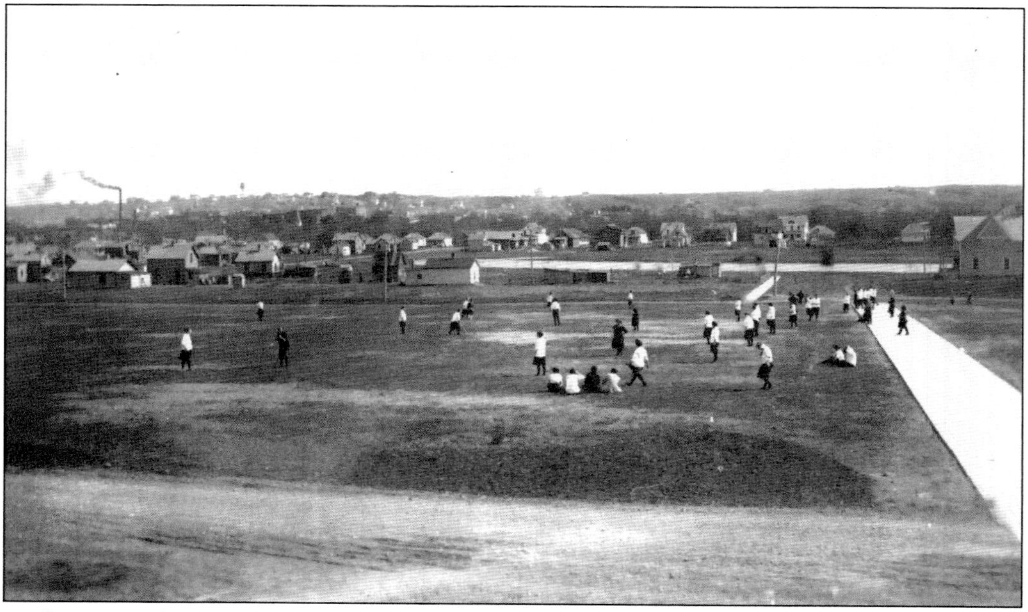

In this 1917 photograph, girls play baseball on the east side of the ellipse in front of Old Main. During the second decade of the 20th century, the lawn had no trees or plants to interfere with play. Having first appeared in the 1880s, girls' baseball remained popular during the period. It lost most of its appeal to the general public during the Great Depression. Lincoln Lake is in the right background.

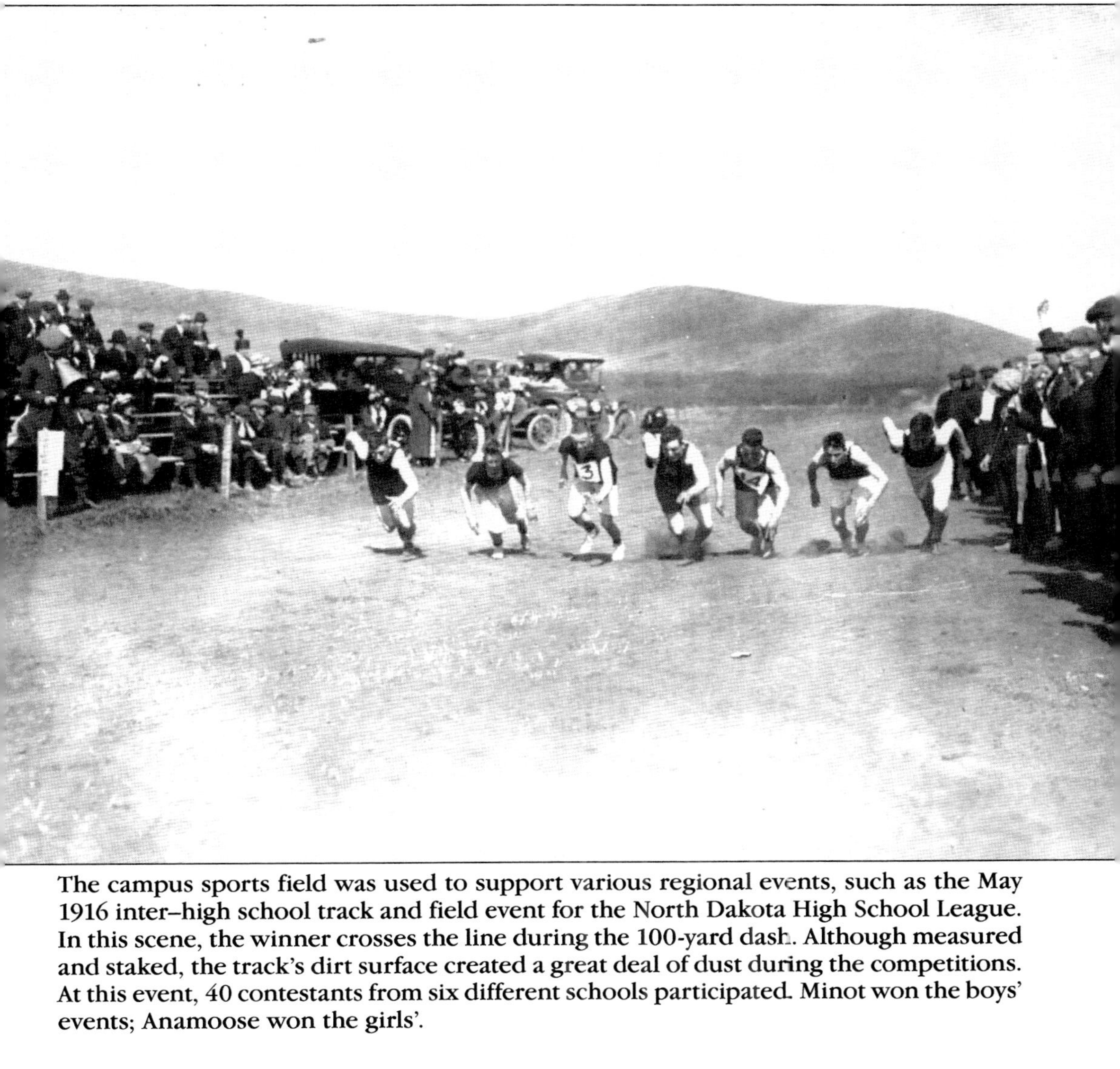

The campus sports field was used to support various regional events, such as the May 1916 inter–high school track and field event for the North Dakota High School League. In this scene, the winner crosses the line during the 100-yard dash. Although measured and staked, the track's dirt surface created a great deal of dust during the competitions. At this event, 40 contestants from six different schools participated. Minot won the boys' events; Anamoose won the girls'.

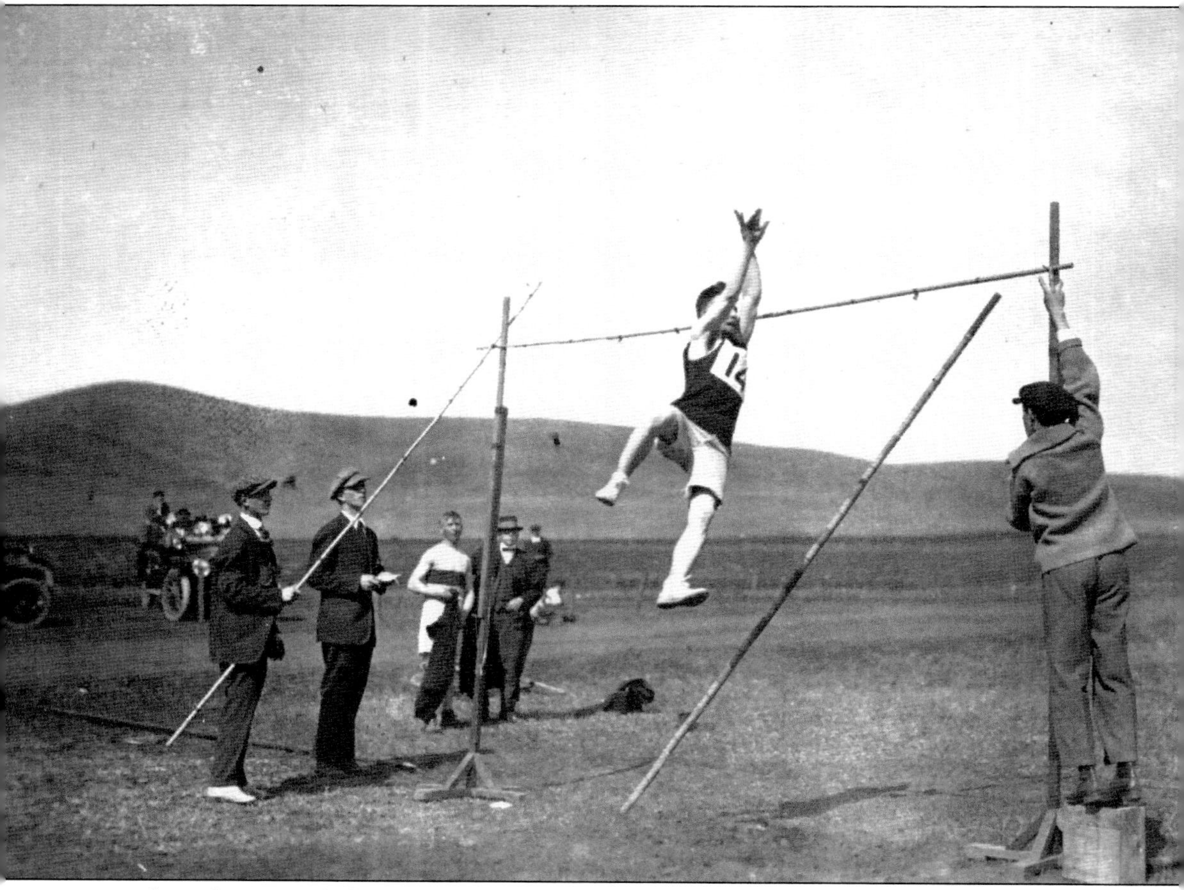

In this photograph from the 1916 inter–high school track and field event, a student participates in the pole vault as judges and bystanders look on. Nothing was provided to break the athlete's fall. The pole vault became popular in the early 1900s.

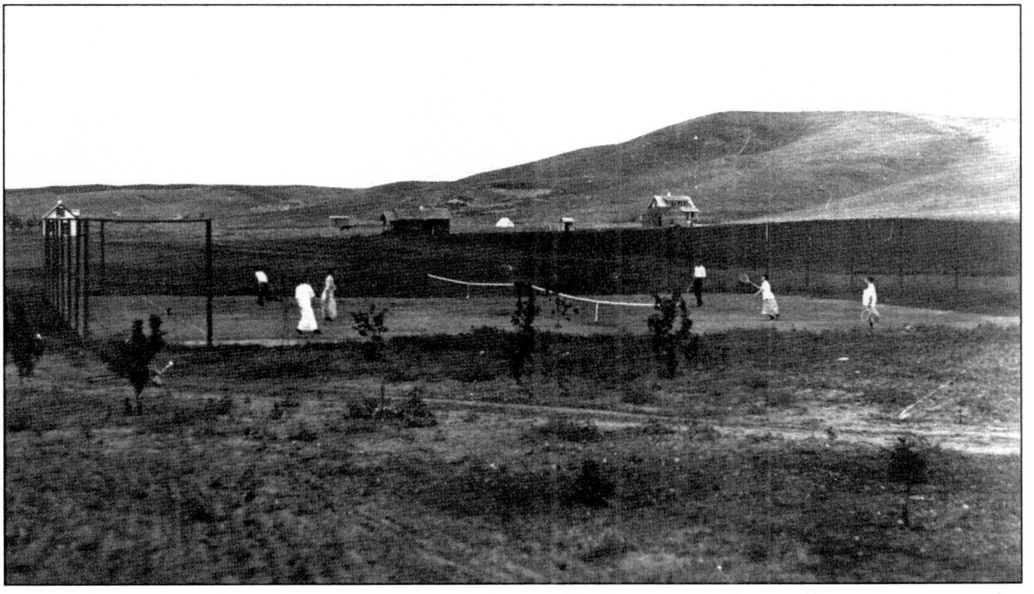

Created in 1915, the tennis courts were located adjacent to the archery range on the present site of Swain Hall. At the start of World War II, the courts were relocated to the east side of campus behind the original student union.

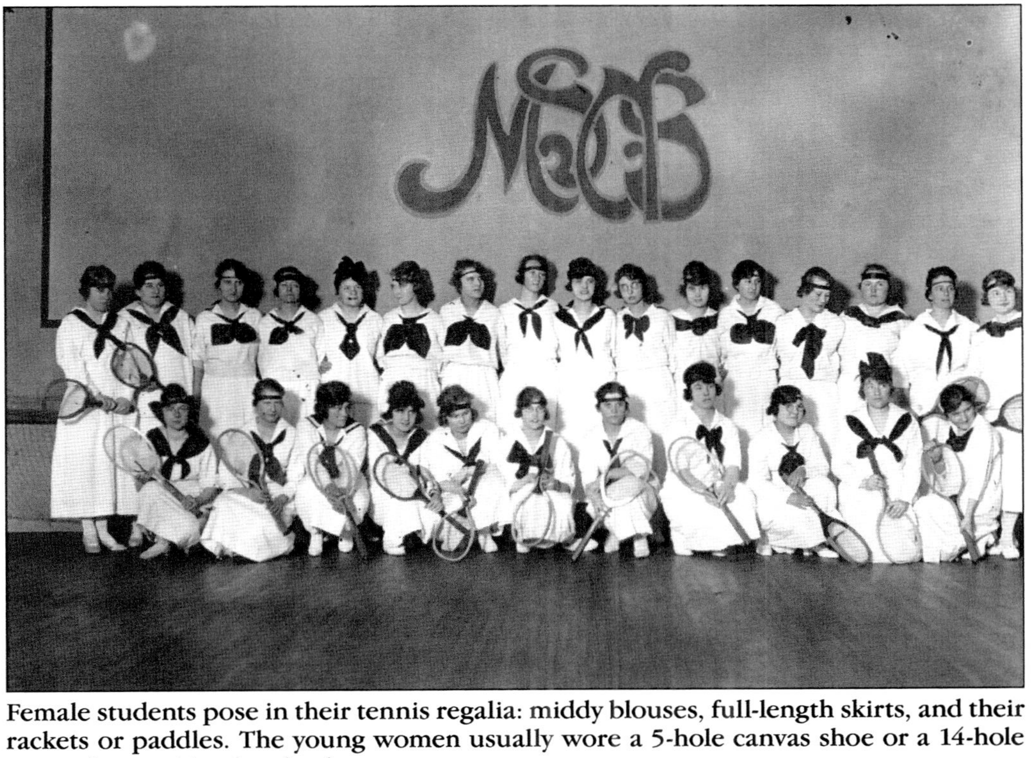

Female students pose in their tennis regalia: middy blouses, full-length skirts, and their rackets or paddles. The young women usually wore a 5-hole canvas shoe or a 14-hole canvas boot with a low heel.

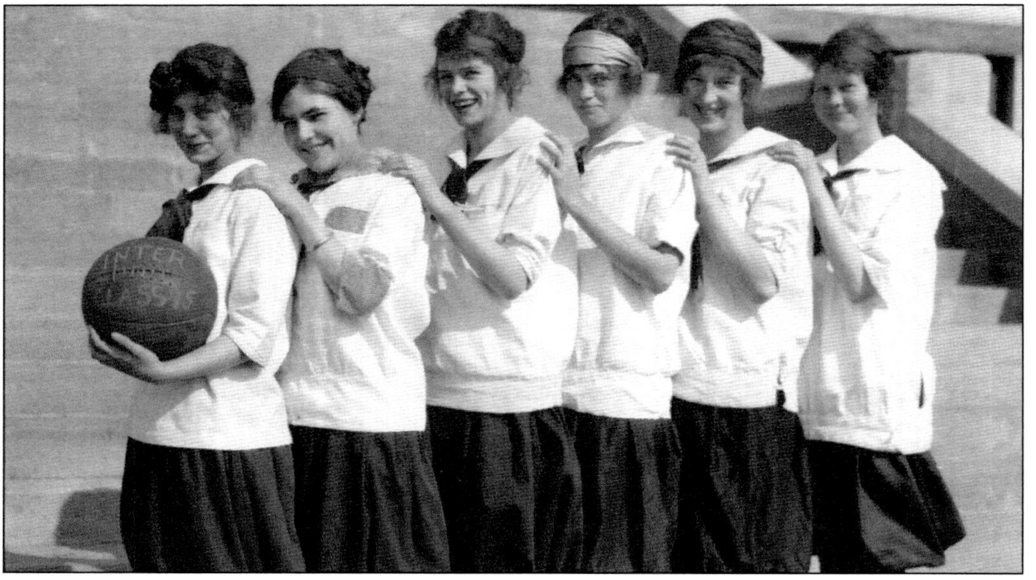

Girls' basketball was an interclass sport on the campus. Uniforms were usually the same, bloomers and white middy blouse. Teams distinguished themselves by wearing different-colored scarves around their necks. The 1915 interclass champions are, from left to right, Ruby Moore, Marjorie Walham, Louise Reishus, Thane Kirkilie, an unknown student, and Thelma Nelson.

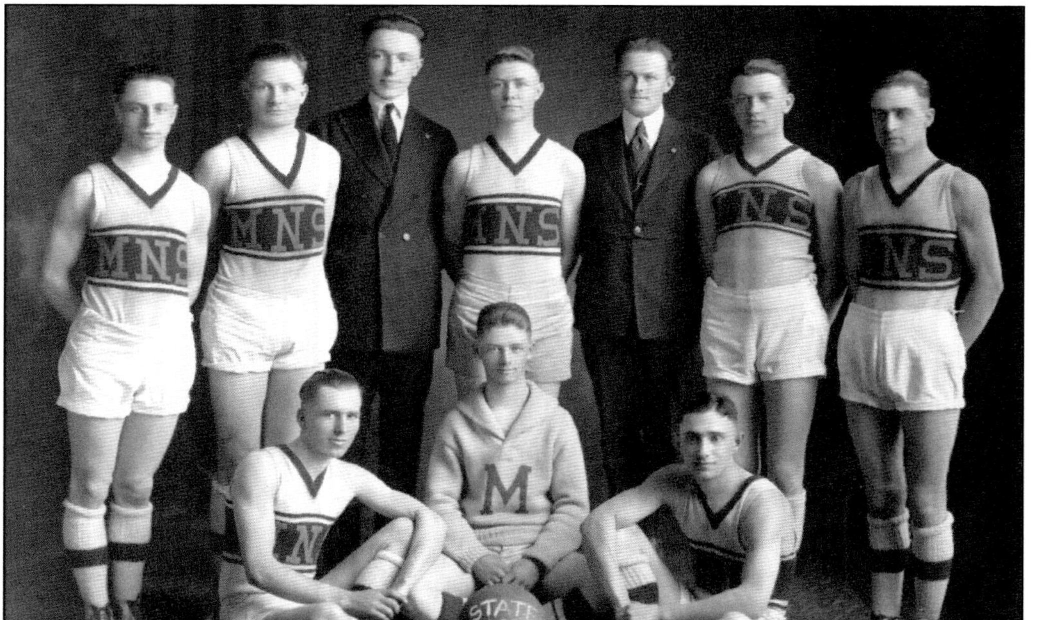

In 1921, the Minot Normal School basketball squad captured its first state championship. The squad includes Roy King, George Bissel, Ted Greenfield, Roy Leighton, Paul Nichols, George Mueller (physical education director), Alfred Opland (captain), coach F. L. Blume, Sam Zaharee, and Paul Malone.

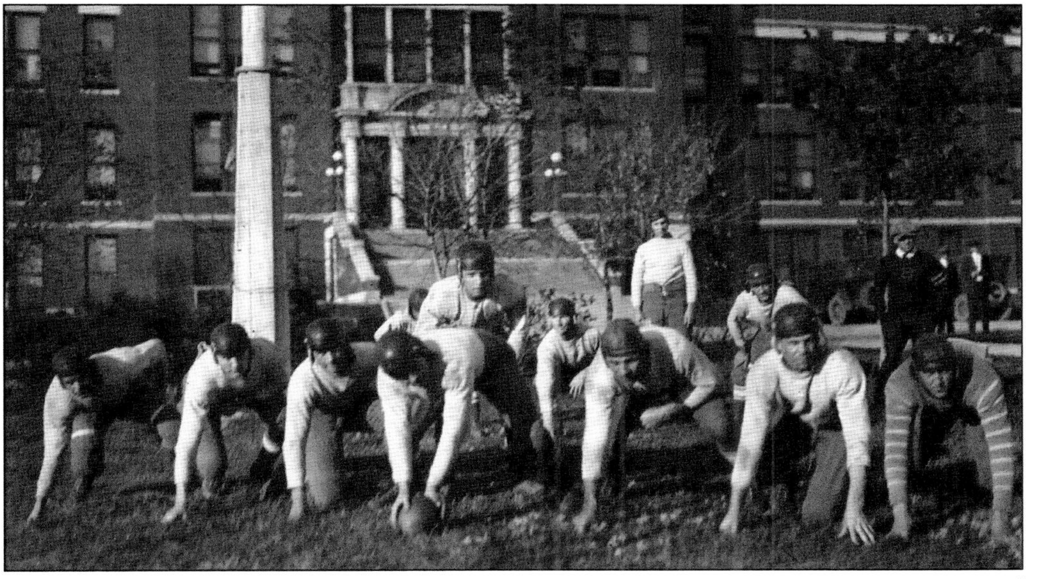

Coach Carl E. Bublitz (right background in sweater and hat) and the 1917 football squad line up at the campus flagpole in front of Old Main for some press shots. The flagpole had recently been donated by the Northern States Power Company.

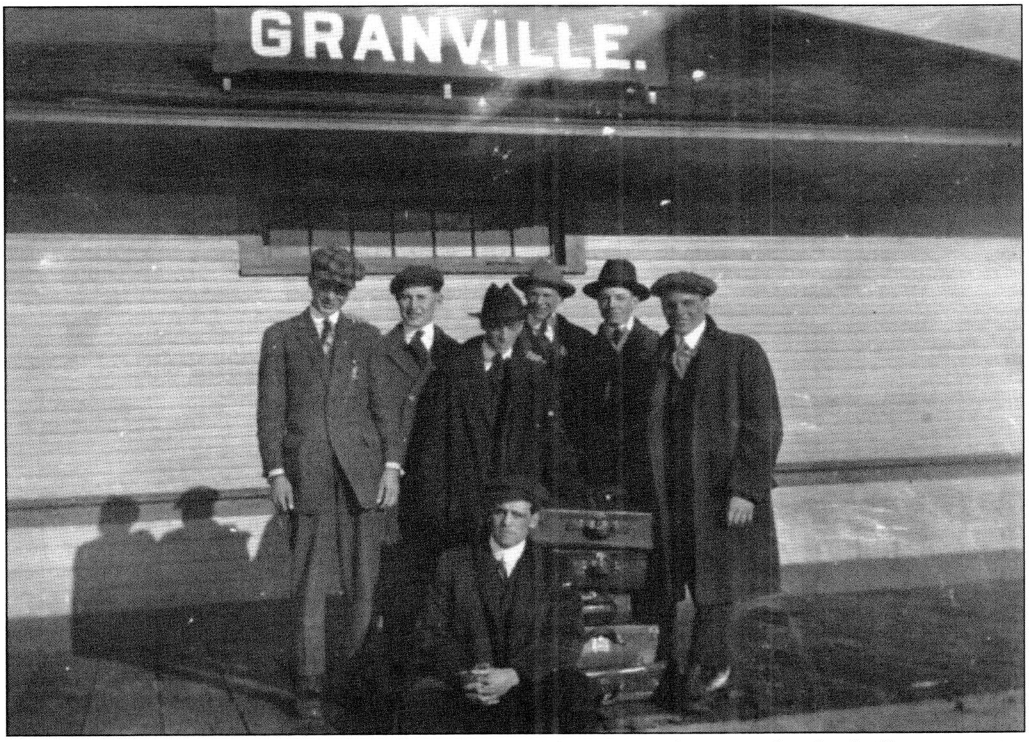

When possible, the early sports teams traveled by train. This 1918 basketball team waits on the platform for its Great Northern train outside the Granville depot.

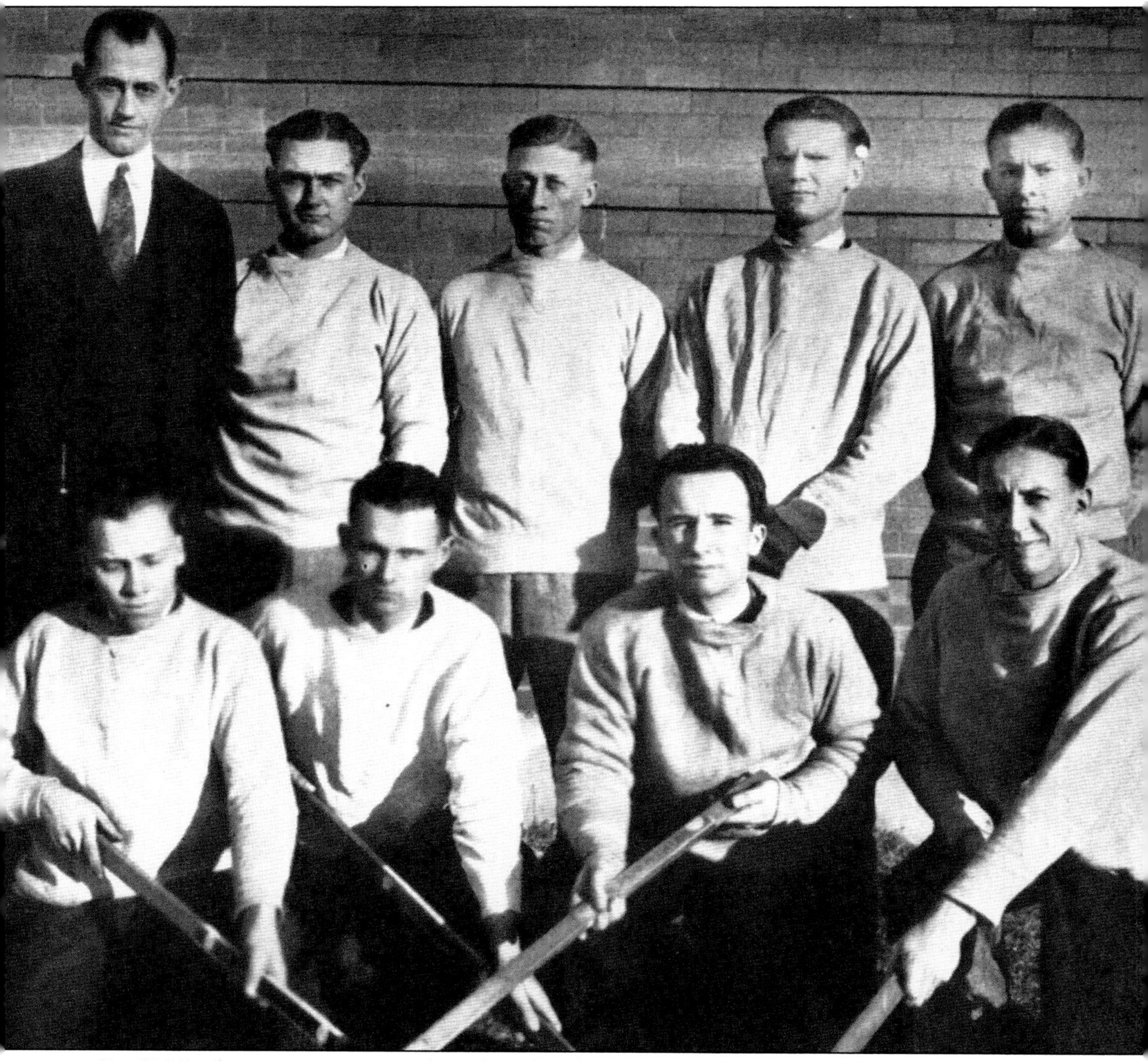

In 1928, the campus created its first hockey team, the Red and Green Pucksters. The campus organized the team to play in intra-city games. The line up includes Allen Burke, left wing; Roy Olson, right wing; Mile Lodoen, utility wingman; Albert Peterson, center; Clayton Bach, left defense; Robley Pitkin, right defense; and Mark Emswiler, utility defenseman. When an all-city team was created, two campus men, Allan Burke and Albert Peterson, earned berths on the team. James W. Coleman, who arrived on campus from the University of Arkansas in 1927, served as coach. Coleman had been the captain and the center for the Razorbacks football squad.

Eight

THE GREAT WAR

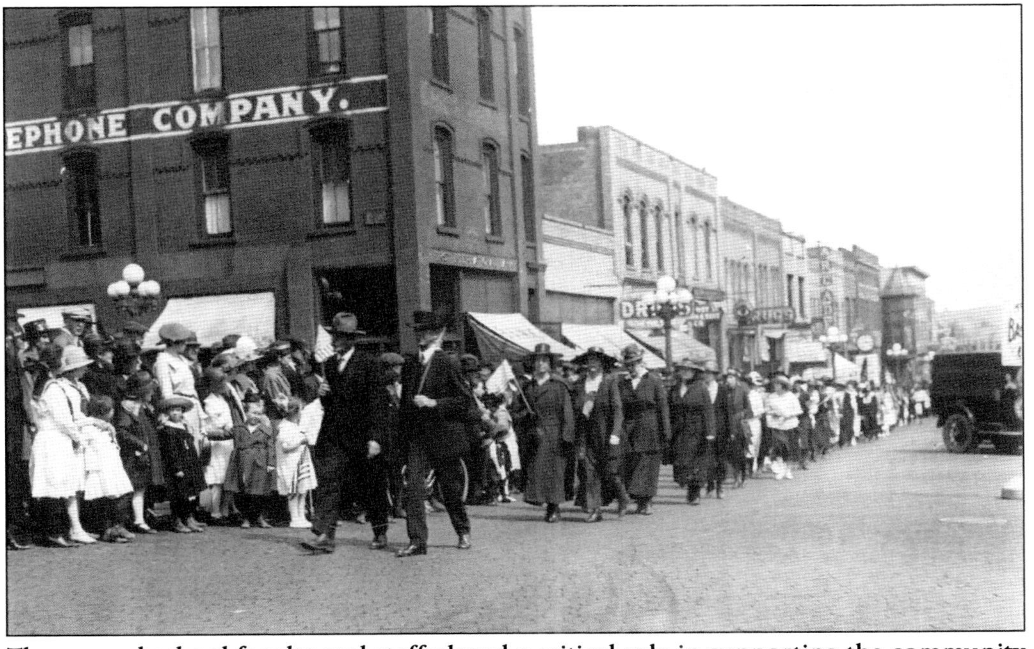

The normal school faculty and staff played a critical role in supporting the community during the Great War, participating in marches, parades, and Liberty Loan campaigns. Acting president William F. Clarke led the normal school faculty, staff, and students in this 1917 march. Many of the marches originated at the campus and wound through the community, ending in the downtown commercial district. Beside the normal school president who served in the U.S. Army Sanitary Corps, other faculty, and students served in the war service abroad and stateside. By the end of the war, two normal school students had perished on the battlefields of Europe.

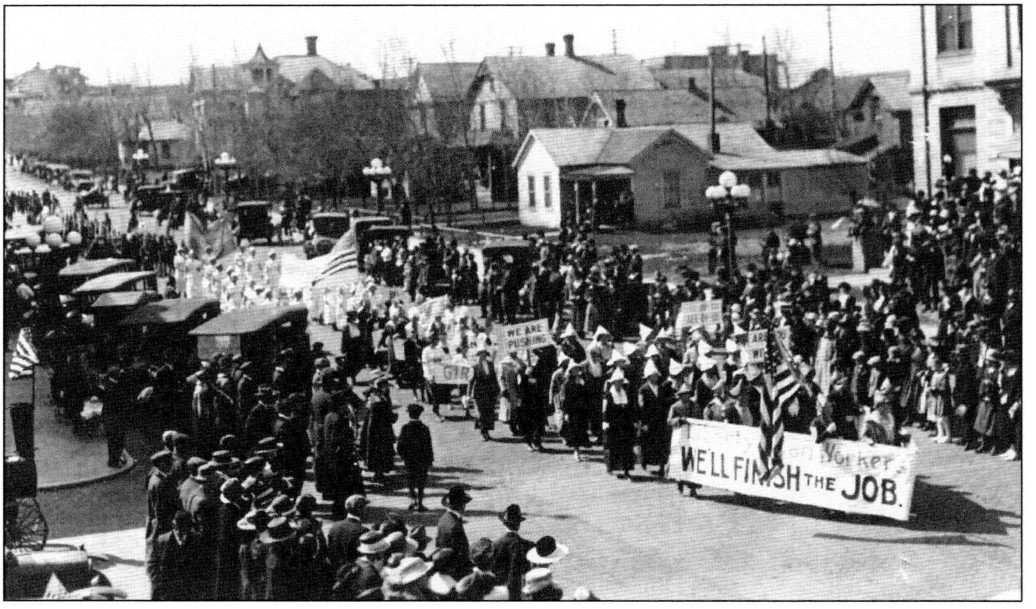

This photograph was taken in 1918 during the first Liberty Loan parade near the Elks Club at the top of South Main Street in downtown Minot. Normal school faculty, staff, and students who served with the campus Red Cross auxiliary can be seen in their white Production Corps uniforms. The city of Minot and Ward County raised more money with the war bond campaigns than any other county in North Dakota, an achievement of which the county and city were justly proud.

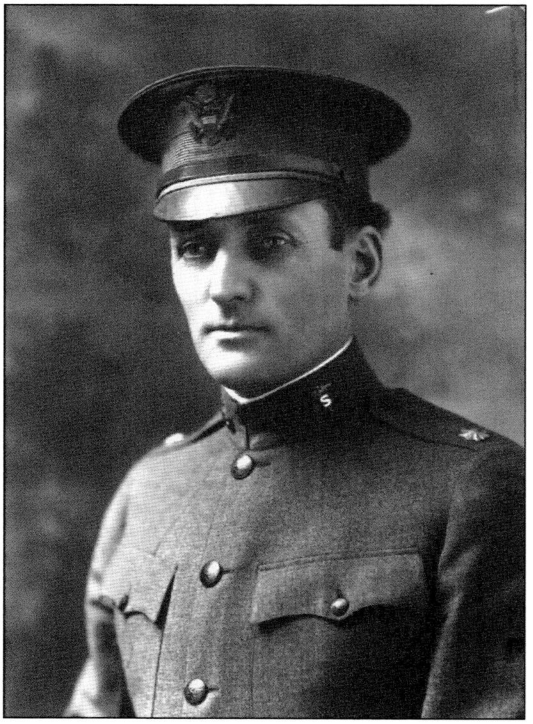

On approved leave completing his doctorate at Columbia University, president Arthur Griswold Crane was called to service in the U.S. Army Sanitary Corps at Walter Reed Hospital, Washington, D.C. He assisted injured veterans in coping with their wartime injuries and learning new workforce skills. He did not return to his post at the State Normal School at Minot until 1920.

In September 1918, president William F. Clarke was informed that Pvt. Henry Finn had been the first student from the State Normal School at Minot to give his life in service of the nation. His citation reads, "The Distinguished Service Cross is posthumously presented to Henry Finn, Private, US Army, for extraordinary heroism in action near Les Franquettes Farm, France, July 23, 1918. Despite the severe bombardment of machine guns, Private Finn went into an open field to administer aid to wounded officers and men. He was killed while rendering aid to these men."

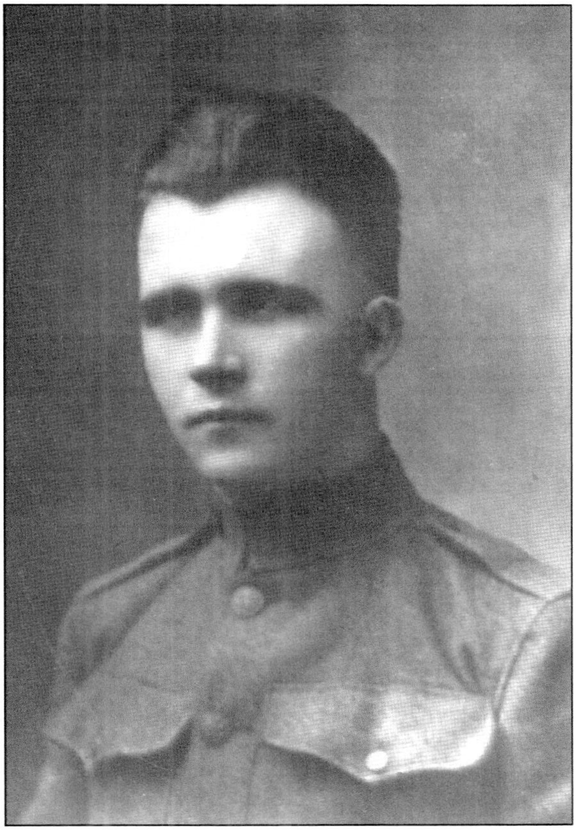

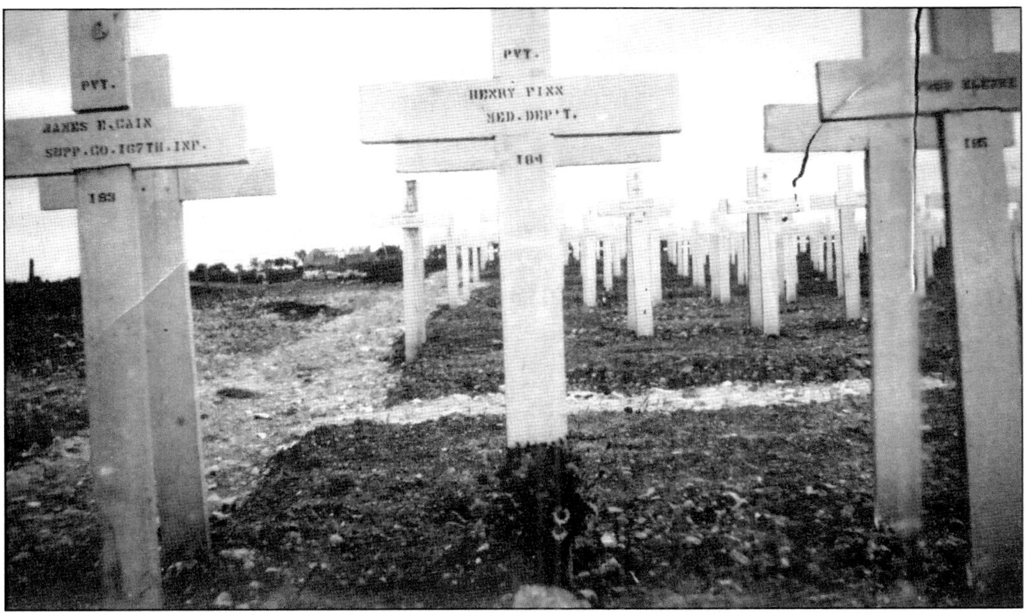

The picture above shows Finn's temporary interment. He was eventually interred in plot A, row 18, grave 27 of the Oise-Aisne American Cemetery at Fere-en-Tardenois, France.

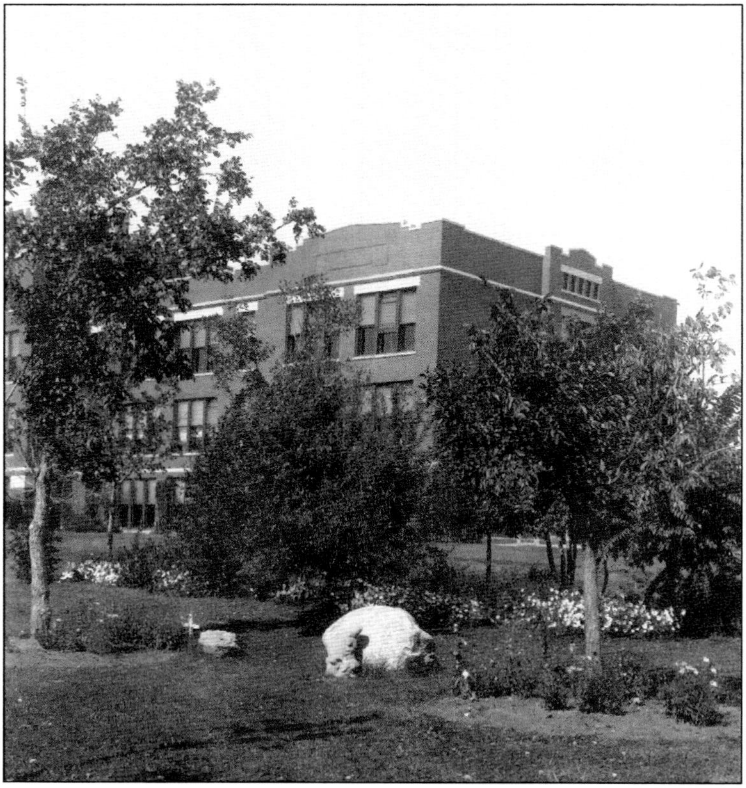

A month later, the campus was informed that a second student, Fred Otis Cooper, had also died. Cooper was seriously injured on the battlefield. He was returned stateside, where he succumbed to his injuries. In honor of Henry Finn and Cooper, the campus planted two trees, a memorial garden with flowers, and two white crosses. The trees remain part of the modern landscape.

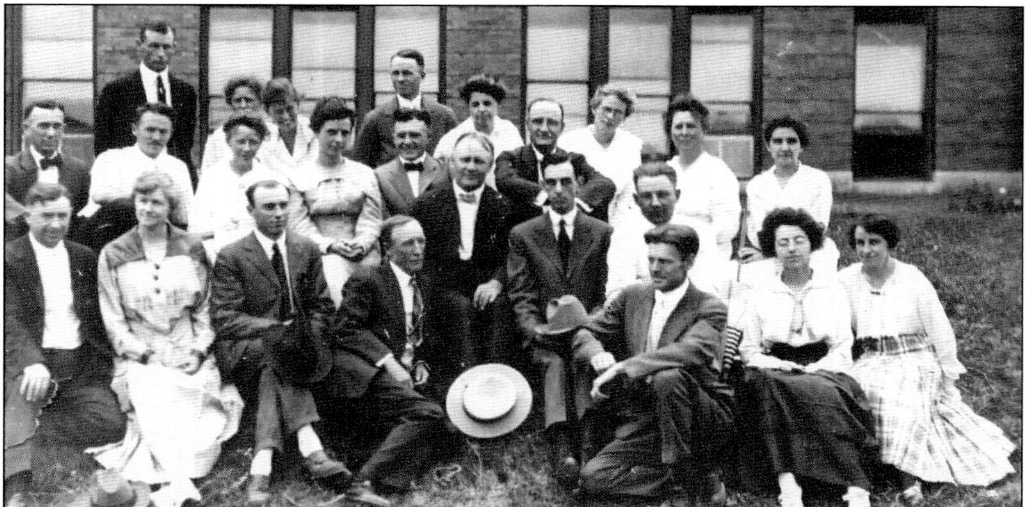

After president Arthur Griswold Crane went to Columbia University to pursue his doctorate and was later called to war service, Dr. Asra Steele (center with bow tie and straw hat at his feet) became acting president (1917–1918). Steele angered local businesspersons during the 1918 convocation with his comments about the progress and financing of the war. Under heavy pressure, he resigned. William F. Clarke (second row, far left) took up the reins of leadership.

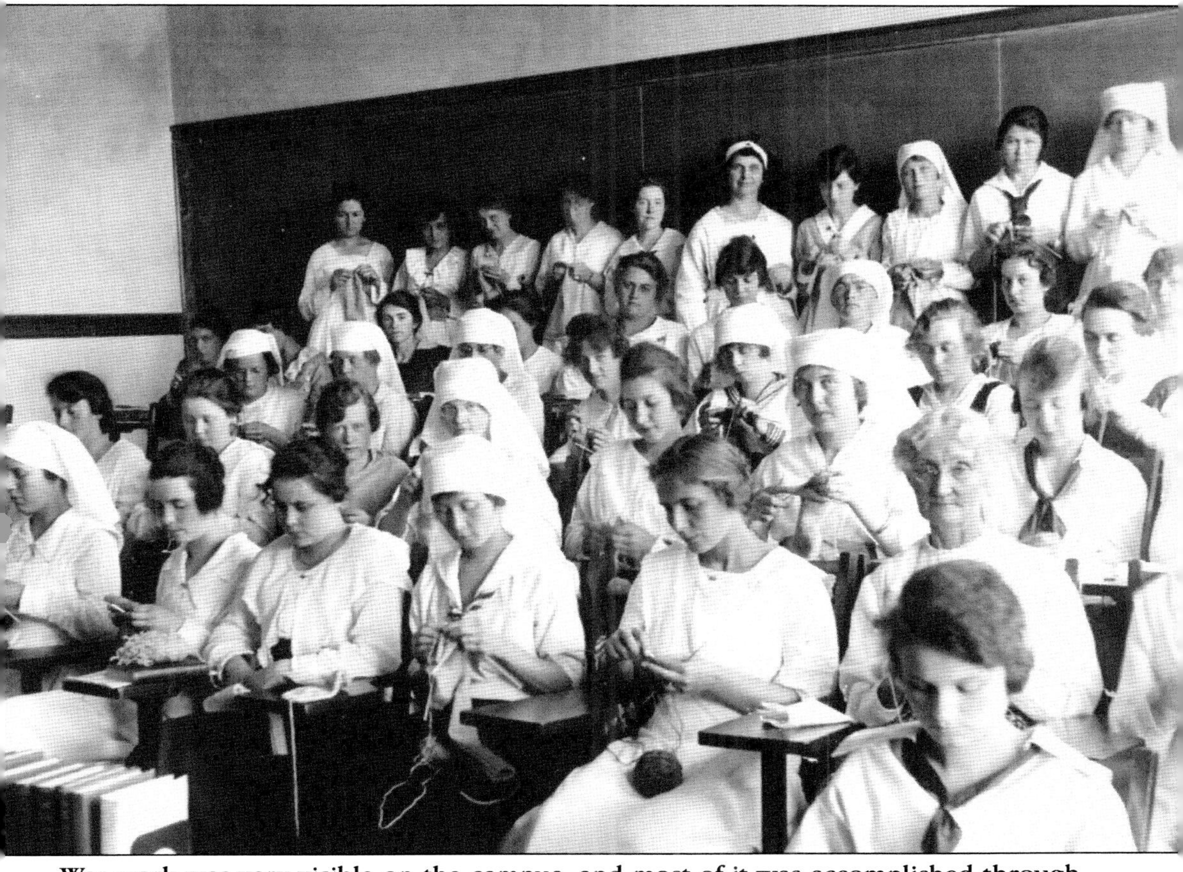

War work was very visible on the campus, and most of it was accomplished through Red Cross knitting campaigns. During the 1917 spring term alone, over 740 articles of clothing and bandages were completed. This represented 3,002 hours of voluntary labor. Work was especially active in the surgical dressing department where work was "cheerfully given and work eagerly done while from the heart of each Christian worker went a prayer that the articles might relieve the pain and suffering" of a soldier "across the sea." Under the supervision of Ethel Lee Detrick, the women in various Christian organizations (above) took up knitting. By year's end, they completed 30 sweaters, 4 knitted socks, 4 wristlets, and 5 dozen various bandages. The home economics classes also made garments for the wounded. Their cooking classes addressed conservation recipes for shortages and rationing.

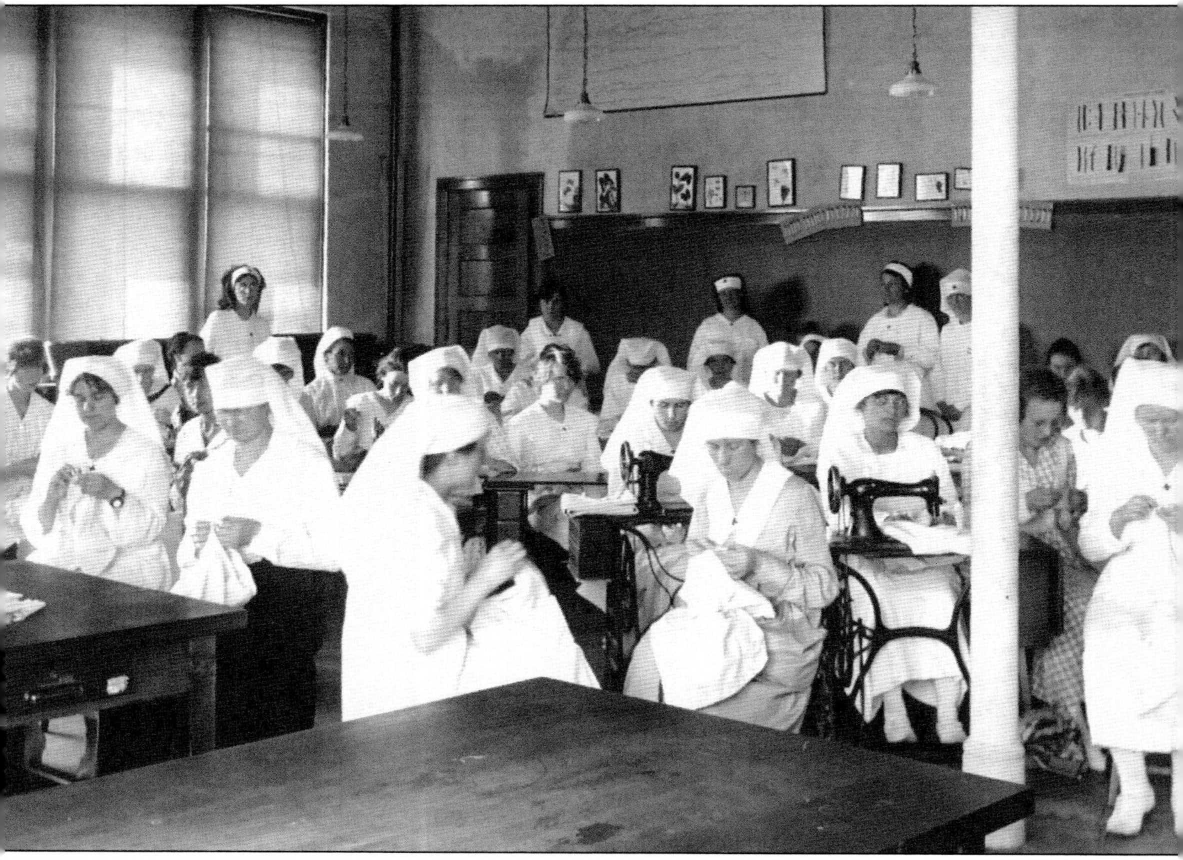

In this 1918 photograph, women in the campus Red Cross Production Corps uniform sewed underskirts for the hospital garment section. A voluntary arm of the Red Cross, the Production Corps was responsible for the production of surgical dressings. They also produced clothing from patterns for soldiers on the front, convalescing soldiers, and refugees of the war. The Red Cross provided the patterns. Every school day, one hour was donated to the effort. The women were divided into a relief garment section, knitting section, and hospital garment section. By the summer's end, the women produced 90 women's chemises, 38 Belgian shirts, 39 Belgian nightgowns, 56 Belgian underskirts, 54 helpless case skirts, 4 day shirts, 18 pairs of socks, and 160 knitted socks. Trench warfare made socks a high-demand item.

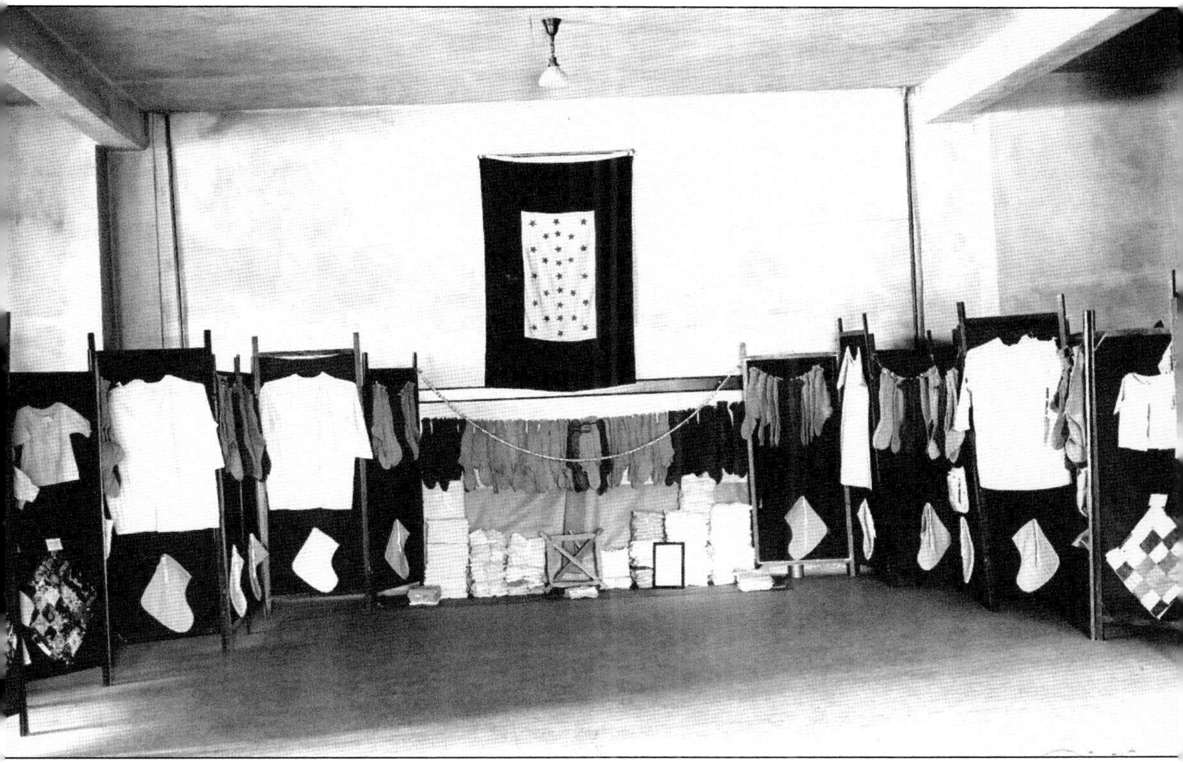

The 1918 summer session produced more clothing items than the spring and fall groups. As they watched the normal school's enrollment plummet and loved ones and friends go off to war, all school members wanted to do their part. Faculty, staff, and students were also active in the community bond drives, marches, community sings, food demonstrations, collection of war saving stamps, and Junior Red Cross drives, all aimed at bolstering community support and morale in dark times. Each star on the flag hanging on the wall represents a member of the institution serving in the war effort.

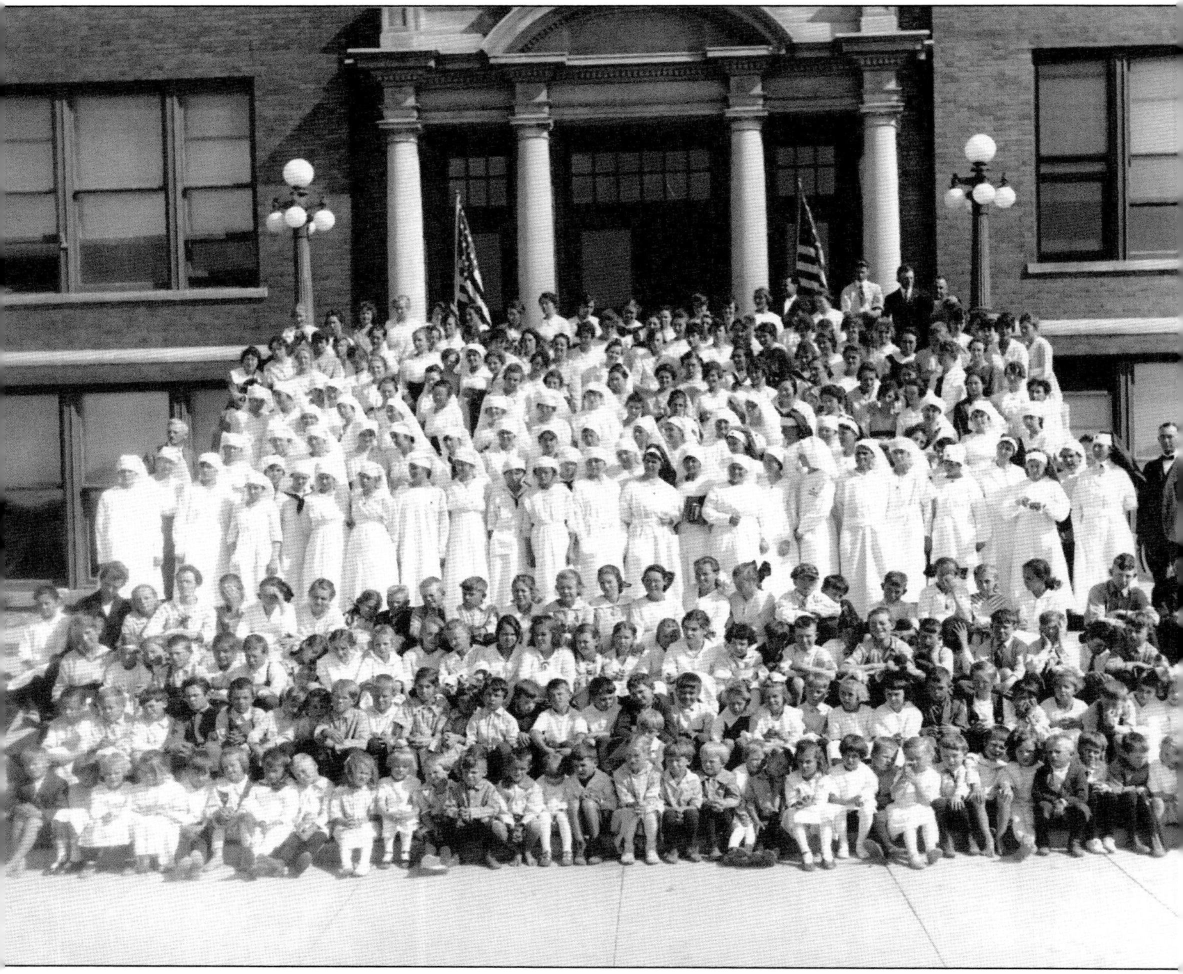

The patriotic summer session of 1918 poses in front of Old Main. Faculty, part-time faculty, and students in their Red Cross Production Corps uniforms cover the upper steps of Old Main. Children who attended the training school for the summer session are seated on the lower steps. William F. Clarke, acting president, stands alone to the right. He coordinated and directed all war service activities, as well as all normal and training school operations.

Nine

The Years between the Wars

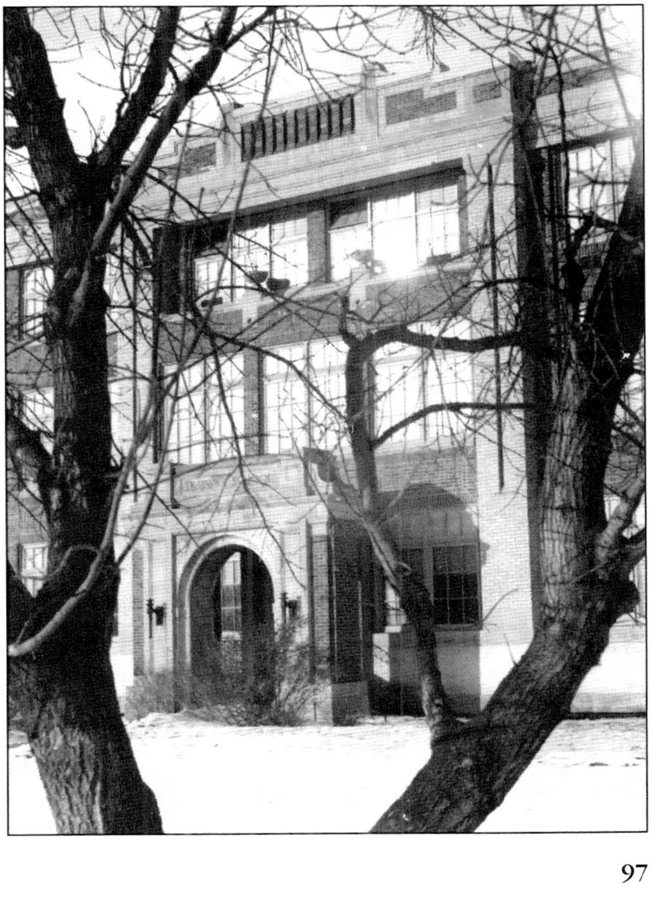

Despite the difficulties of the 1920s and the arrival of the Great Depression, campus leadership managed to carry out several building projects with Pres. Franklin Delano Roosevelt's New Deal. The first new structure built on campus was Model Hall, intended as a long-term replacement for Harrison School—the older training school.

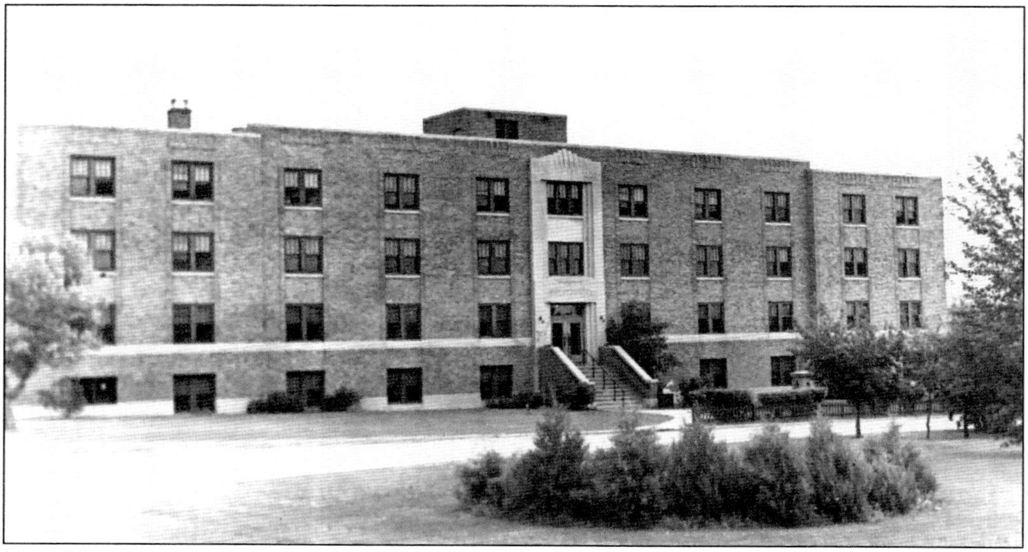

President George McFarland built Dakota Hall, a women's dormitory, in 1930–1931 during the first years of the Great Depression. Unlike the new model school, the dormitory was funded under a $150,000 bond, issued by the local Dormitory Holding Association, under a special act of the 1929 legislature. In front of the dormitory was the old water trough from Main Street. Once used to water horses, dogs, and cats, it was used as a flower planter.

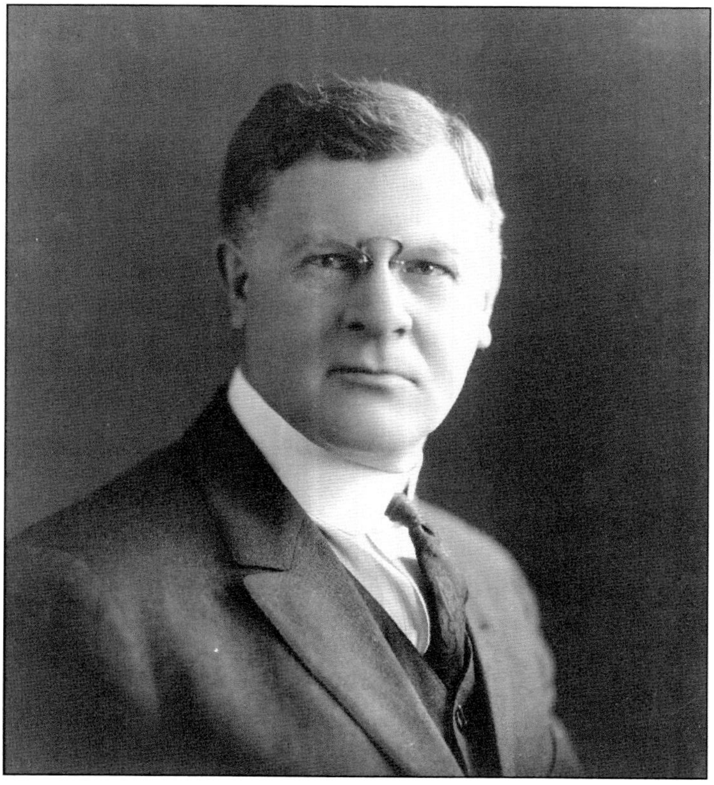

Dr. Levi Beeler served as acting president from 1921 to 1922. He replaced William F. Clarke, who had served as acting president since 1918. His fast talking earned him the nickname of the "Gatling gun speaker."

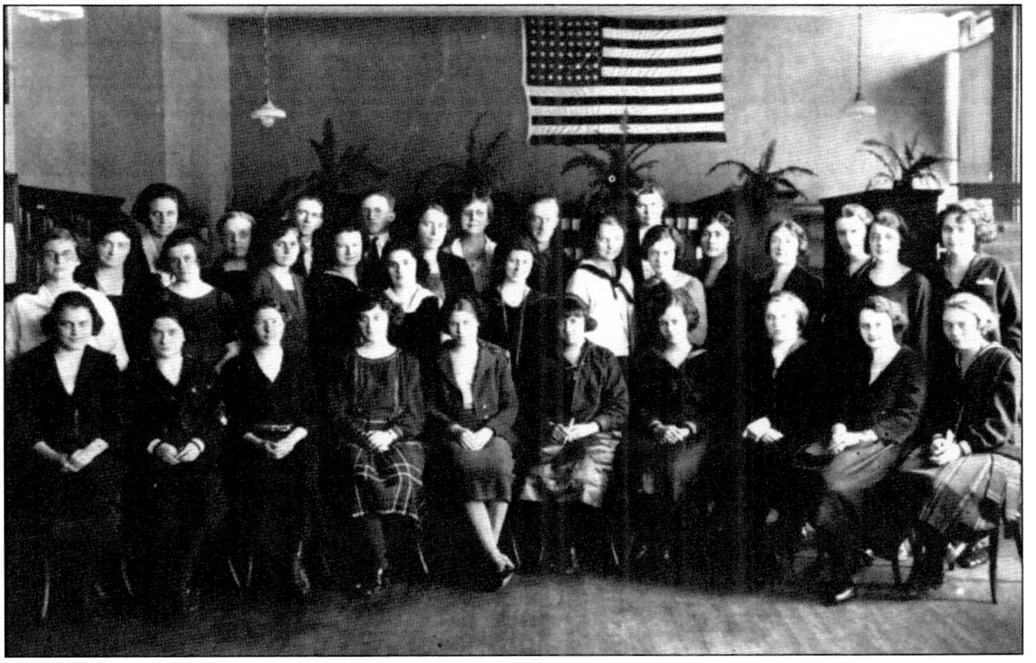

In the fall of 1923, the normal school rhetoric class under the direction of Julia McDonough produced the first normal school paper, the *Echo*. The first edition focused on years past. Before the next publication, the name was changed to the *Normalite*, but after more debate, the name was finalized as the *Red and Green*.

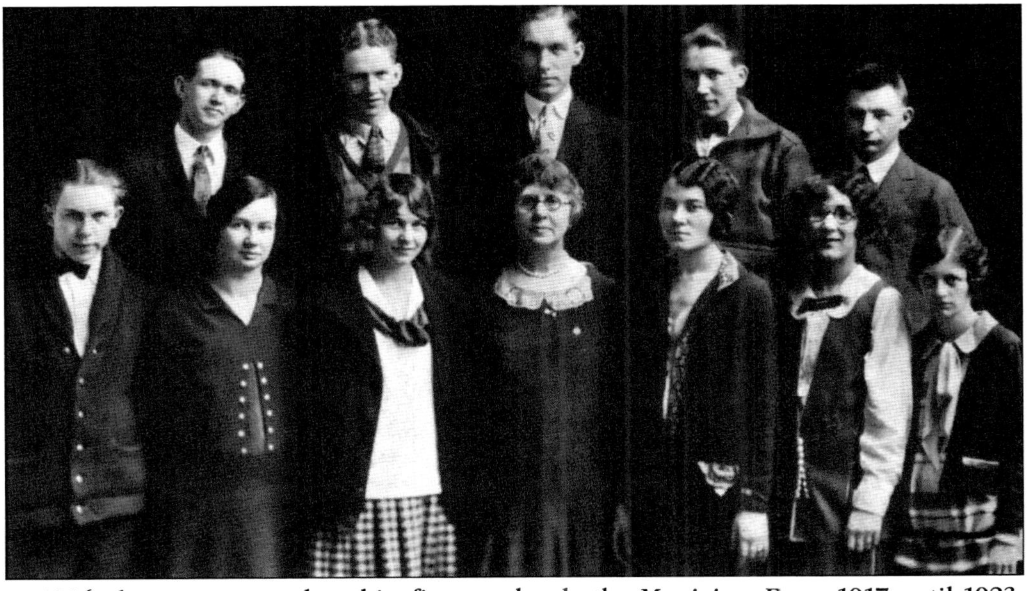

In 1916, the campus produced its first yearbook, the *Magician*. From 1917 until 1923, there was no yearbook. When the campus was awarded collegiate status in 1924, the issue arose again. On January 12, 1926, after a faculty, student, and alumni ballot was completed, the *Magician* staff renamed the publication the *Beaver*, in honor of the campus mascot.

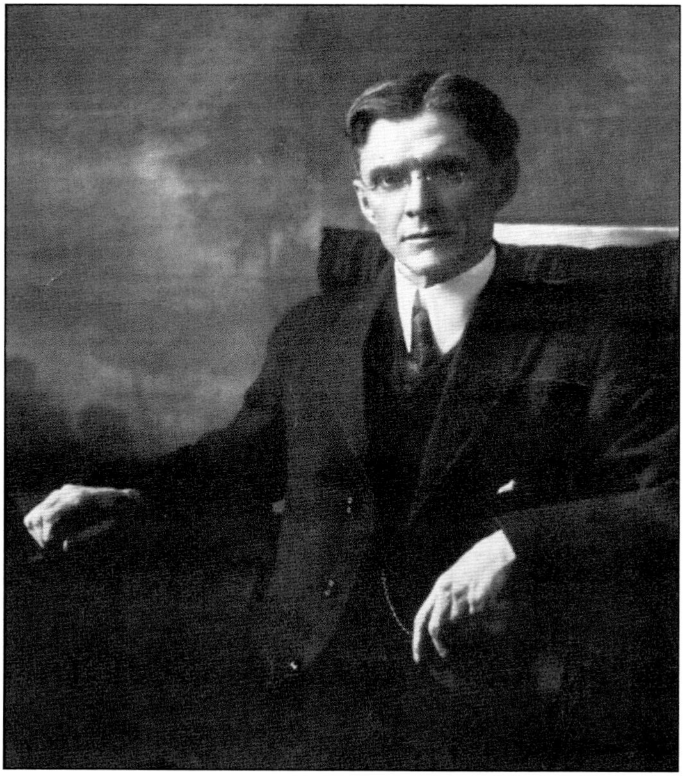

Dr. George McFarland replaced Dr. Levi Beeler in 1922. McFarland served in various capacities, including that of president of the State Normal School at Valley City. Prior to 1892, he served on the Dakota Territorial Board of Education and taught at the state normal school at Madison, South Dakota.

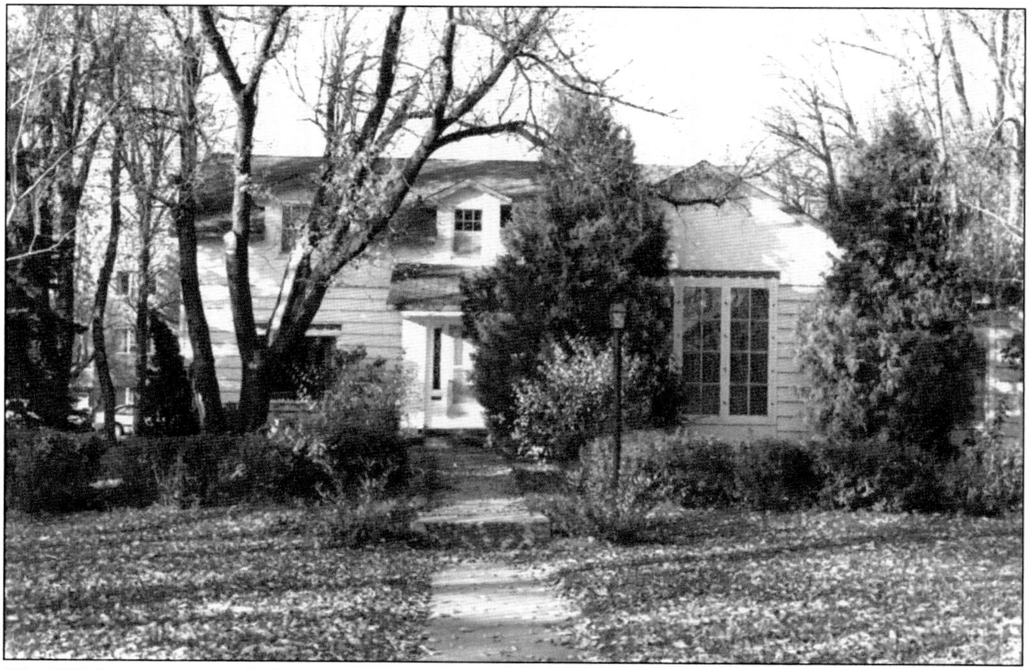

The WPA constructed the president's house on the southeast corner of the campus. The site is currently occupied by a dormitory, Lura Manor.

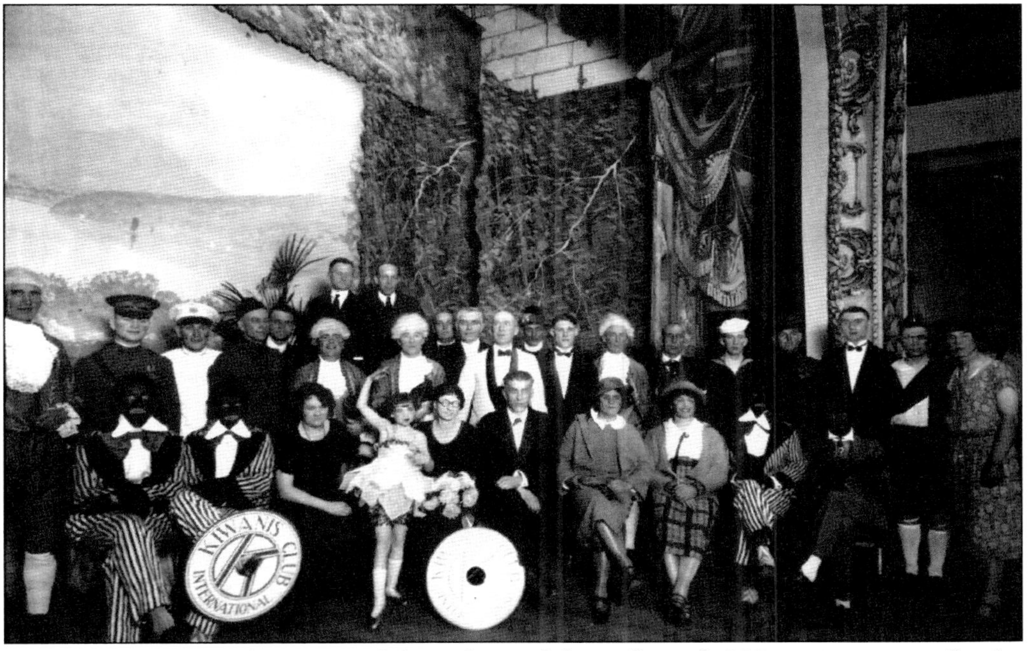

In May 1925, the local Kiwanis Club performed the *Follies of 1925* to raise money for the Kiwanis students' loan fund. The program and other events raised $600. This may be the earliest photograph of the stage in the new main auditorium. Completion was delayed when the west wall collapsed during construction. In 1933, the campus petitioned the state board of administration to name the auditorium McFarland Auditorium.

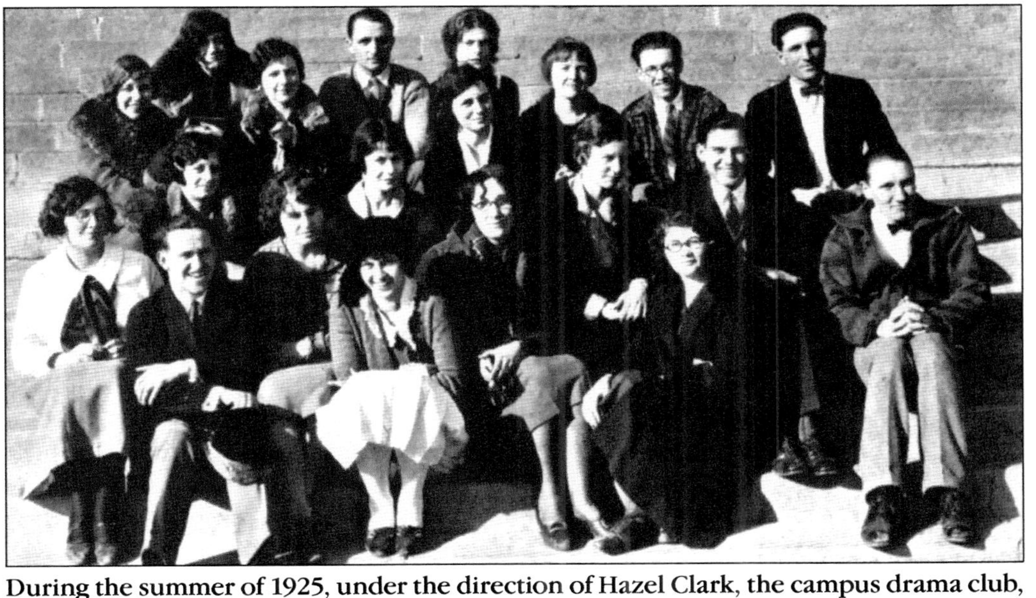

During the summer of 1925, under the direction of Hazel Clark, the campus drama club, Delta Alpha Kappa, organized with 36 members. In November, they reorganized and changed their name to the Campus Players. During their first year, they performed *The Open Road*, *Columbine*, *The Slave with Two Faces*, and a three-act play, *The Gypsy Trail*. The Campus Players are still a very active organization on the campus.

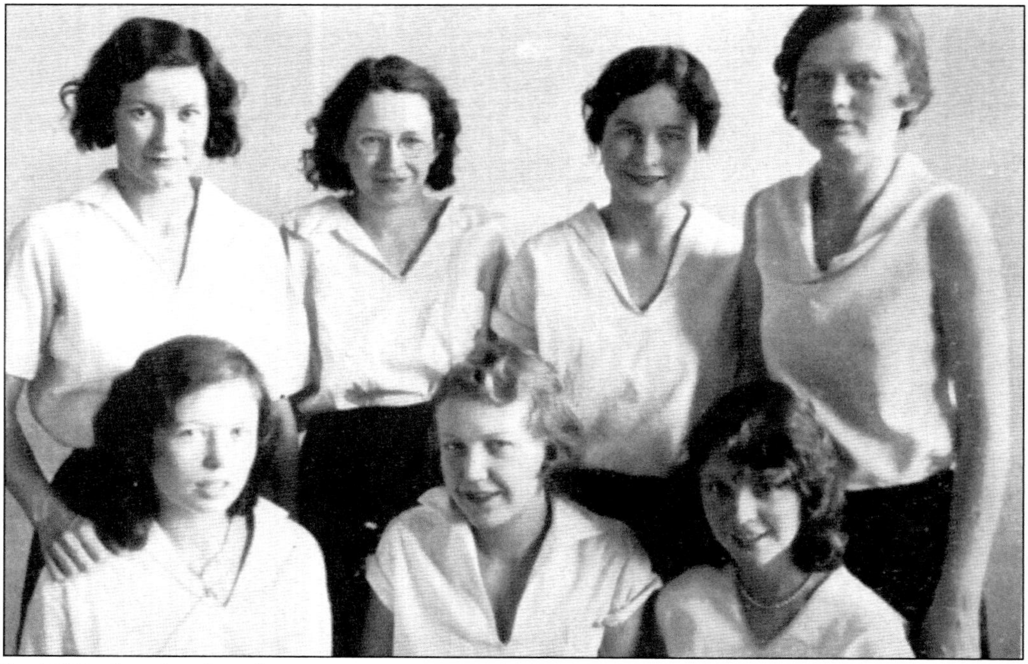

In 1925, shortly after the campus was awarded collegiate status, a student, Pauline Roach (second row, left), proposed the campus adopt a mascot. In a spirited presentation, Roach convinced the faculty and student body to accept the beaver as the institutional mascot. A vote was taken, and the mascot was embraced unanimously. Roach graduated in 1931.

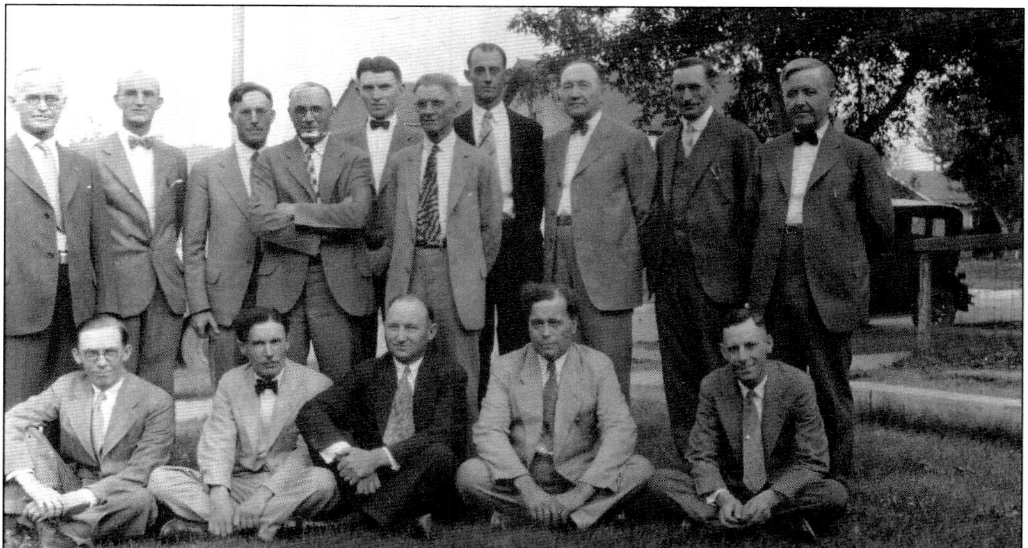

On August 20, 1929, the faculty men's club gathered at Dr. Huebner's house. From left to right are (first row) Paul Seaman, Lester Hartnett, Huebner, W. D. "Doc" Allen, and Morris Webster; (second row) J. W. De La, Charles Scott, Marvin Kirk, George Mounce, Dan Blide, president George McFarland, coach James Coleman, Frank Hicks, Knapp, and L. O. Lantis.

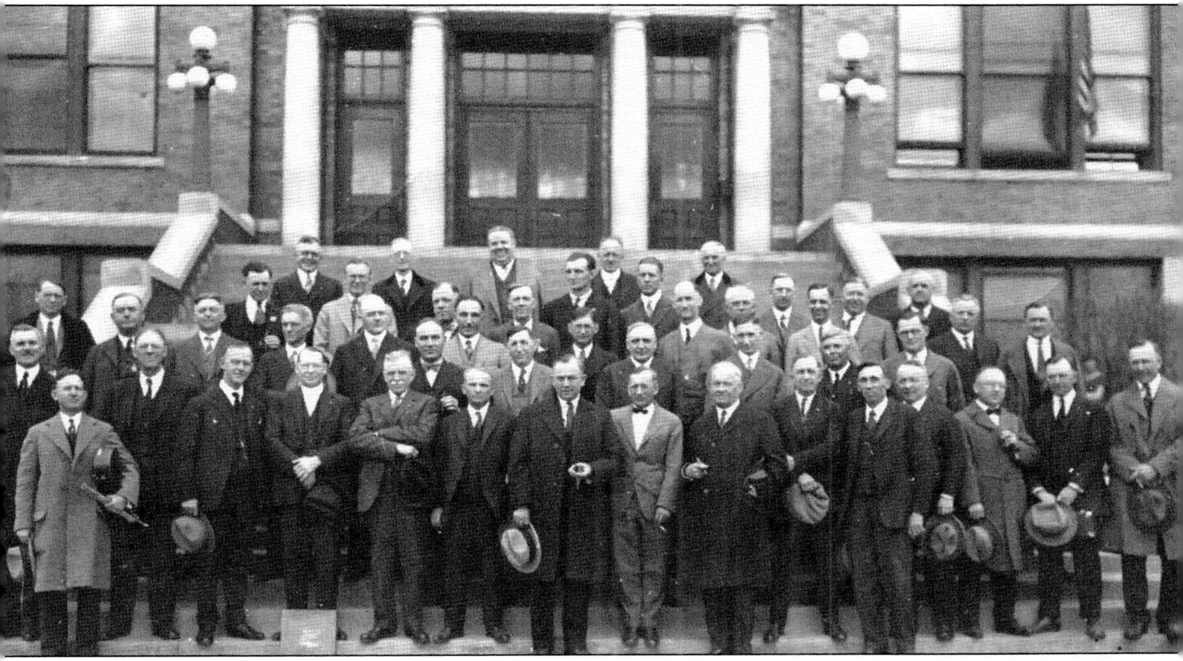

In 1938, Dr. George McFarland died in office. Dr. Carl C. Swain (first row, center, holding his hat) assumed the duties of the president shortly after. Swain prepared the institution for the war years. The presidents from the other state campuses and institutions as well as several local and state politicians, judges, and community leaders attended. McFarland became a beloved educator and servant of the people of North Dakota. Standing in the first row from right to left are Dr. Arthur Griswold Crane, Dr. William F. Clarke, and Dr. Charles E. Scott. Scott was acting president until Dr. Swain arrived on campus.

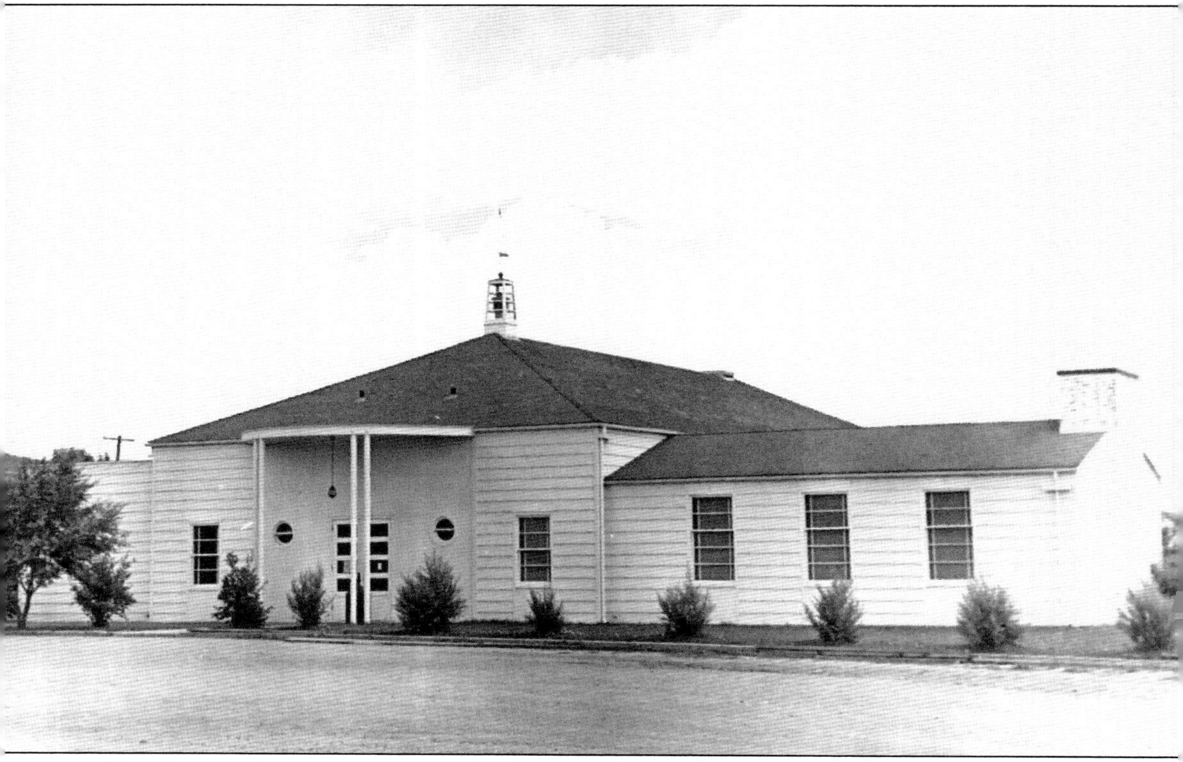

The first student union opened in May 1940 on the present site of the administration and student union complex. It underwent several expansion projects.

Ten

The Impact of World War II

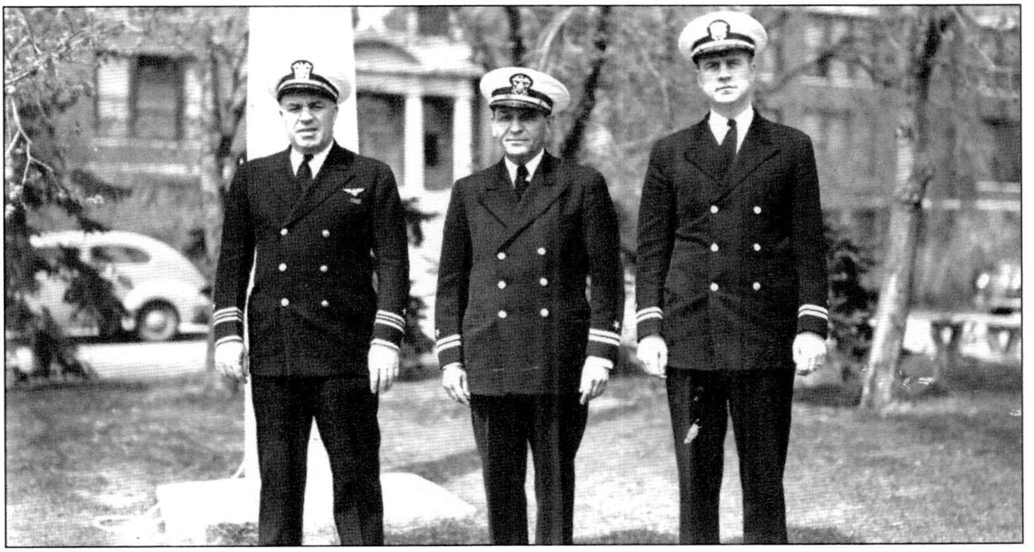

North Dakota State Teachers College at Minot faced enrollment drops as the nation redirected resources and manpower to winning the war. In response, the school opened the campus to the war department. In 1942, the U.S. Navy opened offices in Old Main and Pioneer Hall for the newly formed V-5 program—the Navy Aviation Preparatory Program. The program enlisted students for flight training in the Naval Reserve. Completion led to an ensign's commission and a tour of duty as a naval aviator. The officer in charge of the Naval Aviation Cadet Selection Board, Lt. Commander G. R. MacDonald visited Minot State Teachers College in May 1943 to inspect the facilities. To his right are Lt. R. W. Palda and Lt. George Olson. Lt. R. W. Palda, a Minot attorney, was initially in charge of the Minot V-5 operation.

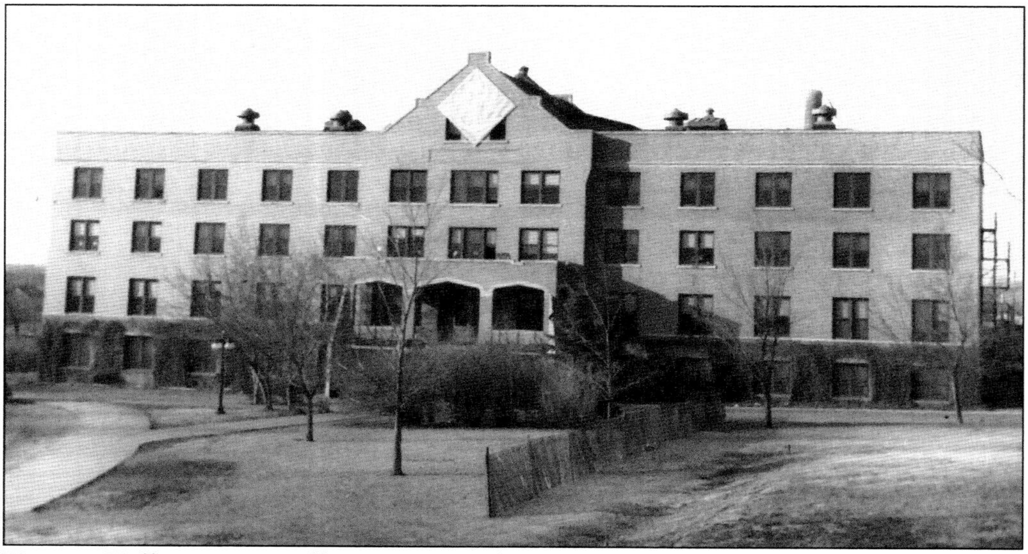

Pioneer Hall was originally a women's dormitory, but effective 1942 it housed the all-male V-5 program student body and instructors. The navy anchor marked the structure as navy housing. The snow fence across the lawn kept drifts off the ellipse drive.

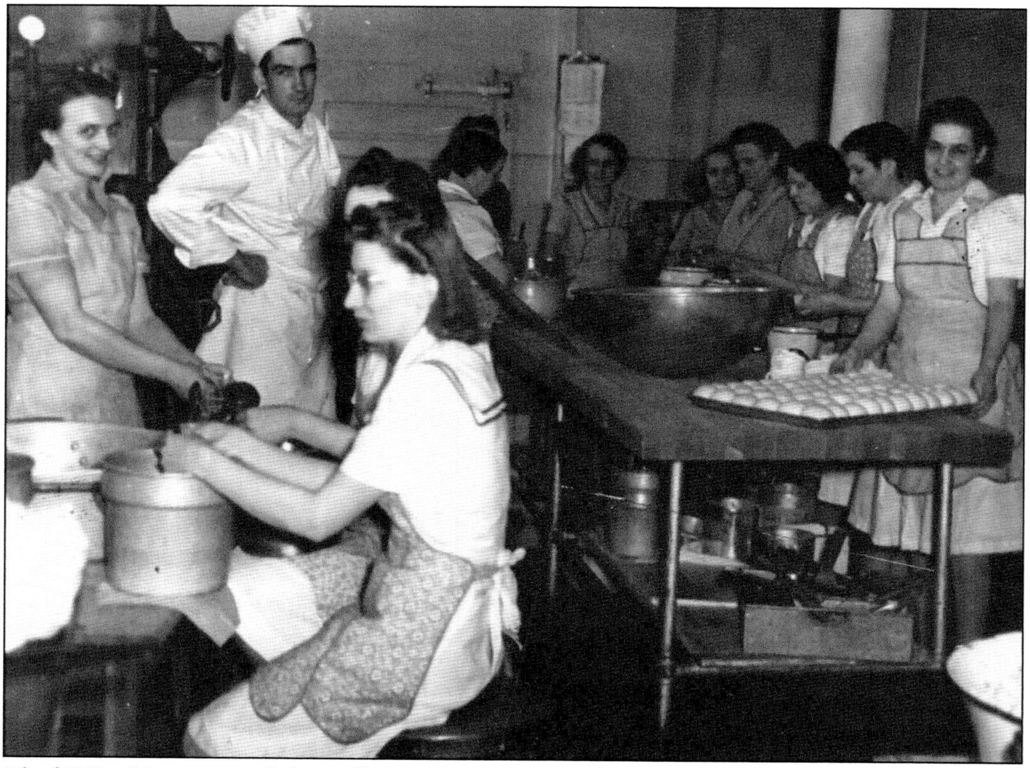

Chef "Slim" Jensen and the galley crew prepare a meal for the students, cadets, faculty, staff, and administrators in the Pioneer Hall kitchen, located in the basement.

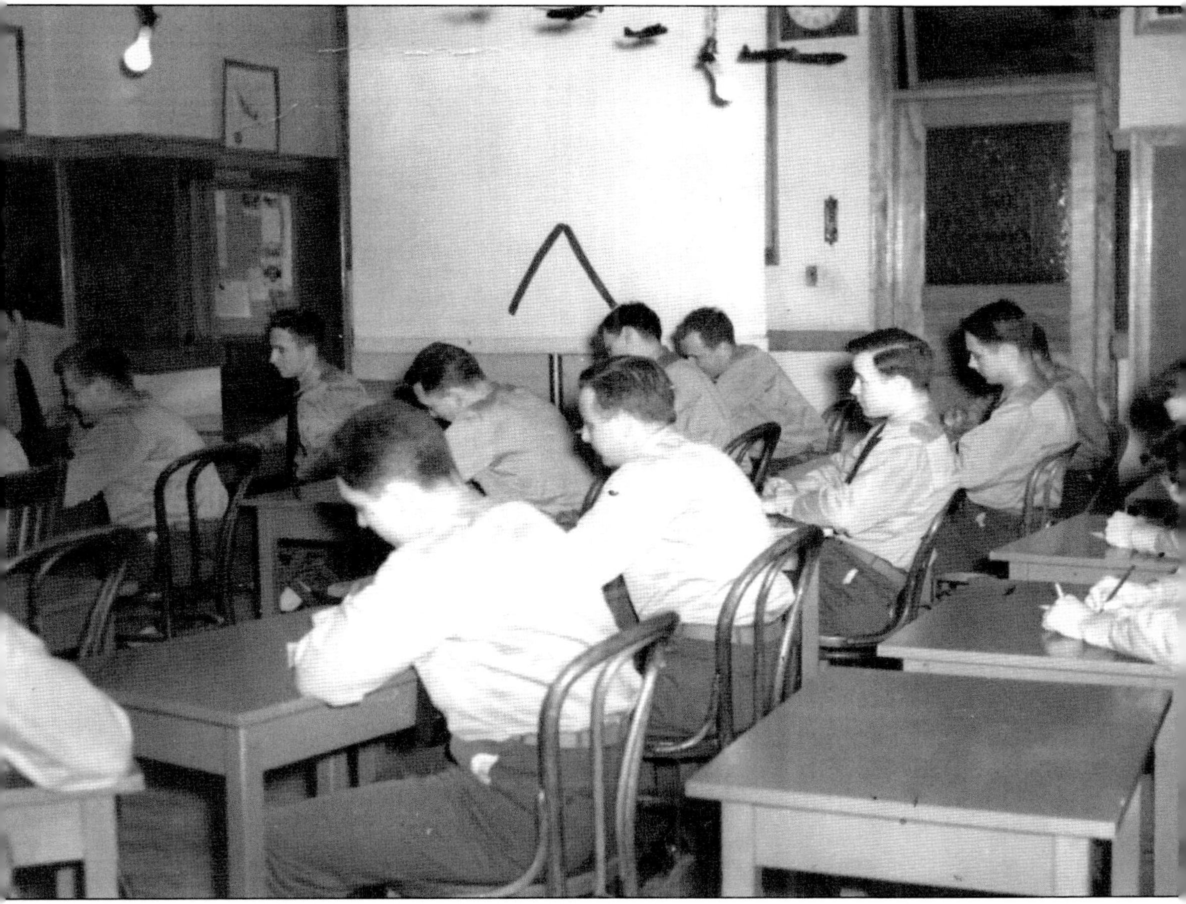

V-5 cadets completed early-morning examinations in the Old Main, room 302. Notice the photographs and models of aircraft about the room. The models were made by students from across North Dakota and Minnesota at the bequest of the U.S. Office of Education. The National School Model Building Program had 90 1:72 scaled kits crafted and reproduced for distribution to high schools. The models were painted black to simulate their silhouette. The finished models were used to train the cadets in aircraft recognition and range estimation. Cadets had to recognize 65 different aircraft from three different views.

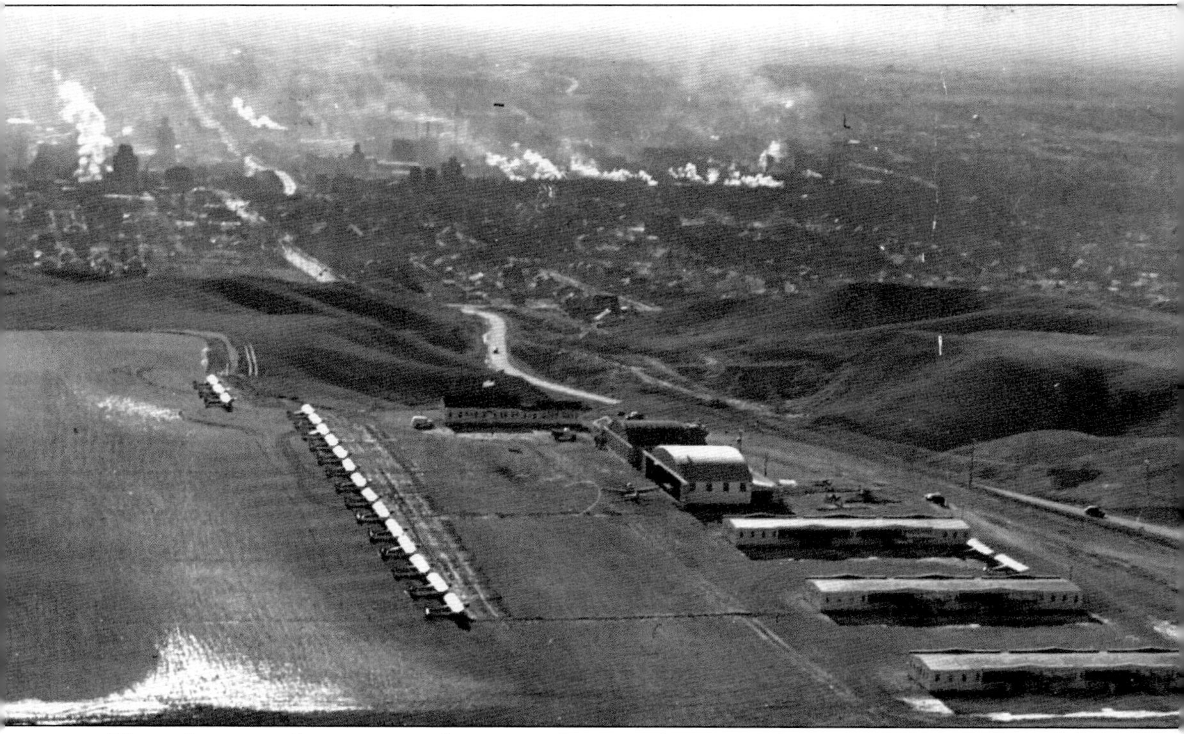

This photograph captures the Port of Minot, home of the Minot Flying Service. The airfield was officially established on July 22, 1928, before a crowd of 30,000 spectators. The Civilian Pilot Training Program (CPTP) was initiated on the field in 1939. In 1941, the WPA enlarged the field to four runways, ranging from 3,400 to 5,200 feet in length. In 1942, the Civil Aeronautics Administration added a radio range station for weather support. Then in the fall of 1942, the V-5 program came on line at the campus with the assistance of the Minot Flying Service, owned and operated by Charles Westlie. Westlie hired 15 civilian aviation instructors to help run the program. Another "rough" airstrip was maintained northwest of Minot to practice landings. In this photograph, the Piper J-3 Cubs and N3N-3 aircraft maintained by the Minot Flying Service are lined up for the day's operations.

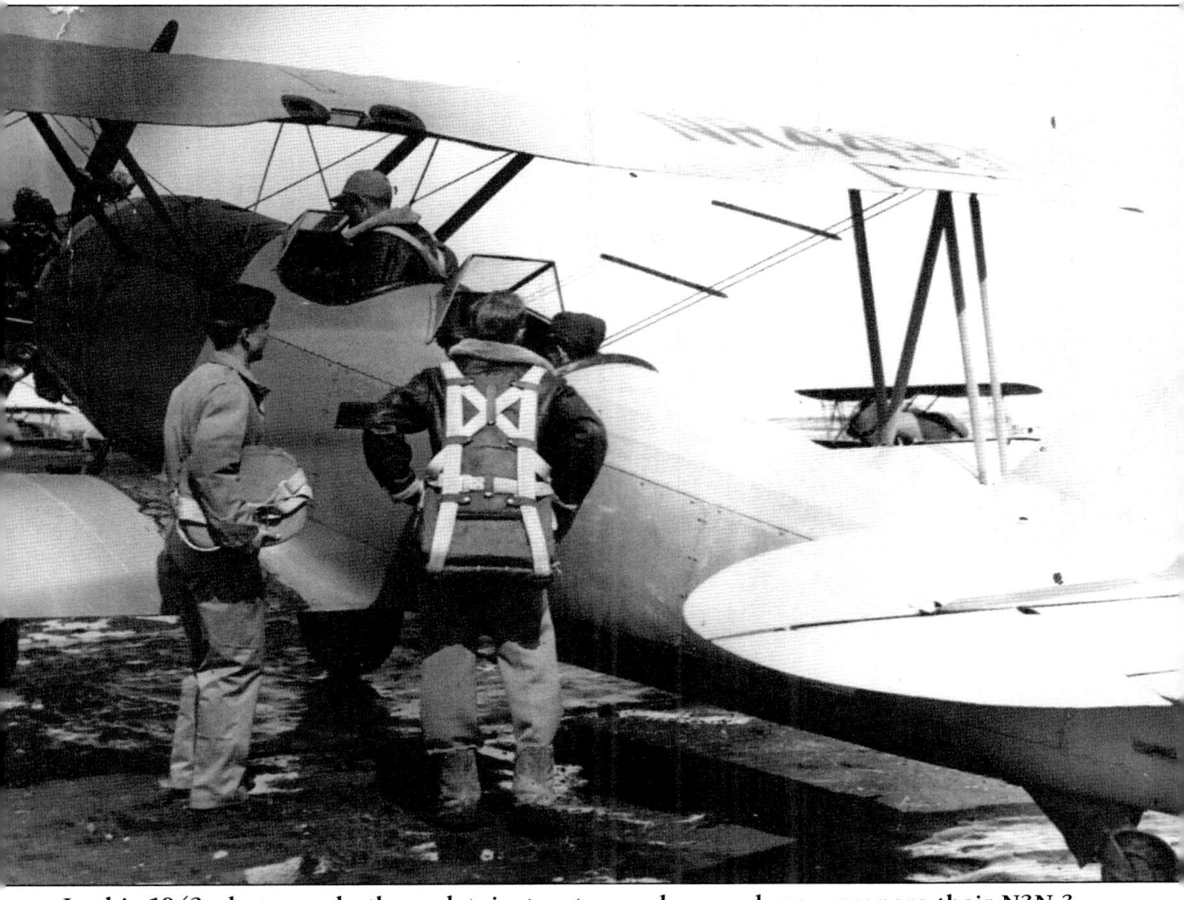

In this 1943 photograph, the cadet, instructor, and ground crew prepare their N3N-3, "Yellow Peril," for takeoff from the Minot airfield. The N3Ns were built at the naval aircraft factory. They were the first and only aircraft built and owned by the U.S. government. It was also the last biplane to see service with the U.S. military. The factory produced 1,407 aircraft, of which 817 (N3N-3) were trainers. It had a 34-foot wingspan, a maximum ceiling of 15,200 feet, and a maximum speed of 126 miles per hour. The nickname Yellow Peril was used by several navy trainers since they were all painted orange-yellow for easy identification. Should the cadet fail to "solo," he would be in peril of not completing the course. The Minot V-5 program's only fatality was James Watts. He was killed on October 9, 1943, during a solo flight when his aircraft crashed in heavy fog one and a half miles northwest of Minot.

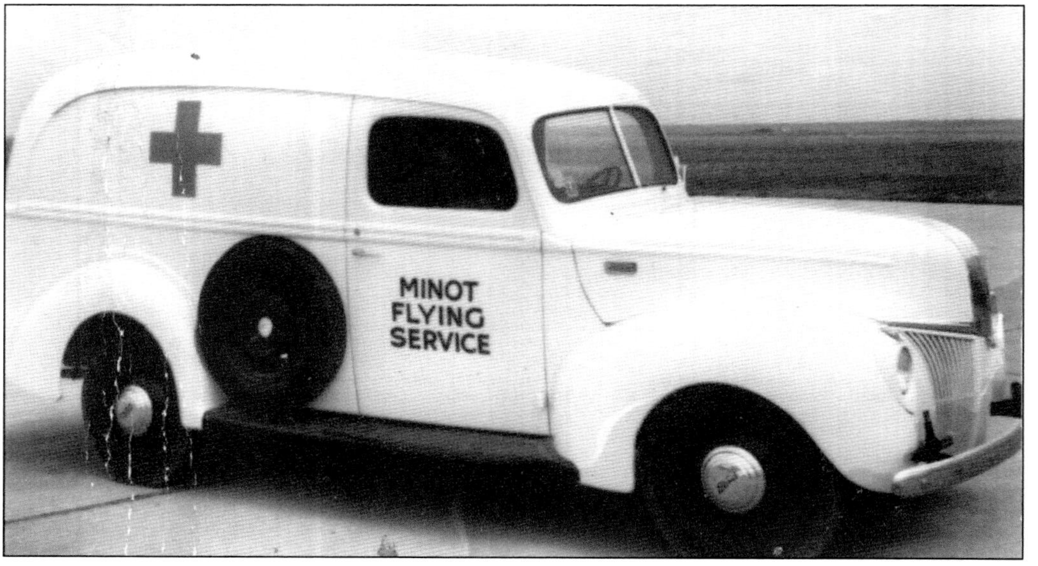

Every V-5 airfield included an emergency response vehicle in case of accidents. Here is the ambulance assigned to the Minot field.

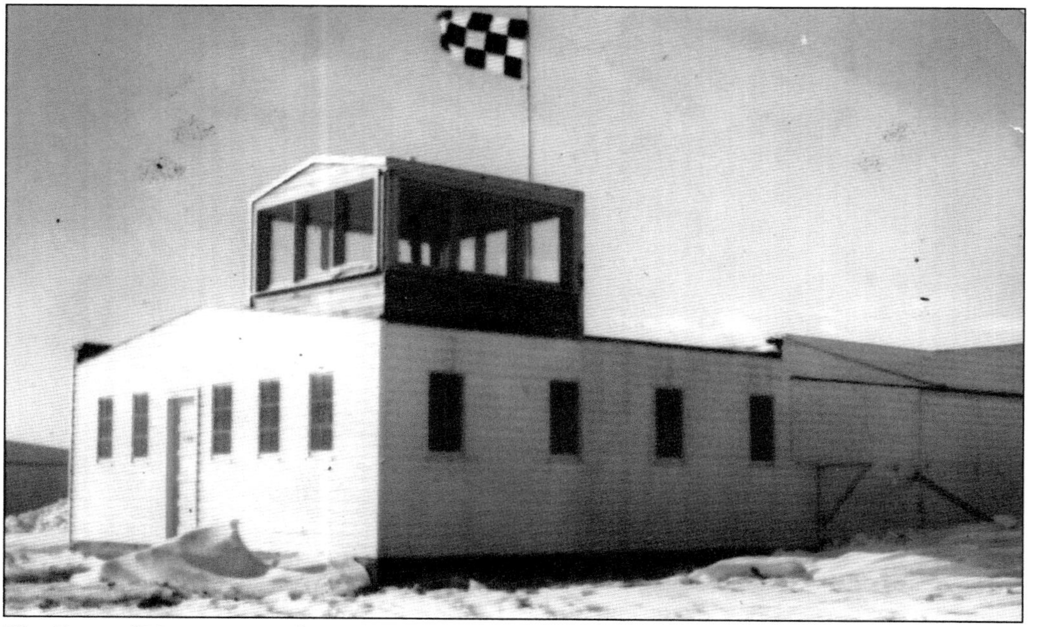
The Port of Minot control tower was used to direct V-5 and CPTP operations.

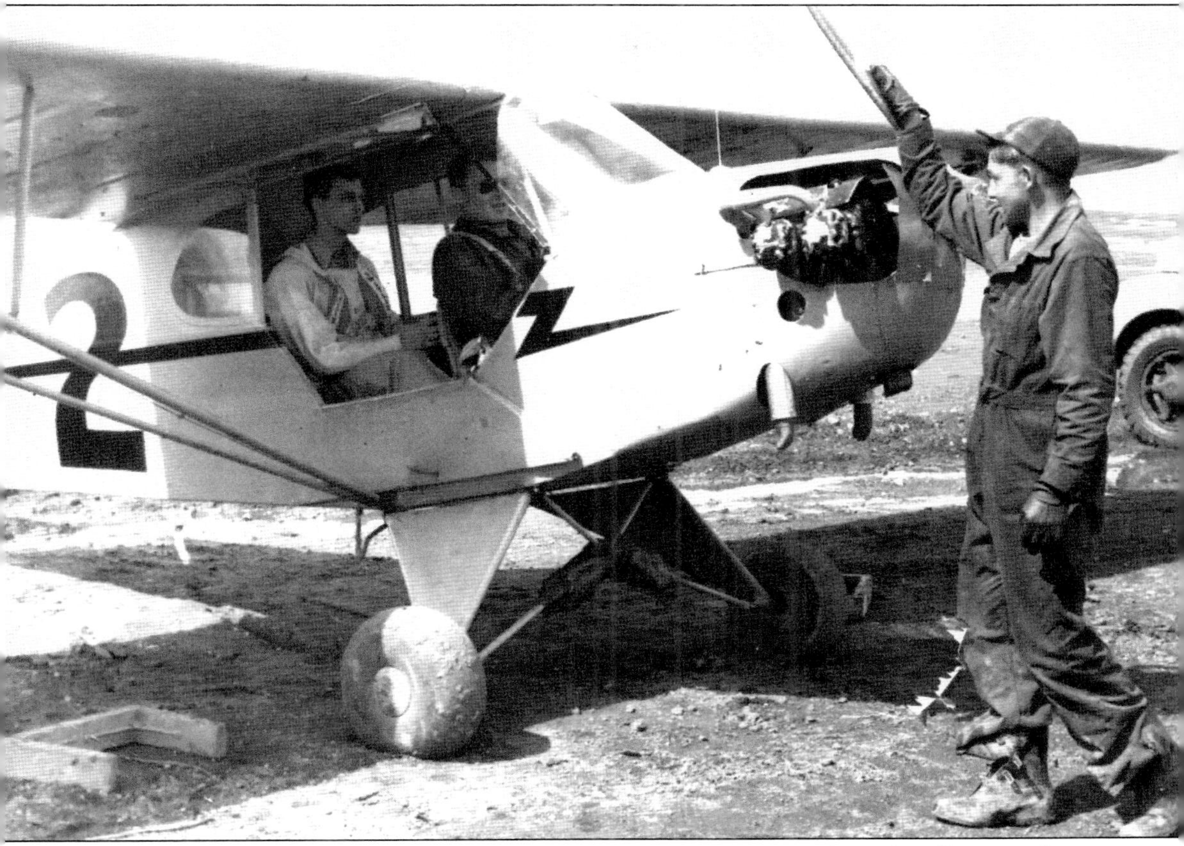

A CPTP cadet and instructor prepare their Piper J-3 Cub trainer for takeoff. V-5 cadets also used Pipers. Charles Westlie maintained 22 of the aircraft at the Minot airport. Between 1937 and 1947, Piper Aircraft built the Cub. As shown in the photograph, it had tandem (fore and aft) seating, ideal for flight instruction. The primary trainer for the CPTP, more than 3,000 were in service by the outbreak of the World War II. It had a maximum speed of 87 miles per hour and a range of 220 miles. It was cheap and easy to fly. Some Cubs actually saw war service as the famous J-3 ("Grasshopper"), which transported wounded troops and Allied leaders around the battlefield and served as an armed reconnaissance aircraft. When snow was on the ground, the wheels were removed and replaced with skis.

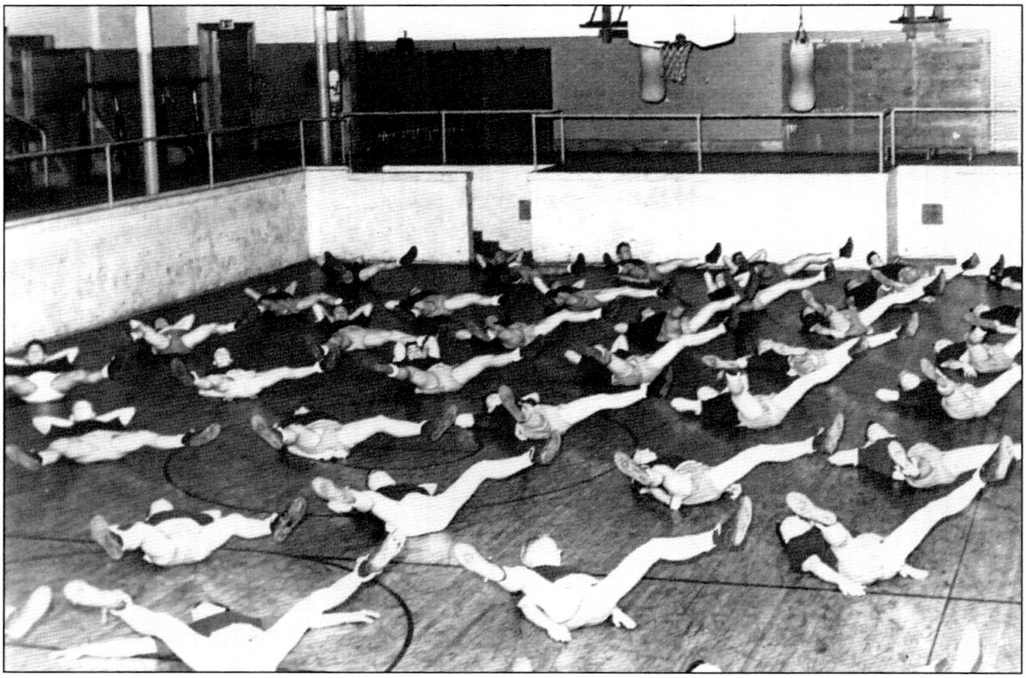

Cadets do leg lifts as part of the daily fitness program. Some fitness events were completed in the gymnasium; others were completed on the obstacle course located adjacent to college field. Weather conditions dictated the amount of outdoor activity.

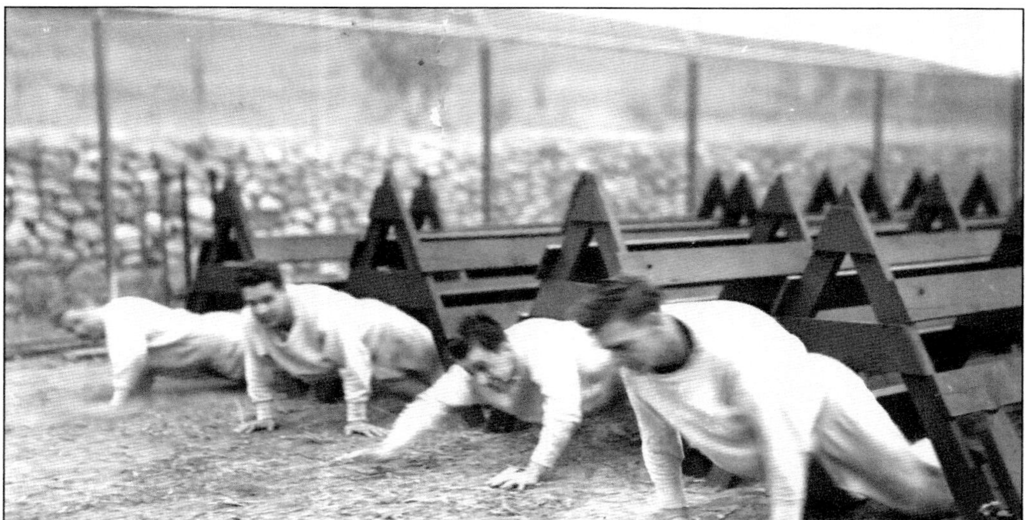

The obstacle course at the college was one of the highest-rated courses in the Midwest. Cadets ran the course and calisthenics daily and regularly completed a three-to-seven-mile hike. From left to right in the photograph above, cadets Harold Connolly, Peter Graff, Edward Hanson, and Clifford Emerson negotiate the "hog run." Lt. Lester Hartnett directed the course. He had returned from training in Iowa City with "plenty of ideas for new instruments of torture."

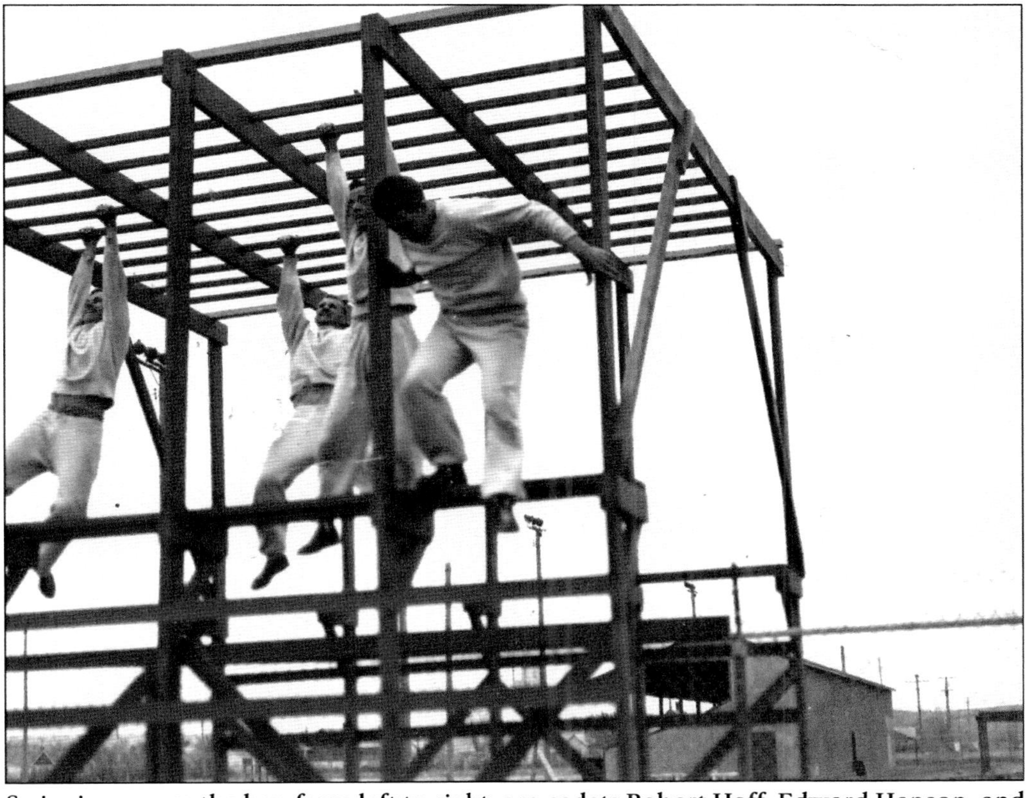

Swinging across the bar, from left to right, are cadets Robert Hoff, Edward Hanson, and Kenneth Henton. Cadet Clifford Emerson has completed the swing and prepares to jump the 8 feet to the ground and complete the last obstacle of the course, the 10-foot climbing wall. The college field can be seen in the background.

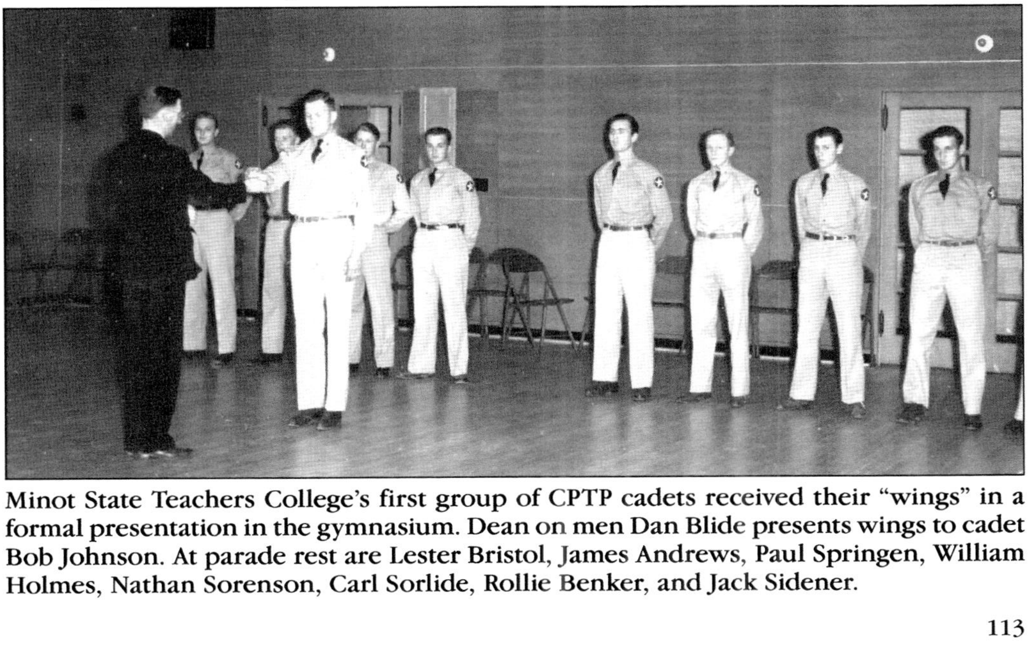

Minot State Teachers College's first group of CPTP cadets received their "wings" in a formal presentation in the gymnasium. Dean on men Dan Blide presents wings to cadet Bob Johnson. At parade rest are Lester Bristol, James Andrews, Paul Springen, William Holmes, Nathan Sorenson, Carl Sorlide, Rollie Benker, and Jack Sidener.

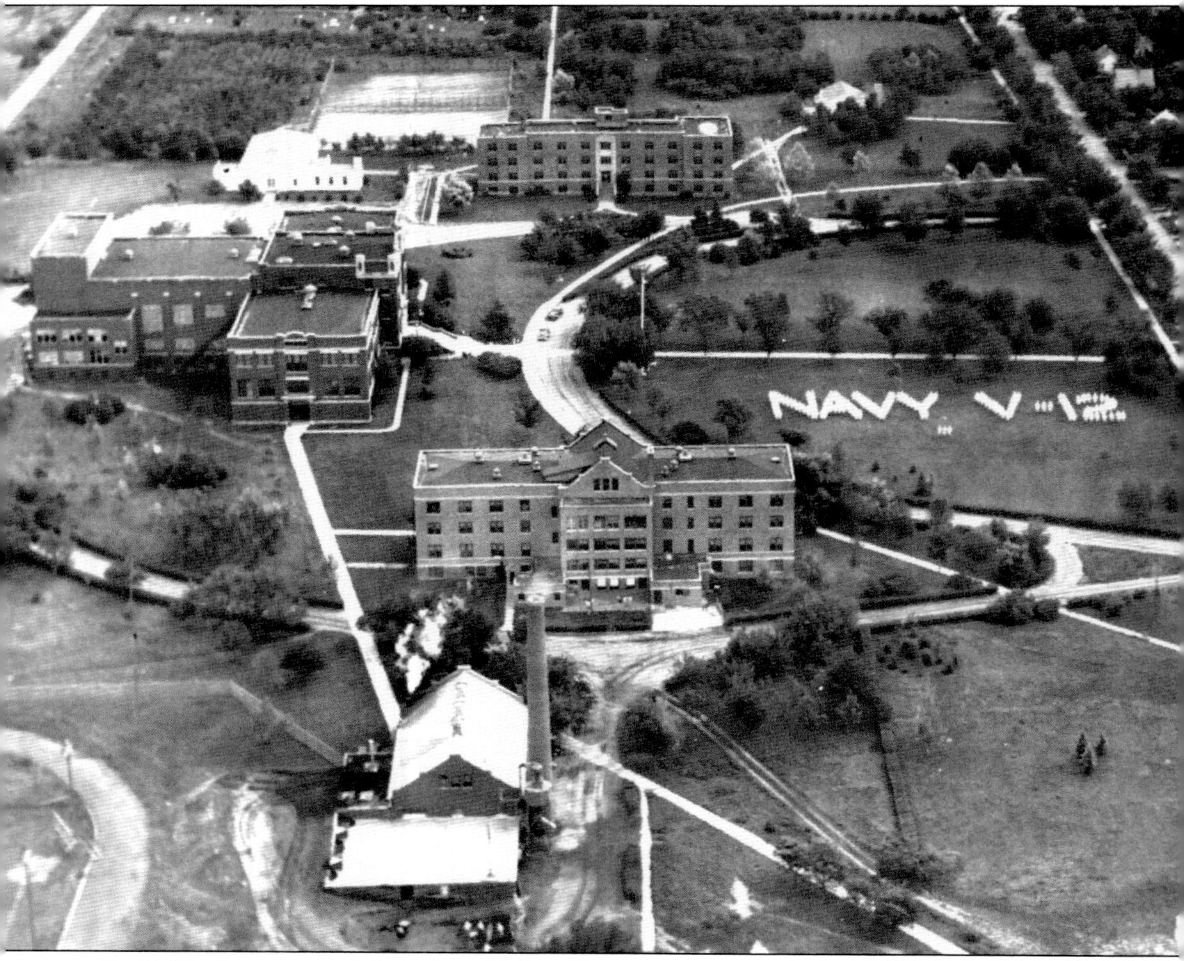

In 1943, the navy established the V-12 college training program to answer the immediate and long-term needs for commissioned officers. The program accepted students from the existing V-5 program, enlisted men recommended by their commanding officers, and eligible high school seniors upon graduation. The program was limited to 131 institutions, of which Minot State Teacher's College was one. Cadets were required to carry 17 semester hours year-round and complete 9½ hours of physical training per week. The cadets were on active duty, in uniform, and subject to military standards and law. Graduates were sent to a 4-month reserve midshipmen's training school or the 12-week Officer Candidate Course at Quantico, Virginia. In the fall of 1943, Lt. M. G. Sousa took this photograph of Minot State Teachers College from a V-5 aircraft. (*The Navy V-12 Program; Leadership for a Lifetime.*)

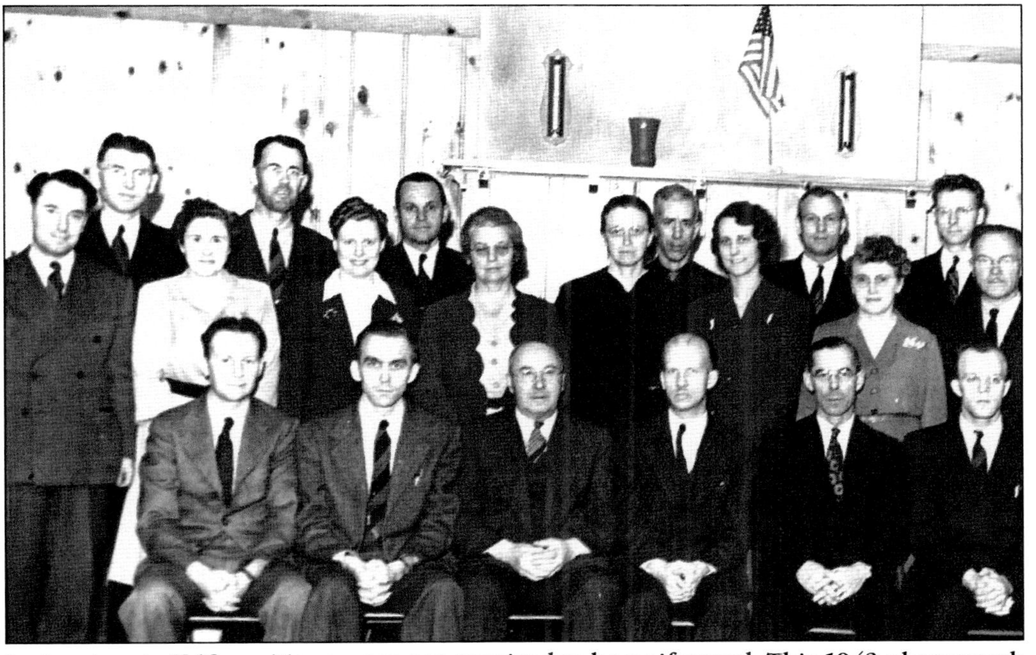

Instructors in V-12 positions were not required to be uniformed. This 1943 photograph captures some of the faculty in the student union. From left to right are (first row) M. Betterley, Robert Bernsten, George Mounce, Carl Pearson, F. R. Manning, and Cyril Moore; (second row) Curtis Yeager, Lyla Hoffine, Edna Gilbert, Hazel McCulloch, Nellie Swanson, Agnes Beckstrom, Ruth Dillavou, and William Bublitz; (third row) Dan Bilide, C. Hoffman, Alexander Paterson, John Scheffer, Reyond Wik, and Grant Norem.

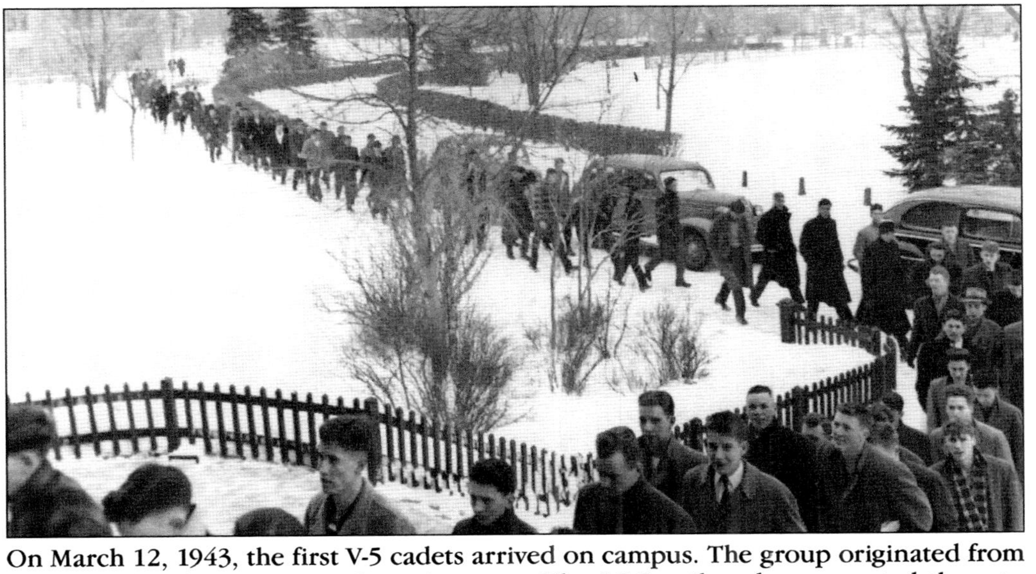

On March 12, 1943, the first V-5 cadets arrived on campus. The group originated from Minneapolis, the region's V-5 staging area. The SOO railroad transported them to Minot. Their arrival was delayed several weeks because of a mumps outbreak. Most of the 200 cadets hailed from Iowa, Minnesota, and Wisconsin. A four-day blizzard with 50-mile-per-hour winds had raced through the area several days earlier.

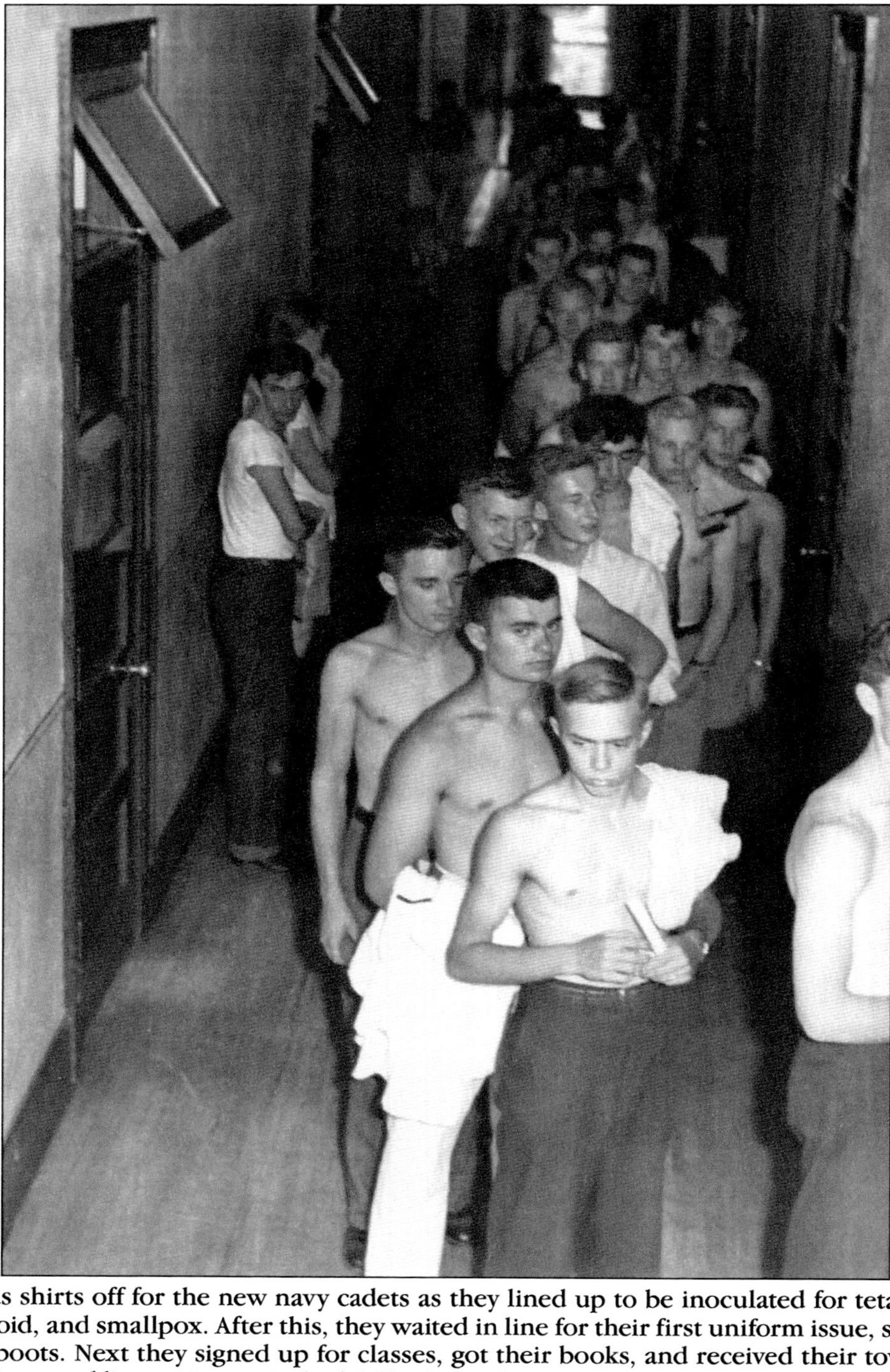

It was shirts off for the new navy cadets as they lined up to be inoculated for tetanus, typhoid, and smallpox. After this, they waited in line for their first uniform issue, shoes and boots. Next they signed up for classes, got their books, and received their towels, blankets, and linen. Most units had difficulty with sizing footwear. The lack of uniforms often delayed inspections and public formations. Men without the appropriate gear "fell in" with civilian attire until properly suited up. The photographs shows that the Minot V-5 and V-12 units encountered few uniform problems.

Reveille was played at 0530 hours. The men were expected on the field for calisthenics within 15 minutes. After the 0700 hours muster, where they were inspected and received instructions for the day, the men were marched to the mess hall for breakfast.

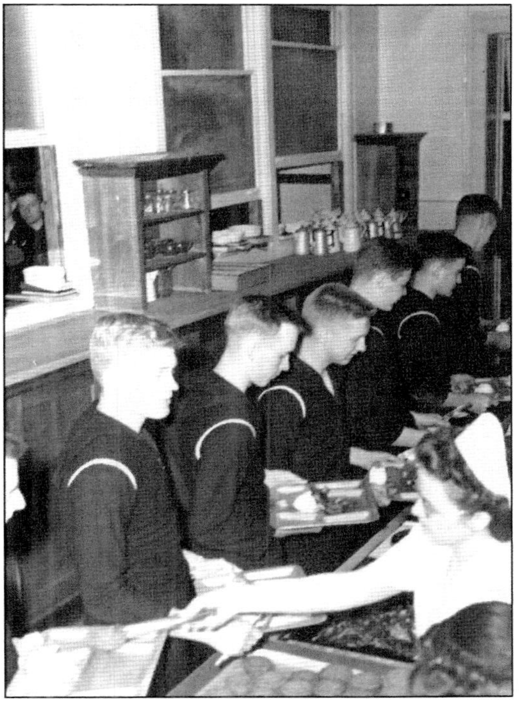

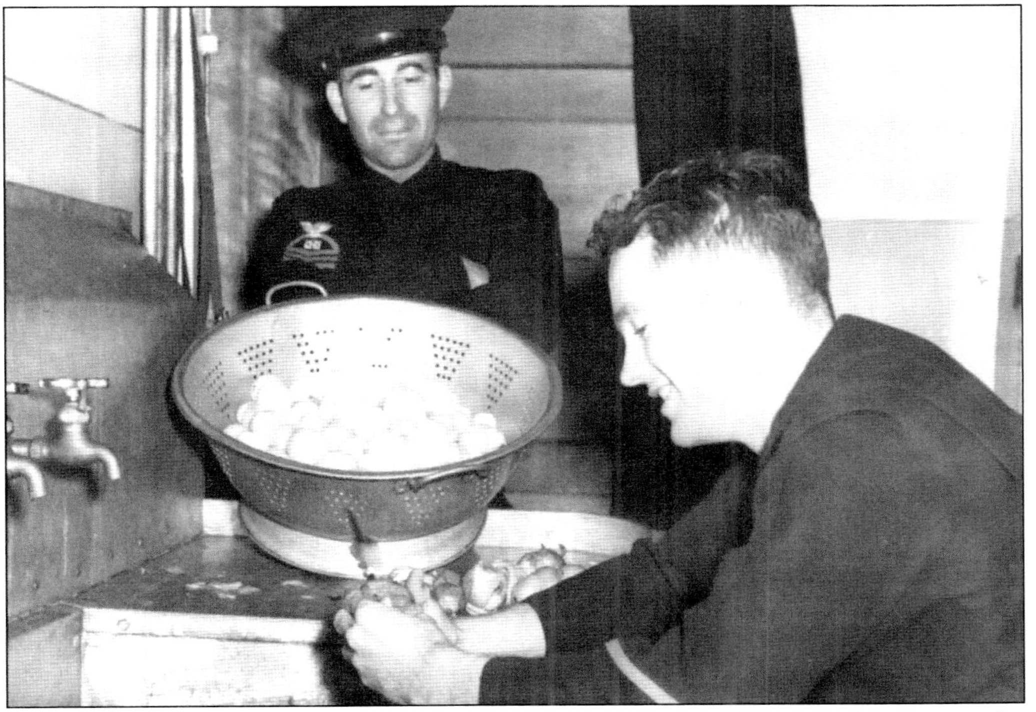

KP duty really existed, and this photograph is proof as the "chief" watches over cadet Henry Price as he peels the spuds. Minor problems with discipline were handled with additional duties, watch duty, fire watch, and early reporting times.

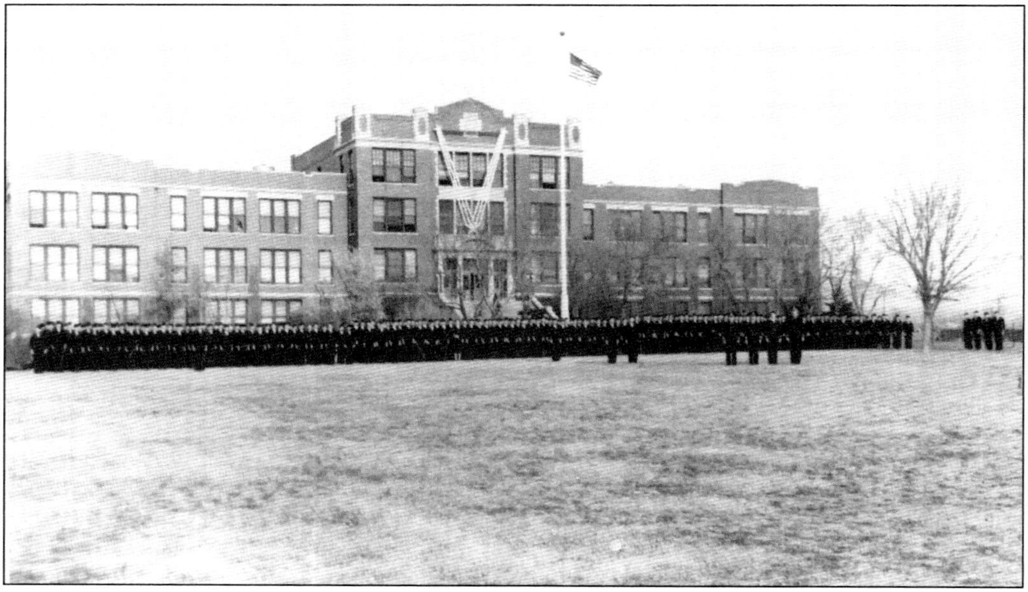

The 1943 V-12 battalion stands at attention at the Old Main flagpole for its first outdoor muster. When it was exceptionally cold, muster was conducted in the second-floor hallway of Old Main and occasionally in the gymnasium. Some units delayed the use of formations until uniforms were available for all new recruits. The Minot battalion was well staffed and equipped.

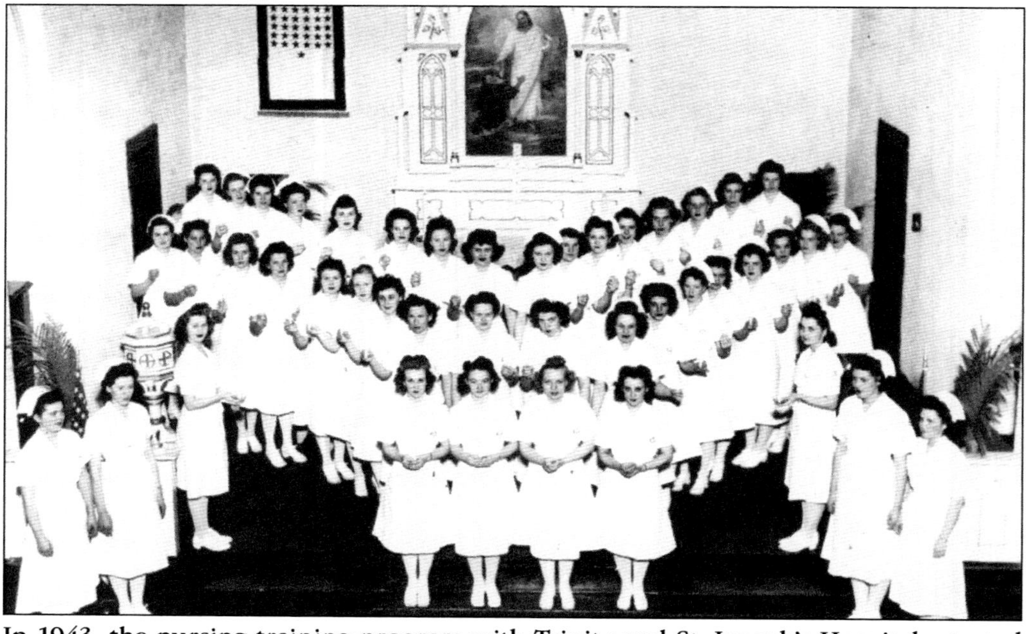

In 1943, the nursing training program with Trinity and St. Joseph's Hospitals started with an enrollment of 100 student nurses. The nurses attended chemistry, bacteriology, psychology, and other courses at the college in the afternoon. Classes were held in the training school and Old Main. This 1943 photograph shows the capping service at the Minot Bethany Lutheran Church.

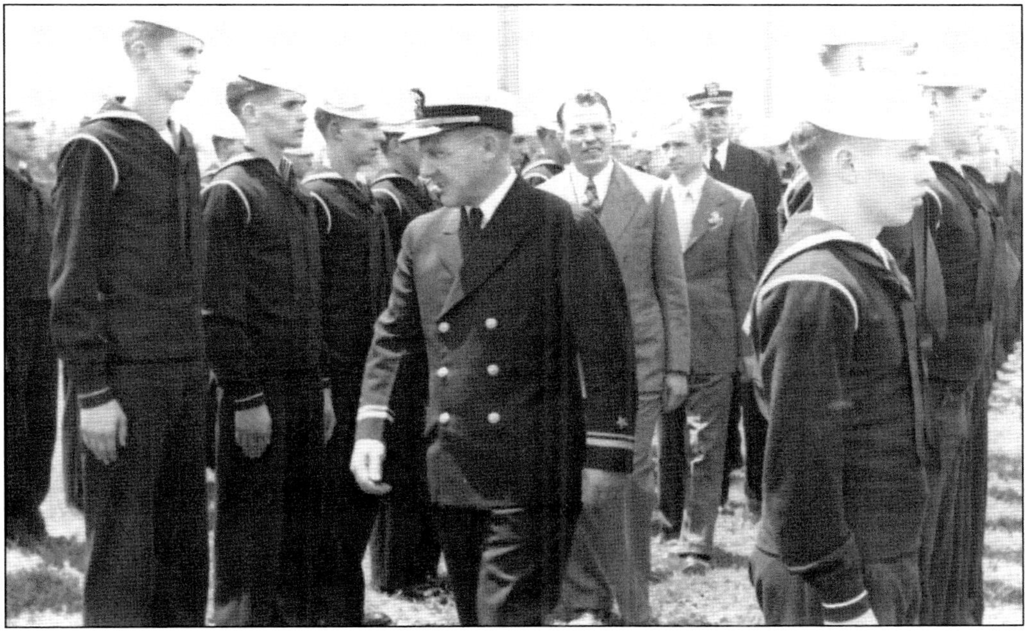

Lt. H. O. Ashton, officer in charge of the Minot V-12 unit, inspects the troops during the July 1944 review by North Dakota governor John Moses. A popular governor, Moses tried to attract war industries to the state, but the state remained last in war spending. In July 1944, Lieutenant Ashton replaced Lt. R. C. Perry as V-5 officer in charge of the program at Minot.

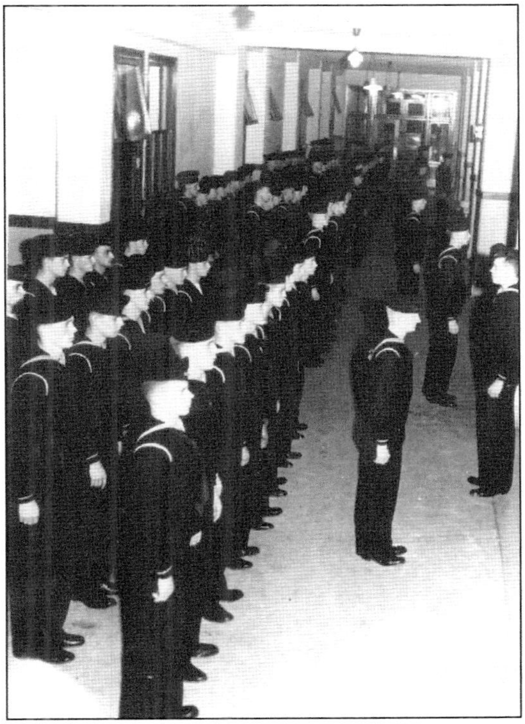

On occasion, freezing temperatures and snow prevented early morning muster on the ellipse. As shown here, when this occurred, formation and inspection was held in the second floor hallway of Old Main, which had wider hallways than the dormitories.

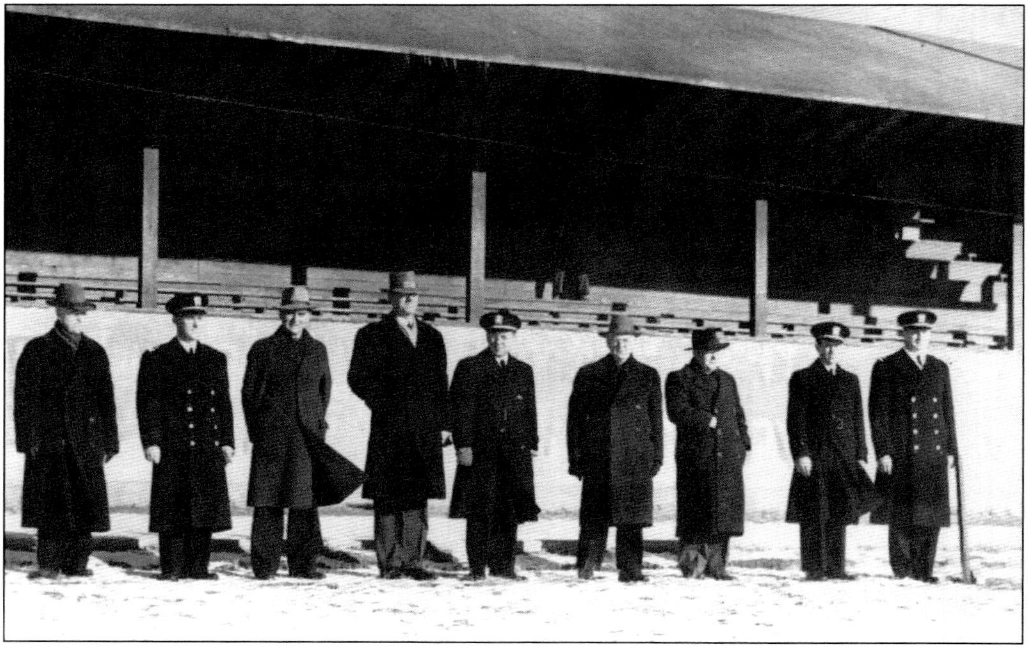

North Dakota senator Gerald P. Nye inspects the V-12 battalion. First elected in 1925, Nye was an isolationist who urged Franklin Roosevelt to negotiate peace in Europe. However, when Japan attacked Pearl Harbor, he voted for the declaration of war with the rest of the U.S. Senate. He visited the campus twice during the program's existence.

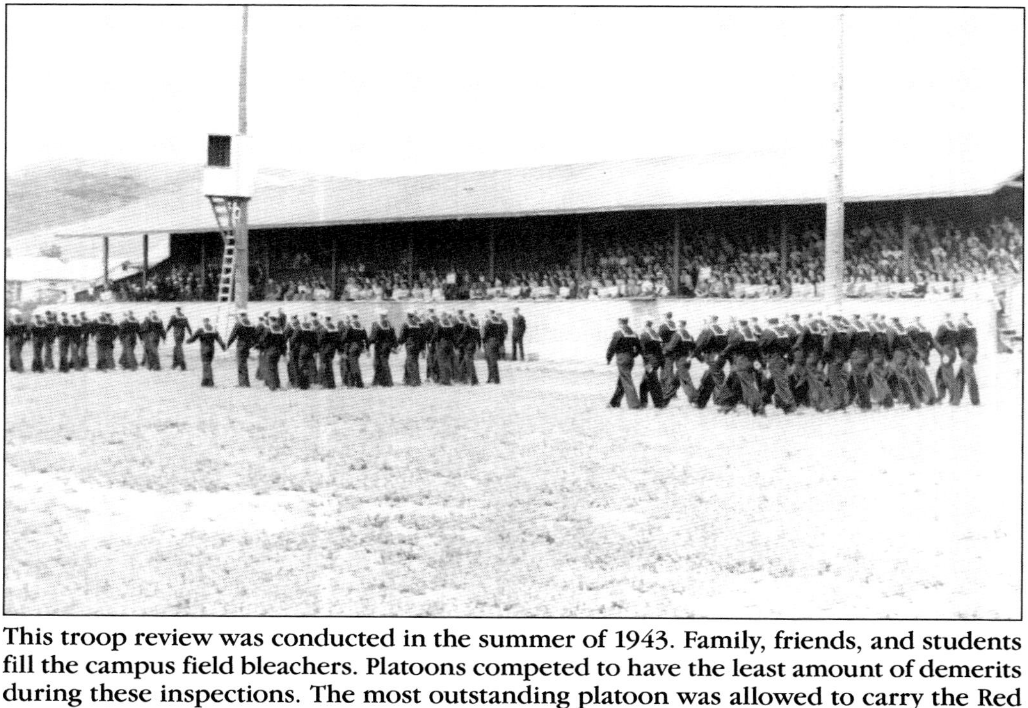

This troop review was conducted in the summer of 1943. Family, friends, and students fill the campus field bleachers. Platoons competed to have the least amount of demerits during these inspections. The most outstanding platoon was allowed to carry the Red Rooster flag.

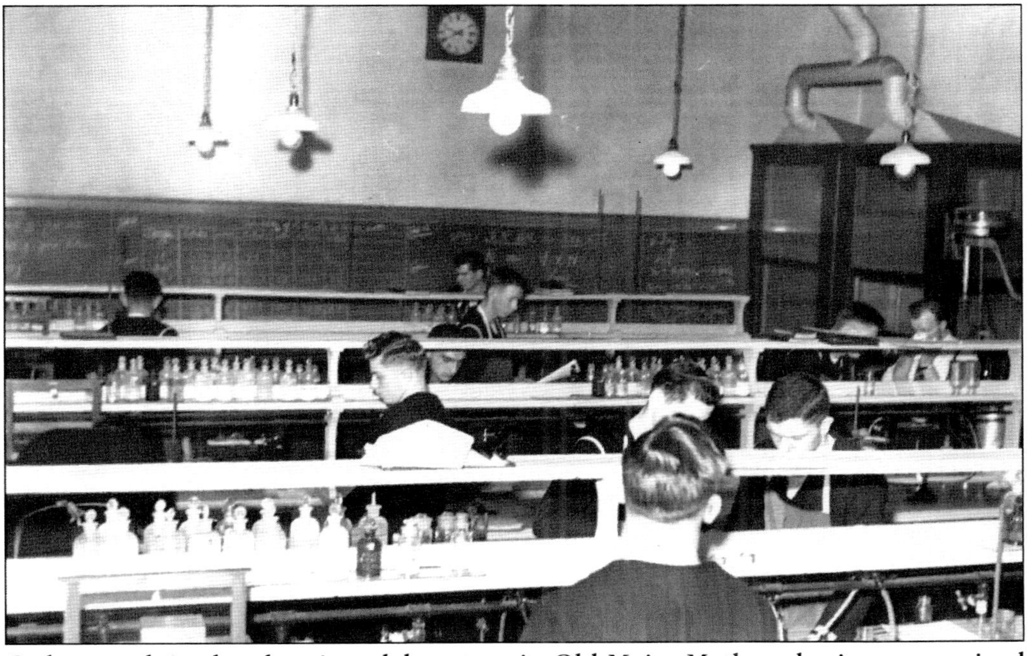

Cadets work in the chemistry laboratory in Old Main. Math and sciences received emphasis in the V-12 curriculum.

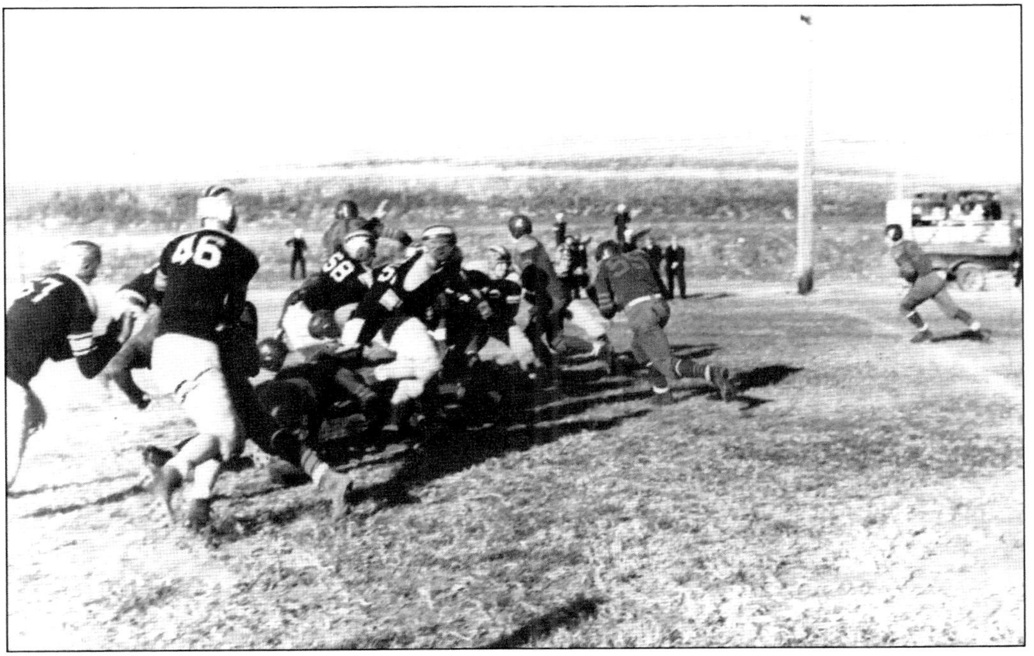

Navy cadets constituted the entire 1943–1944 and 1944–1945 football teams. This photograph captures the action in the 1944 game between the Minot State Bluejackets and the Dickinson State College Savages, also a navy contingent team. Minot won 7-0. The 1945 team went undefeated. The navy did not use the beaver nickname for any of its sports teams.

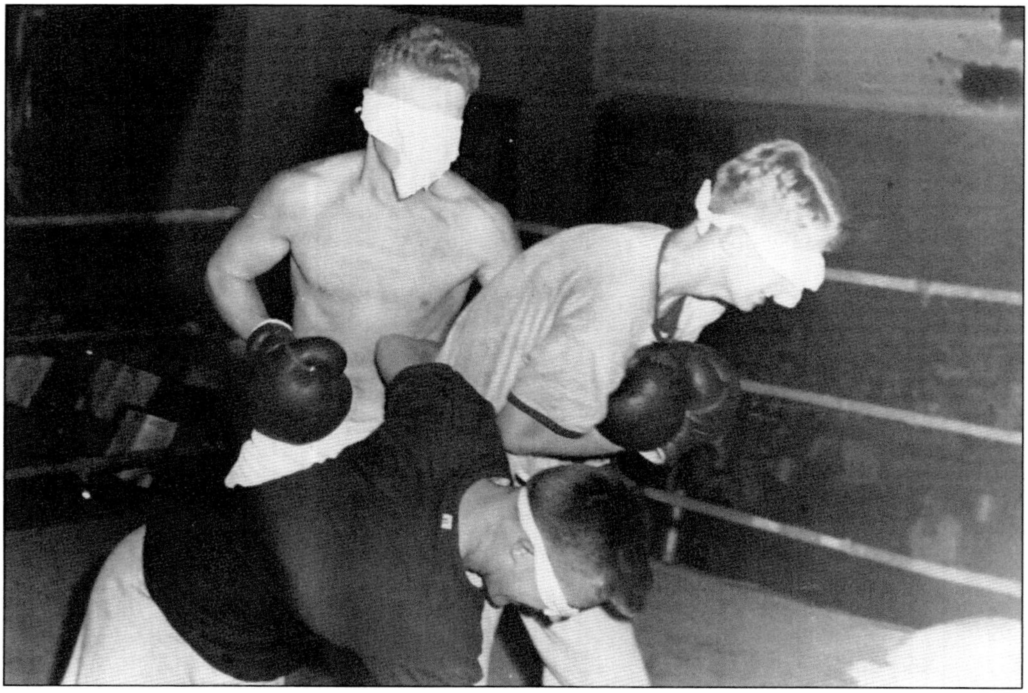

This a photograph of a three-way "blind staggers" match in Swain Hall between cadets Paul Stoms, Hagen, and Williams. The last man standing (staggering) was the victor.

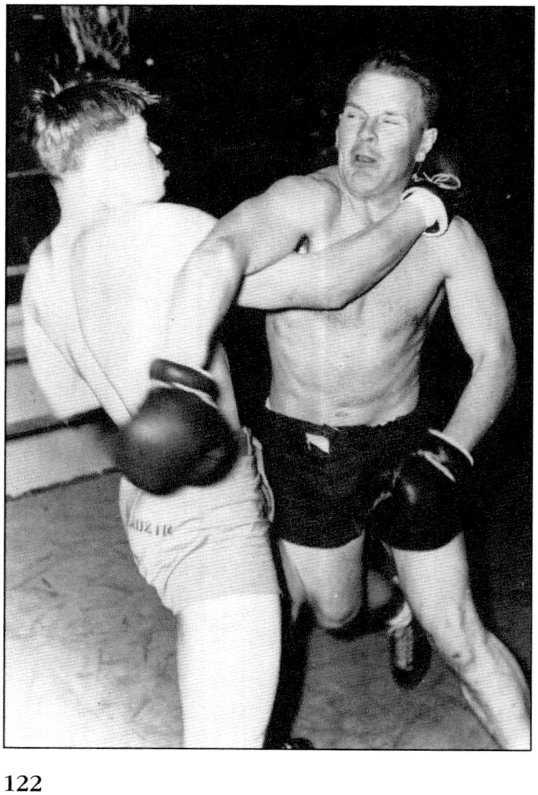

Boxing was a favorite sport for the navy battalion. Most of the matches were held in the old gymnasium. In this bout, cadets Joe Radzik and Wallace Larson are tied up.

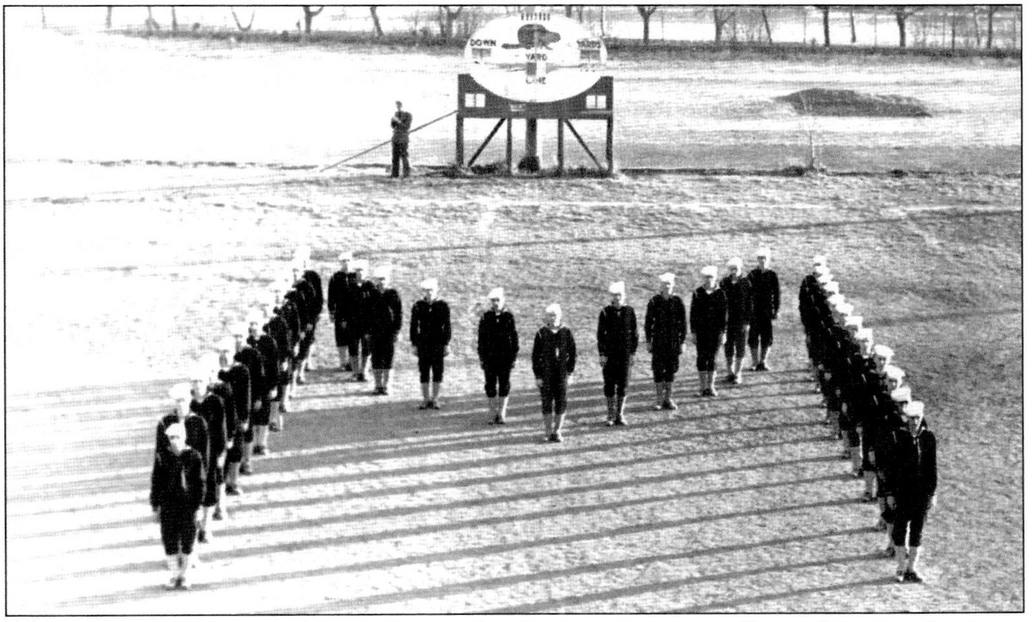

Chief M. G. Sousa managed a drill team for the battalion. It performed during dignitary visits and sporting events where navy teams played. The mighty *M* was a favorite formation. This particular formation was formed during halftime at the 1944 football game against Dickinson State College.

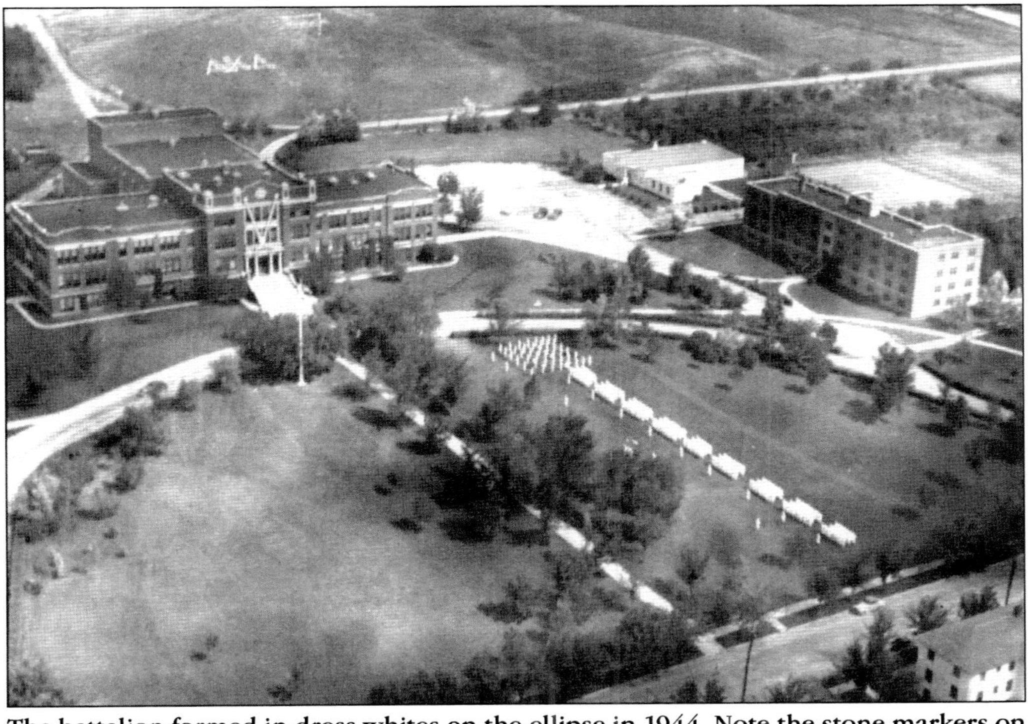

The battalion formed in dress whites on the ellipse in 1944. Note the stone markers on the hillside behind and to the right of Old Main (see the next page).

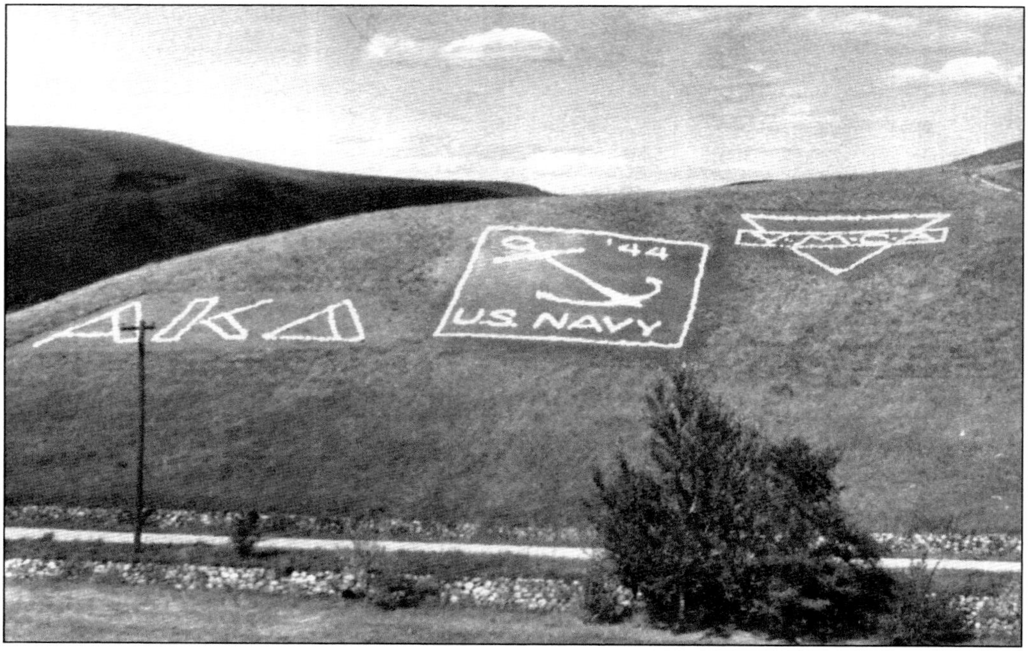

The navy cadets class of 1944 made its presence known in Minot by constructing a white stone logo on the prairie landscape behind Old Main. This is the present site of the Minot State University dome's east parking lot (see the photograph above). Alpha Kampa Delta and the YMCA had already made their mark on the landscape.

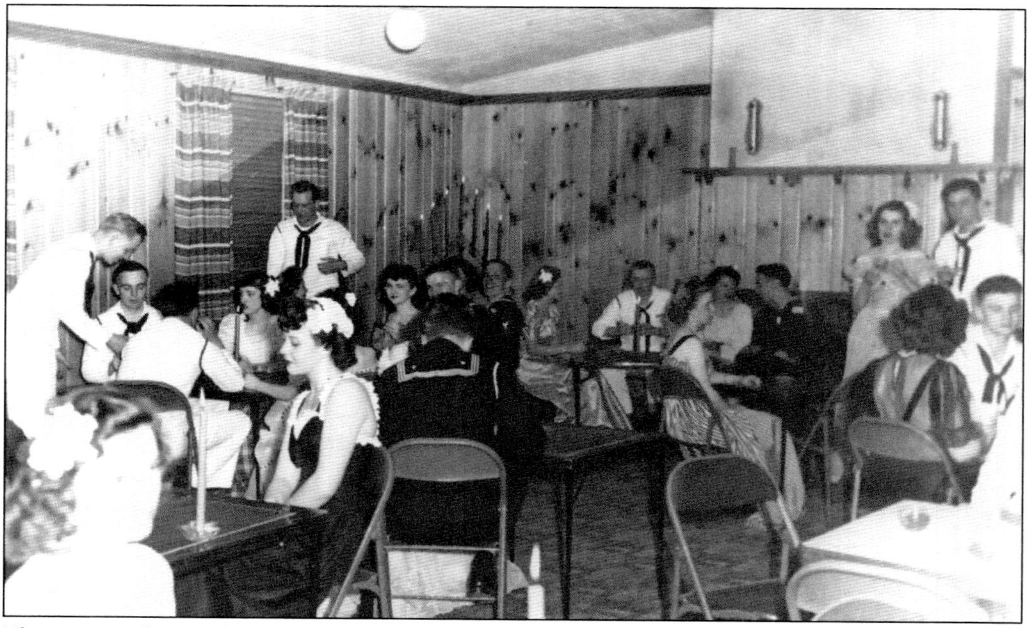

The navy cadets and their dates met in the student union for refreshments and conversation during the 1944 spring prom. Their dances were held at the student union most weekends, and every semester there was a Seaman's Ball and Navy Farewell Formal. The Navy Swing Band performed on campus for several events.

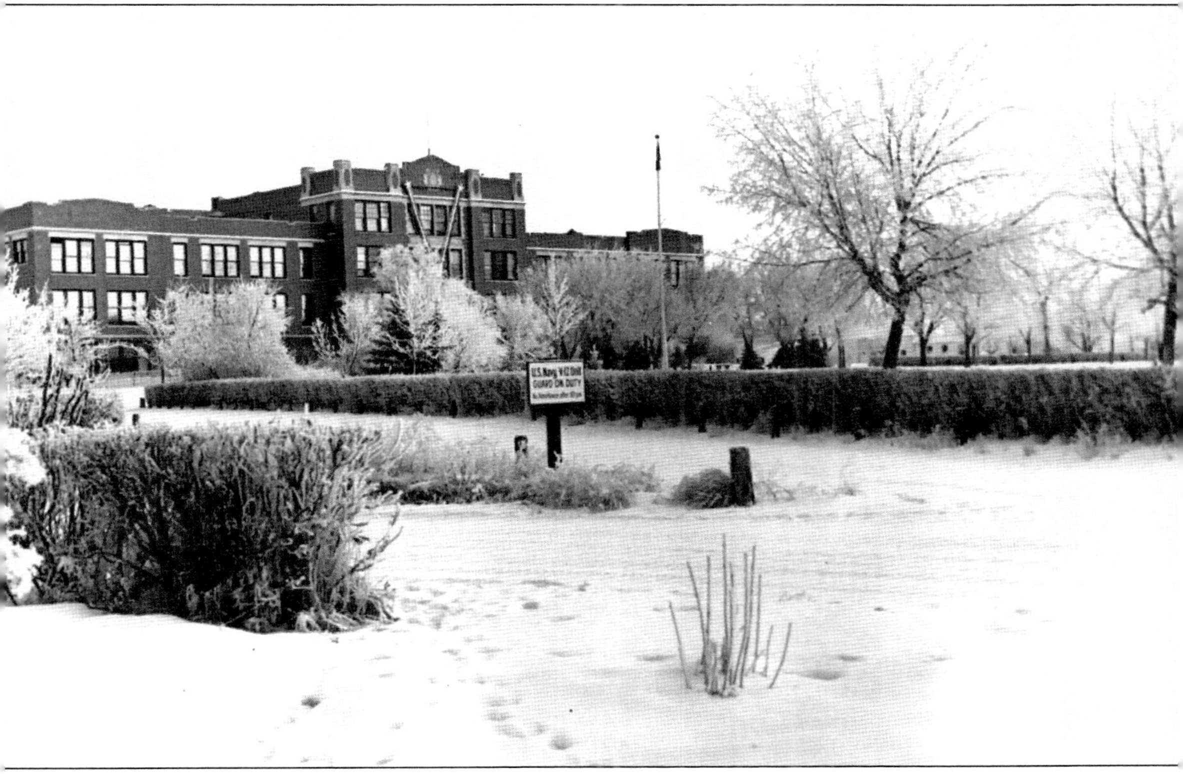

Several security and watch guards were maintained on campus to ensure the security of the V-5 and V-12 cadets and campus facilities. Nonmilitary students not from the area were required to reside in apartments across the community. The dormitories were reserved exclusively for military personnel. The sign at the entrance to the ellipse warned visitors to the campus that a U.S. Navy V-12 unit guard was on duty.

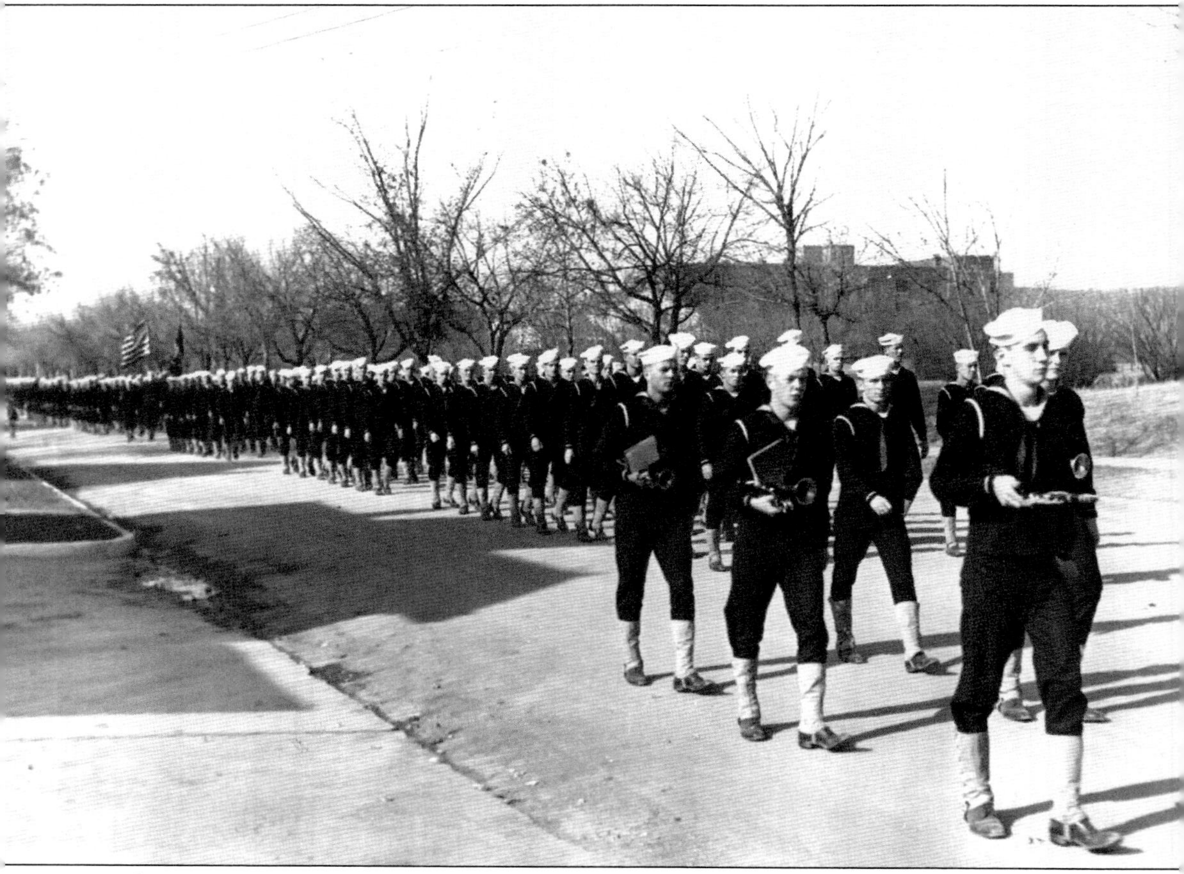

"The Navy Hymn" by Rev. William Whiting reads, "O Trinity of love and power / Our brethren shield in danger's hour / From rock and tempest, fire and foe / Protect them where so ever they go / Thus evermore shall rise to Thee / Glad hymns of praise from land and sea." Many of Minot's naval cadets, V-5 and V-12, marched off to fight in the war. The overall program proved very effective for the navy. Both programs produced an educated cadre for the U.S. Navy's officer corps. The State Teacher's College at Minot produced 479 V-5 graduates and 789 V-12 graduates.

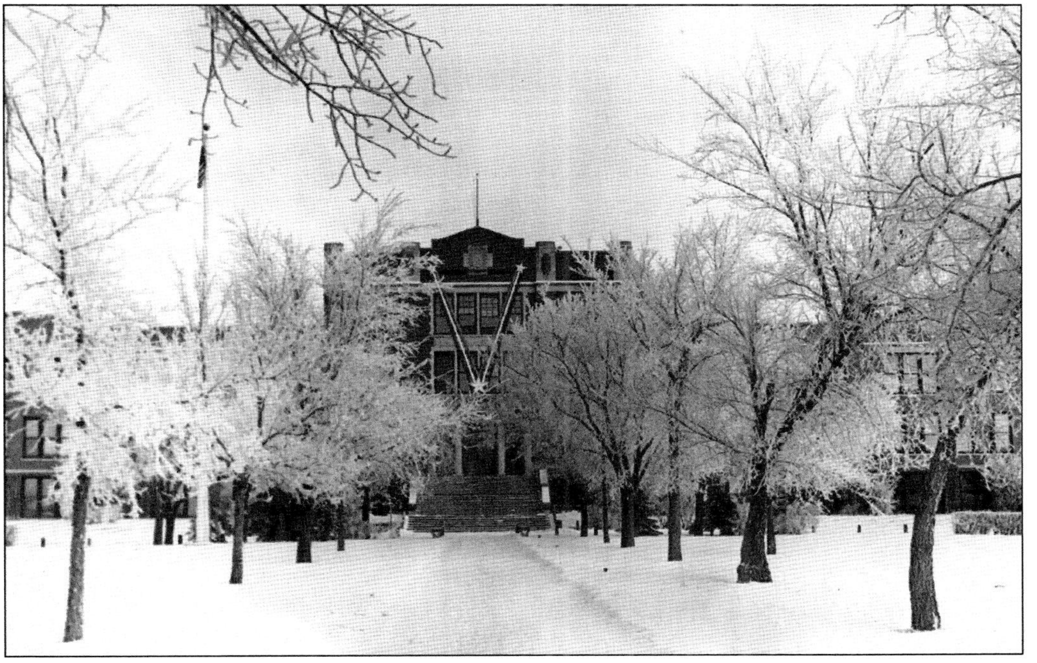

After V-E and V-J Day in 1945, the victory symbol that adorned Old Main for three years was happily removed. In the year that followed, campus operations slowly began to return to normal. Under president Carl C. Swain's leadership, the campus would finish the 1940s with a renewed vigor, prepared for the arrival of the World War II veterans under the newly formed GI Bill. The campus was prepared for the challenges that lay ahead. The progression to university status was set in motion.

Minot State UNIVERSITY